STRENGTH FROM THE WATERS

Confluencias

SERIES EDITORS

Susie S. Porter
University of Utah

María L. O. Muñoz
Susquehanna University

Diana Montaño
Washington University in St. Louis

Strength *from the* Waters

A History of Indigenous Mobilization in Northwest Mexico

JAMES V. MESTAZ

University of Nebraska Press

LINCOLN

Some sections of chapter 2 first appeared in James Mestaz,
"Sweetness and Water Power: El SICAE Sugar Cooperative
and Mayo Struggles for Water, 1943–1955," *Journal of
Latin American Studies* 52, no. 1 (February 2020): 1–25. ©
Cambridge University Press. Reprinted with permission.

The University of Nebraska Press is part of a land-grant
institution with campuses and programs on the past, present,
and future homelands of the Pawnee, Ponca, Otoe-Missouria,
Omaha, Dakota, Lakota, Kaw, Cheyenne, and Arapaho
Peoples, as well as those of the relocated Ho-Chunk, Sac and
Fox, and Iowa Peoples.

⊗

Library of Congress Cataloging-in-Publication Data
Names: Mestaz, James V., author.
Title: Strength from the waters : a history of indigenous
mobilization in northwest Mexico / James V. Mestaz.
Description: Lincoln : University of Nebraska Press, [2022] |
Series: Confluencias | Includes bibliographical
references and index.
Identifiers: LCCN 2022003494
ISBN 9781496228826 (hardback)
ISBN 9781496232564 (paperback)
ISBN 9781496232892 (epub)
ISBN 9781496232908 (pdf)
Subjects: LCSH: Mayo Indians—Economic conditions. |
Mayo Indians—Religion. | Mayo Indians—Politics and
government. | Water resources development—Mexico—
Fuerte River Region. | Water rights—Mexico—Fuerte River
Region. | Irrigation—Mexico—Fuerte River Region. | Fuerte
River (Mexico)—History—20th century. | Fuerte River Valley
(Mexico)—History—20th century. | BISAC: HISTORY / Latin
America / Mexico | NATURE / Natural Resources
Classification: LCC F1221.M3 M39 2022 | DDC
972/.320049745—dc23/eng/20220414
LC record available at https://lccn.loc.gov/2022003494

Set in Minion Pro by Laura Buis.

I dedicate this book to the Mayo people of the Fuerte valley. From my first day of research in northern Sinaloa, Mayo villagers were gracious enough to open their homes to me and happy to share their stories in hopes that it would help create positive change in their communities. It is my hope that sharing stories of Mayo mobilization will help garner them the respect and allies they deserve in their struggle to secure their rights and be an inspiration for Indigenous people globally.

CONTENTS

ILLUSTRATIONS

ACKNOWLEDGMENTS

I am delighted to thank all of the amazing people who assisted me in writing this book. The wonderful staff at the University of Nebraska Press have been very supportive throughout this process, especially Bridget Barry and Emily Wendell, who I appreciate a great deal. Christopher Boyer has been a huge inspiration as my former PhD adviser—thanks for that. Even after completing the PhD, he has stood in my corner, read countless drafts, and advised me in everything imaginable. I am proud to call him my friend. Thank you to Jeffrey Banister for challenging me to think critically throughout the process, and his publications on water and development studies served as a benchmark for this project. Enrique Ochoa was kind enough to offer useful feedback on several occasions. Mikael Wolfe read numerous drafts, left thoughtful comments, and his book was a constant inspiration. Joaquín Chávez was a huge help in allowing me to grasp how to integrate oral histories into the manuscript. Sterling Evans gave great feedback and support. Ben Fallaw offered productive feedback from early drafts. I also had a great support staff in Peter Hohn from Amend Editing and Ben Pease of Pease Press Cartography, and I appreciate their talents and professionalism.

I could have never accomplished this without the help of my family. They kept me on track and also gave me their honest opinions on the project. Mom, you are my rock and I cannot fully put into words what your support means to me. Thanks for teaching me how to use my words to help foster a more equitable society. I promise to continue this work. Danny, I always aspire to become as great of a writer as you. Thanks for showing me how to reach my potential. Kristine, thank you for reading portions of the book and offering feedback, and for reminding me of the importance of my voice in this world. And to the rest of my family, this achievement is yours too—thanks for your love and support.

This long journey was made easier by my colleagues at the excellent institutions where I've taught. At the University of Iowa I learned how to write while struggling with an overwhelming teaching load. I want to acknowledge in particular Lisa Heineman, Jacki Rand, and Mariola Espinosa for your help. My time at Claremont McKenna College was my most productive, and I will forever be grateful for the funding to continue research and guidance my colleagues there offered me and the time they put into my scholarship. I want to thank Daniel Livesay and Sarah Sarzynski for reading drafts and Diana Selig for her continued support and of course the rest of the history department faculty. Tomás Summers Sandoval and Char Miller at our sister school of Pomona also helped me a lot with this project, so thank you. Teaching at Harvard University was a remarkable opportunity, as I got to learn from incredible colleagues and students. I thank Lauren Kaminsky and the rest of the history and literature faculty for allowing me to thrive. Thanks to Central State University colleagues for your support and commitment to social justice. I also thank my new colleagues at Sonoma State University for offering me my dream job. You have all inspired me to be a better educator and scholar, and I am looking forward to learning more from you, teaching great students, and collaborating with the local community.

Great professors and graduate school colleagues in the history department at the University of Illinois Chicago helped me navigate difficult challenges as a PhD student and beyond. Thanks to Javier Villa-Flores and John Monaghan for being influential in shaping the project's overall arguments. I also thank Robert Johnston and Jeffrey Sklansky for offering feedback. Thanks to

Corey Capers who helped me formulate my arguments early on. Thank you, Michael Goode, for offering helpful advice, especially on the introduction. Graduate students in the department (who are now off doing amazing things in this world) offered incredible advice and support, so thank you especially to Tom Alter, Tom Dorrance, Sarah Koning, Jenna Nigro, Maria Ritzema, Benn Williams, Sam Mitrani, Juanita Del Toro, Peter Strickland, Jeff Nichols, Erik Kalweit, Ian Darnell, Michał Wilczewski, and Eliot Fackler. I also thank my colleagues in the Latina/o Graduate Student Association.

I would like to thank the archivists at all of the incredible and vast archives in Mexico City, in particular the very helpful workers at the Mexican General National Archive (AGN), Agrarian Archives (AGA), and Historical Water Archive (AHA). I appreciate the great advice I received from established professors of Mexican history such as Ignacio Almada Bay and Luis Aboites. To my colleagues also teaching, researching, and writing about Mexican history, Jonathan Graham, David Wysocki, Beau Gaitors, David Reid, and Shayna Mehas, thanks for reading drafts. I thank all of the workers and archivists at the local archives in Culiacán, Sinaloa, particularly the state archives and municipal archive of El Fuerte. Rosario Heras Torres assisted me in locating useful sources at both of these archives and helped me understand the history of Sinaloa better, for which I am forever grateful. Thanks to Maria de los Angeles Hernández Rodríguez for helping me to understand literature on the river systems of northwest Mexico.

Last but certainly not least I want to thank my second "family" in my adopted home of Los Mochis, Sinaloa. Thank you to Loreto Coronado, your family, and the Universidad Autónoma Indígena de México for everything. To all of the Indigenous elders and local experts who allowed me to interview you, thank you. I hope my work does your extraordinary stories some justice. To Henrique and the rest of my great friends in Los Mochis, thanks for opening your homes to me and helping me understand the region better. Thank you, Oralia Inzunza, for setting up interviews and helping me appreciate Yoreme culture as much as you.

STRENGTH FROM THE WATERS

Introduction

I n 1957 Antonio Bacosegua, an Indigenous farmer from northwest Mexico's Fuerte River valley, claimed God appeared to him
on the banks of the Fuerte River. In his vision, God, who took
the form of a diminutive elderly man, told Bacosegua to revive the
religious fiestas that were essential to Indigenous Catholic spirituality in the region.[1] But as word of Bacosegua's prophetic vision
spread through the area, including in neighboring valleys, the vision
quickly became enmeshed in controversy over the region's changing hydrological landscape.[2] For decades the federal government
had been siphoning water away from Indigenous and small farmers in this region and giving it to large, corporate farms. Whether
God visited the Fuerte valley in the late 1950s is an open (perhaps
unanswerable) question, but it is clear that many Mayo farmers—
the Indigenous inhabitants of the area—saw divine intervention as
the only solution to the inequity that plagued them. Indeed, as this
book shall explain, several Mayo people interpreted the vision as
a prophecy that God, in a righteous defense of the indignities suffered by the Mayo people, would send down an apocalyptic flood
to sweep away the hydraulic infrastructure that had marginalized
them in their own homeland. At the same time, other Mayo farmers rejected this interpretation and rallied their Indigenous brethren to protect the dams, canals, and pumps that they had worked
so hard to access.[3] The real question is why the Mayo people, who

had lived along the Fuerte River since before recorded history, found themselves in a literal and figurative place where a mystical vision could hold so many real-world implications. What had happened in such a short period of time to make the Mayo people, who as late as the nineteenth century still carried on largely traditional cultural and economic practices, become so desperate that they would disagree among themselves over one man's prophecy?

Strength from the Waters seeks to answer these questions by framing economic development, environmental concerns, and Indigenous mobilization around one of today's most pivotal issues: access to water. It looks to a particular region of Mexico—Sinaloa's Fuerte valley—to answer questions of global concern: Who can access water? How and why? What are the consequences of this unequal access?[4] For though they are a distinct people, the Mayo—struggling to retain their identity and remain in ancestral lands—are far from alone. The global struggle for equity and water justice for native people and other marginalized groups is an issue the modern world is finally acknowledging on a broader scale. Transforming a prophetic vision into a call for water justice was only an extreme example of what I label "hydraulic social mobilization"—a popular movement to secure water rights.[5] Typically, hydraulic social mobilization did not rely upon acts of divine providence and was more commonly characterized by efforts to resist corporate control over communities by collectively asserting Indigenous rights, forming alliances with government functionaries and local non-Indigenous power brokers, and, on occasion, taking direct—even violent—action. Its immediate goal centered on access to irrigation. But in the case of the Mayo people, the larger goal was to preserve local autonomy and their culture.

At the center of that culture flowed the largest body of water in the region, the Fuerte River. This book highlights the historical relationship of the Mayo people with this river system. Between the 1920s and 1970 some Mayo farmers deftly wielded what little political and economic leverage they had in order to maintain a deep and meaningful connection to the Fuerte River. This was not a matter of mere production; Indigenous villagers used tech-

nologies like pumps, dams, and canals to protect cultural practices such as religious ceremonies that, in their minds, defined
them as different from Yoris, as they call non-Indigenous people.

The history of the arid Fuerte valley in the twentieth century centers on the struggle for water—who has command over it and how it
is used.[6] The massive Fuerte River runs through the historic homeland of the Mayo people, and the valley's original *milpa* cultivation
of maize, beans, and squash depended upon its annual floods.[7] The
cycle of flooding, planting, and harvesting defined life for a mil-
lennia in the valley, but beginning in the late nineteenth and early
twentieth centuries, large landowners and corporations claimed
large swaths of the most fertile parts of the valley and installed
canals and pumps along the river. The new hydraulic technology
that Yoris constructed reduced the river's flow and ended the flooding. In a very short period of time—a single generation really—the
crucial relationship that had defined Mayo society for as far back
as any elder could remember had been severed. Not only had the
floods that brought life to the valley stopped coming with predictable regularity, but most Mayo farmers had been pushed back to
marginal lands further from the river. This cultural trauma and how
Mayo villages responded is at the heart of this book.

Strength from the Waters revises twentieth-century Mexican
hydraulic and ethnic histories by demonstrating how Indigenous
tactics not only contested but helped shape state development
plans.[8] For instance, this story opens with Mayo people joining an
army to assert their claims to land, cultural autonomy, and water
rights.[9] In other periods, Mayo farmers overcame their political
and economic marginalization to collaborate with *campesino* (rural
farmer) and labor organizations to shake off an oppressive, fed-
erally sponsored economic agency in the valley.[10] These periodic
assertions, examples of hydraulic social mobilization, ensured an
Indigenous voice within local development decisions. Popular
assumptions aside, post-Cardenista Mexican national development in the mid-twentieth century did not completely undermine
campesino rights; in the case of Mayo villages, Indigenous people stood up and demanded a voice in crucial political matters.[11]

Attention to the use of water, when seen as a linchpin of native Mexican resistance, provides a new framework that promises to recover campesino actions and voices.[12] On the one hand, this book's focus on water justice reveals how Indigenous people viewed these local waterways as integral members of their communities rather than profitable commodities and how they worked hard to maintain access.[13] Yet from a global perspective, Mayo farmers are far from alone, and hydraulic social mobilization can also help scholars to appreciate how other marginalized groups have used similar strategies to defend their identity, material wealth, and health. *Strength from the Waters* employs an environmental history approach to expose how, as has been the case in so many riverine systems where Indigenous ecological systems have been replaced by private and corporate technology, the Mayo villages of the Fuerte valley invented practical stratagems to maintain access to their river.

Land policies and hydraulic infrastructure did more than change the land in the Fuerte valley, it challenged the very notions that underwrote Mayo identity, for the land—and especially the river— was central to Mayo cosmogony. Because of this fact, *Strength from the Waters* also employs an ethnohistorical approach that analyzes how Mayo people adapted and invented new cultural practices within their communities. In fact, because water is rarely a mere commodity for those who have been marginalized and pushed away from their traditional relationships with it, hydraulic social mobilization weaves together environmental and ethnohistorical approaches. This book manifests environmental history in its exploration of outside influences on the Mayo homeland and how they reacted in terms of political and economic strategies, while its ethnohistorical component analyzes how Mayo society adapted culturally. Combining these methods answers the question of what it meant for Mayo villages to witness outsiders employing new technologies to control their river and then to fix it.

Government and corporate archives help to answer how Mayo people responded politically and economically to environmental changes, but questions of culture require different, unexplored sources. Historians have written much about the Fuerte valley without including many native voices in their work, but *Strength from the Waters* aims to correct this. This work uses oral histories to investigate how native people in the valley reacted to, thought about, and even felt toward the changes they faced. While I strive to elevate Indigenous voices, this work does not view them uncritically or present their views as indisputable historical fact; rather, they serve as a record of historical memory, providing an Indigenous perspective of events.[14]

Likewise, it is important to approach archival documents with equal skepticism, especially since authors usually wrote them with the intent of protecting their own interests. Various Indigenous studies scholars have pointed out that archives often marginalize and terrorize native communities by relating subjective information about them, reflecting a Western viewpoint that erases Indigenous voices through key omissions.[15] For instance, corporate development records and state documents of water sources, while useful, reveal the actions of only a fraction of stakeholders and typically do not include Indigenous users. However, tucked within government records are petitions from native communities requesting river resources that provide perspectives revealing Indigenous agency and knowledge. By interrogating these petitions, we have a chance to see how representatives of Indigenous communities presented themselves to the Mexican state and broader society.[16]

Strength from the Waters begins in the years after the Mexican Revolution, when the federal government enacted laws that sought to realize the promise of equity in land and water to all Mexicans. As is explained below, the story is more complicated than that. But irrespective of how matters turned out for Mayo farmers, in this initial period some took advantage of changing laws and official attitudes to integrate hydraulic technology into their river usage practices. Far from an act of cultural colonization, some Mayo farmers welcomed modern irrigation infrastructure as a means to maintain and even increase access to the Fuerte River. Hydraulic social mobility was never, for Mayo farmers, a wholesale rejection of modern life but rather a crucial strategy of cultural and physical survival for Indigenous people in the twentieth century. It should encourage scholars of cultural resilience to see the importance of water access, use, and management in political and cultural movements and the ways in which certain socio-natural landscapes shaped relations between individuals and the state.

Certainly, like other marginalized Indigenous communities around the world, Mayo people were never full and equal partners with the state—a problem that became painfully obvious as the Mexican government embraced invasive developmentalist programs in the late 1940s—yet they leveraged what influence they had in creative and effective ways. Often this meant searching out tactical alliances with Yori neighbors and institutions that could shift with stunning regularity. Sometimes Yori and Mayo interests could overlap but more often they were in conflict. In some instances Mayo farmers joined Yori campesinos against corporate and state capitalist control of the river, yet there are far more episodes in which Mayo farmers could only rely on the cultural affiliations of other Mayo farmers and communities in their mutual opposition to non-Indigenous initiatives. Mayo activists proved very adept at staying abreast of the quickly changing political climate, constantly searching for the most advantageous position or partnership that would help them to achieve their objectives.

This fascinating mix of change and continuity that defined Mayo communities in the twentieth century is best explained by Mexican Argentinian anthropologist Néstor García Canclini's concept of "hybridization." In his view, Latin American cultures are "hybrid" in that they blur the border between traditional and modern.[17] All cultures in this sense are hybrid, and it becomes increasingly difficult to distinguish cultures from one another as they constantly appropriate practices and traditions. Indigenous cultures in Latin America, in particular, have historically adapted by integrating outside practices into their traditions as a means of survival, affording them the opportunity of being "modern" in some contexts and "traditional" in others. When a newly constructed canal, which carried the sacred waters of the Fuerte River, became the stage of an ancient ritual it is difficult to say whether culture had coopted technology or technology had transformed culture.[18] As Canclini's ideas suggest, it could be both simultaneously. In the end, hybridization is simply a way of acknowledging that Mayo people had to continually adjust. Surrounded by change, they creatively adapted.

The Indigenous people of the Fuerte valley embraced new technologies not in order to pursue commercial farming but instead as a subsistence strategy that helped them protect their identity as self-reliant farmers tasked with reproducing their society. Such strategies also accounted for longstanding traditions of religious rituals that repaid the socioecological landscape—and the Fuerte River specifically—for keeping them alive. The acceptance of new technology was integral to campesino subsistence. As historian Cynthia Radding describes it, "The complement of resources necessary to ensure both material existence and the social and ceremonial needs of community life."[19] Mayo integration of new technology therefore assisted in crop production and other practical needs as well as the protection of Indigenous cultural practices such as the religious ceremonies that they conducted on the banks of and within the Fuerte River itself.

While change and adaption was a constant in the Fuerte valley in the twentieth century, *Strength from the Waters* shows that there is no easy way to generalize about either. Mayo people have a long history centered on very localized, even village-based action, and painting with too broad a brush covers up nearly as much as it reveals about Indigenous agency in the region. Some Mayo villages like La Misión adapted by relying more heavily on old traditions like rain-requesting ceremonies or took up new practices such as using purified drinking water systems. In other Mayo communities, such as Los Goros, disagreements arose over whether new hydrological technology could be used for sacred purposes. That said, while how they did so varied, all Mayo villages adapted. Though some appear, to outsider eyes, to be more forceful and active than others, they all sought to maintain their identity and survive in their own way. To be Mayo was to care for, and desire to be close to, the Fuerte River.

Yet while this overarching goal is the common denominator for

Mayo identity, *Strength from the Waters* reveals that native communities were not always as cohesive as one might imagine. The availability of new irrigation technologies resulted in employment opportunities for some and uneven water access for all, creating further inequities within Mayo villages that resulted in social, economic, and ecological stress. The distribution of hydraulic resources caused internal dissension as communal factions questioned who had the authority to anoint new practices as a tradition. These factions often broke down along the lines of who had access at a given moment and who did not. All could agree that they wanted to protect the river and, in so doing, preserve their cultural identity, but how to protect the river and what determined the key components of Mayo identity could be contentious questions as resources dwindled and Indigenous influence waxed and waned.

This shifting Indigenous identity and how it shaped natural resource management in the agricultural heart of Sinaloa is this book's main contribution to contemporary Mexicanist scholarship. Building on the insights of scholarly works such as Paul Liffman's *Huichol Territory and the Mexican Nation* and George Collier's *Fields of the Tzotzil*—both of which establish a link between land, identity, and rituals—as well as Christopher Boyer's *Political Landscapes*, which discusses the importance of natural resource management in Mexican Indigenous community dynamics, *Strength from the Waters* delves further into Indigenous responses, exploring how Mayo cosmology shaped their resistance to the Mexican state's attempts at controlling natural resources.[20] This book centers the history of water not just because it was—and remains—a critical resource but because water, and in particular the Fuerte River, was at the center of the Mayo people's spiritual *and* physical world. To study the Mayo people's shifting traditions and culture in the twentieth century is to study the nonhuman (or more than human) environment and vice versa. In this respect, it offers an expansive take on Indigenous history.

Strength from the Waters also challenges recently published works analyzing changes to water access over time in northern Mexico. Shaylih Muehlmann's *Where the River Ends*, for instance, focuses on an Indigenous group's cultural struggles as access to their river was cut off, but tells only one side of the hydraulic story.[21] In the case of the Mayo people, they adapted their cultural practices by embracing irrigation infrastructure on their own terms. Similarly, Mikael Wolfe's *Watering the Revolution* analyzes Mexican engineers'—or *técnicos* as he terms them—unsuccessful attempts to control nature through their river development initiatives on the Nazas River. *Strength from the Waters* tells a different story—or perhaps a similar story but from a wildly different perspective.[22] Whereas the local and Indigenous people along the Nazas River appear primarily as foils to the frequent challenges and occasional achievements of Wolfe's técnicos, here the roles are reversed. This study privileges the central role Mayo farmers played in mediating the relationship between themselves and their water.

Strength from the Waters fits into a relatively new current of Mexican environmental history that includes such works as Matthew Vitz's *A City on a Lake*, Emily Wakild's *Revolutionary Parks*, and Sterling Evans's *Bound in Twine*. Each of these books interrogate how the modern Mexican state's often capricious development policies substantially affected the physical environment and the way some Mexicans viewed nature. In the case of the Mayo people, despite all the radical transformations to the ecology of their homeland, they held true to a core understanding of themselves—an understanding predicated upon their relationship to the natural world around them. Developmentalist policies impacted Mexico and Mexicans greatly in the twentieth century, but there were some things policy makers could only obliquely influence and not completely transform.

This book breaks new historical ground by showing how hydraulic social mobilization enabled some Mayo farmers to thrust themselves into political decision-making processes and have their interests and demands incorporated in official policies. Not all attempted to do so and fewer succeeded, but some villages and networks of Mayo activists did make their political presence felt, not only in the "golden years" of campesino farming from the 1920s to the 1940s but even into the period of Mexican developmentalism of the 1940s to the 1970s, when conventional wisdom suggests the state silenced and constrained campesinos.[23] By using irrigation technologies to increase crop production and protect lands from outsiders trying to claim it as fallow, Mayo farmers of northern Sinaloa not only made their material existence marginally better but also secured their spiritual and cultural existence. Only by staying physically and culturally close to the river could they be assured that they carried on their ancient reciprocal connection with the sacred river that underwrote Mayo identity. The story of perseverance flowing through *Strength from the Waters* is an inspiration to the global struggle for water justice, and it is my hope that the Mayo perspective of water as a human right and not merely a commodity might ensure the equity of water availability and distribution today.

Physical Geography of the Fuerte Valley

If asked, a Mayo villager today would explain that to understand them, one must know their valley, for the diversity of the Fuerte valley's climate, subsoil, rainfall, and river flow helps to explain the vastly different experiences and relationships of those who have historically inhabited the region. The Fuerte valley was as inhospitable to newcomers in the sixteenth century, when Spaniards colonized it, as in the late nineteenth century when large-scale agriculturalists moved in to exploit its resources. Mexican historian Mario Gill suggests that when the latter groups arrived, the basin, "with his fiery deserts, aggressive flora and venomous wildlife, could not exactly be considered a hospitable place."[24] Soon hydraulic development turned the formerly "fiery" deserts into one of the most productive agricultural sectors of Mexico, but it also grafted a new racial hierarchy predicated on unequal access to water resources onto older notions of order.

All three of the valley's subregions were unpromising places before the advent of industrial irrigation, and the contrasts between them best illustrate the diversity of the area's ecosystems and topography. Starting at the river's headwaters and moving downstream, the sparsely populated eastern subregion includes the municipality of Choix and a small western portion of the state of Chihuahua. It covers two-thirds of the valley's surface area but is the least economically developed. Its uneven rainfall and mountainous, rocky terrain make even raising livestock, let alone more water-intensive agricultural pursuits, difficult. Further downstream, the intermediate subregion containing El Fuerte and parts of Sinaloa and Choix municipalities is a land of transition between the mountains and plains. A large number of hills, a dry climate, and limited rainfall make seasonal agriculture difficult but raising livestock possible. Finally, furthest downstream, encompassing the Ahome and Guasave municipalities, the fine-textured, fertile soil and abundant flat areas of the western subregion have led it to become the most economically successful, yet only because reliable irrigation has overcome the dry climate and low rainfall.[25]

Many crops, if they spoke, would call the Fuerte valley home, but the most lucrative one—the crop that has commanded the most attention since the advent of large-scale, commercial agriculture in the late nineteenth century—is sugarcane. The ideal soil pH for vegetables and sugarcane is from 5 to 7.5. With a pH level ranging between 6.5 and 7.5 under normal conditions, the land along the Fuerte River lays safely within that range.[26] Soils that have become salinated usually have pH levels of 8.5 and higher, making horticulture difficult. The usually neutral acidity of Fuerte valley soils and flexibility of sugarcane (it can thrive in soils with pH levels rising as high as 8.5) brought in outsiders, their capital, and their oversized political influence in the early decades of the twentieth century. Where Mayo people had raised a variety of subsistence crops for centuries, the Yori agriculturalists envisioned an empire of sugar.

The lifeline of both the Mayo homeland and massive Yori agricultural operations is the Fuerte River. The 180-mile river flows at an annual rate of nearly five million cubic meters, providing water for the majority of the Fuerte valley. During the region's two rainy seasons, June through September and December through February, the Fuerte River usually flows smoothly and sometimes floods, but it is often reduced to a mere trickle in the drier months.

Like many of Mexico's rivers, the Fuerte's unencumbered flow is irregular, but it still provides enough water to irrigate one million acres of land, or roughly four thousand square kilometers.[27] In fact, even though it is one of eleven rivers in Sinaloa, the Fuerte River is responsible for providing almost one-third of the state's irrigation water. Through the combination of federal and private investment in hydrological technology, the Fuerte valley contained almost 10 percent of all the nation's irrigated land by the 1960s, making it the fourth-largest irrigated agricultural zone in Mexico.[28] Only by diverting water from this massive river could the Fuerte valley grow from an arid desert with a sparse population in the late nineteenth century to one of the most important agricultural hubs in Mexico by 1970. Yet the cost would be high.

Fuerte Valley Mayo Villages in the Early Twentieth Century

As the center of their spiritual and economic life, the shores of the Fuerte River have always housed Mayo villages. Mayo people refer to themselves as Yoremes, or sometimes as Mayos-Yoremes, and they view all non-Indigenous people as outsiders, or Yoris. But while Mayo villages traditionally claimed the river as home, not all Yoremes live on the Fuerte. Mayo people are joined in a broader Yoreme cultural-linguistic group with the Yaquis of Sonora as well as other Mayo populations situated along southern Sonora's Mayo River.[29] All three groups share a common language and culture with slight regional variations. The current population of Sinaloan Mayo people stands at around fifteen thousand, a number that has remained steady since the early 1900s.[30]

The potential productivity of the Fuerte valley terrain (combined with generous tax incentives) motivated entrepreneurs to annex Mayo ancestral properties in the late nineteenth century. What ensued in the Fuerte valley happened to Yoremes elsewhere, as in the case of the neighboring Mayo valley, where geographer Jeffrey Banister describes the late nineteenth-century dispossession of Mayo land as, "the earliest sustained effort to de-territorialize the valley, and separate the thick history between a people (Yorem) and a place."[31] In the arid Mayo valley, according to Banister, "deterritorialization" required irrigation and diversion dams. By that measure, the process began in the Fuerte valley in 1880 when Mexican entrepreneur Zacarías Ochoa built the valley's first irrigation ditch, diverting water from the Fuerte River to his sugarcane fields. His efforts would commence a wholesale transformation in the region.

Other large landowners followed Ochoa's example and began installing irrigation ditches and diversion dams in not only the Fuerte valley but the Northwest more broadly. Of course, the ostensible aim of these efforts was economic, but the cultural implications were nearly as important. Those like Ochoa who undertook massive hydraulic infrastructure projects saw themselves creating a new history for the region, one that broke from what they perceived as its backward, Indian past. They envisioned a region that would one day be celebrated for its order, accomplishments, and riches.[32] Such construction forever changed the area's economic and social trajectory. Until that time, the region had remained relatively isolated from large scale industry and lagged behind other areas of Mexico in technological development. Indeed, as late as the 1880s, river flooding and capturing rain water were the two chief forms of irrigation for the kind of small scale, subsistence agriculture most Indigenous farmers pursued. For new arrivals looking to grow enormous amounts of profitable sugarcane, such time-honored strategies would be pitifully insufficient.

None of the new arrivals did more to transform the Fuerte valley and usher in a new era than Benjamin Johnston. A native of the United States, Johnston founded a company in the early 1890s that would become the nucleus of a sugar conglomerate, the United Sugar Companies, which would soon dominate the valley through a near monopoly in irrigation. The canal system Johnston helped to create allowed Yori farmers to turn their focus to sugarcane, a crop which demands inordinate amounts of water. He began expanding the irrigation network by funding the construction of lateral ditches and diversion dams in the late nineteenth century.[33] Along with pumps, these canals drew enough water from the Fuerte River to reduce its flow, ending the predictable schedule of flooding that Mayo farmers had depended on for centuries to water their crops and deliver nutrients to the soil. With unreliable irrigation, Mayo farmers found it hard to keep with traditional practices and their harvests suffered. In a vicious cycle, as their yields fell, they found themselves forced to seek employment from entrepreneurs like Johnston and his United Sugar Companies.

From the early 1890s on, landowners like Johnston dominated the economy of the Fuerte valley, even after legislation passed in the wake of the Mexican Revolution of 1910—such as the progressive articles promulgated in the 1917 Constitution—aimed to amend this.[34] Despite the adverse effects of this stranglehold on the region, some Indigenous farmers learned from Johnston and other local hydraulic entrepreneurs the advantages of using modern technology to access water from the Fuerte River. Yet even as they copied him, Johnston and his United Sugar Companies had another lesson to teach Mayo farmers about the new, transformed Fuerte valley: like water rushing downhill, the right to take irrigation water flowed to the most powerful. If Mayo farmers were to beat his monopoly, they would have to be creative and tenacious.

Mayo Adaptation to Land and Water Laws

One tool that Mayo farmers deployed in their efforts to break through Johnston's monopoly was a series of legislative reforms that took place after the military phase of the revolution. Article 27 of the 1917 Constitution states that since land and water within national territory was owned by the nation, state functionaries in pursuit of the "public interest" had the right to transfer this ownership to private parties. However, in the following decade, while the state made at least some effort to redistribute land equitably, large landowners like Benjamin Johnston continued to accrue water rights. Though the framers may have had grand intentions, the lack of political will and the resistance of powerful landowners mostly postponed the execution of these laws until the 1920s and 1930s. Presidents Venustiano Carranza (1917–20), Álvaro Obregón (1920–24), and Plutarco Elías Calles (1924–28) held back much of the progressive legislation set forth in the 1917 Constitution and dragged their feet on subsequent legislation. This meant for those living in the Fuerte valley that from 1917 until the mid-1920s that Johnston and United Sugar, who should have been pressured into being a more pliant partner with their Indigenous neighbors, continued on as though the revolution had never happened. State officials generally ignored requests for irrigation water from smaller farmers and what deals did occur were often exorbitant.

Only in 1926 did the federal government implement the Law of Irrigation with Federal Waters, which gave the constitution teeth and ensured that all would receive equal consideration in their requests for water rights.[35] At that point, individuals, corporations, and Fuerte valley villages petitioned the Secretaría de Agricultura y Fomento (Ministry of Agriculture and Development, or SAYF) for water concessions.[36] Here was the first chance for all players in the Fuerte valley to carry on as equals. For small farmers, that meant they would, at least in theory, have access to plentiful and uninterrupted irrigation access.

Article 27 of the 1917 Mexican Constitution also held another, equally important clause. With an eye to appeasing the small farmers who were largely the backbone of revolutionary armies, the constitutional convention granted rural communities the right to apply for a *dotación* (grant) of an *ejido* (communally managed land), where *ejidatarios* (land reform beneficiaries) enjoyed usufruct rights to raise their own crops. For decades after 1917 this constitutional power lay nearly dormant as the nation's leaders doled out limited land grants, until President Lázaro Cárdenas began approving ejidos around the nation at an unprecedented rate, with a wave of thirty-five in the Fuerte valley in 1938 alone.[37] The majority of these ejidos received an irrigation concession, though some gained more than others. The logic of the concessions was hardly a science (let alone fair), and how much irrigation and the quantity and quality of land ejidos received could depend on such disparate factors as when they put in requests, how persuasive their argument was, and, perhaps most importantly, who they knew. As time would prove, it could be economically disastrous to try and farm too much land with too little water. But in the 1930s that point was a mere technicality, and Mayo ejidatarios could celebrate that they had land—some of it along their sacred river—and the right to irrigate from it. In any case, they saw the benefit of new hydraulic technology and understood it was in their own self-interest.

As beneficial as they were, the formation of ejidos in the Fuerte valley in the late 1930s complicated the meaning of the term "Mayo community." Indigenous villages in the Fuerte valley applied for ejidos and were sometimes granted communal property located on their ancestral land, but their neighbors were often ejidos made up entirely of Yoris.[38] By 1938 the population of the Fuerte valley was so mixed between Yoremes and Yoris that some of the ejidos created in the initial wave started out as "mixed," a circumstance that proved to be so beneficial that other Mayo ejidos would integrate Yori outsiders over time. Yoris often had more and better political connections than Yoremes, and they commonly rose to ejidal leadership positions. Yet this influx of outsiders did not dilute Indigenous identity, for the Mayo people's sense of community extended beyond ejidal affiliation.[39] Indigenous ethnic identity and self-recognition arose not from where one precisely lived alongside the river but rather from how one approached and understood the river, Mayo language fluency, and participation in religious ceremonies. Particularly in "mixed" ejidos, Mayo people could be both members of an ejidal community alongside Yoris that they did not interact with often and part of a broader Mayo community in which riverine religious rituals and other shared practices united them across ejidal boundaries. Being an ejidatario did not necessarily mean that one was Indigenous in the Fuerte valley, but the overwhelming number of Mayo farmers there became ejidatarios. This meant, in practice, that most Mayo farmers relied on the official backing and support of the state to right the wrongs of the previous generation.

As the Indigenous villages of the Fuerte valley received dotaciones in the late 1930s, much of the power that had been bestowed on the traditional village governor, or *cobanaro*, shifted into the hands of a six-person, member-elected executive ejidal committee. This restructuring of power signaled an important transition in Mayo life, but gendered structures of power remained. Previously, the cobanaro position reflected the status and respect that those who took the title held in the community. Those who were selected possessed qualities revered in Mayo culture: command over traditions and ceremonies, consensus building, and oration. Being fluent in Spanish was a useful talent as well.[40] Since traditional villages tasked cobanaros with negotiating and communicating with Mexican state officials and large landowners who were overwhelmingly male, it is no surprise that men continued to fill this role in the early twentieth century.

This gendered notion of power carried on from the traditional village into the modern ejido. Mexican law stated that only males could be ejidatarios, so Mayo village/ejido formal leadership positions remained exclusively in the hands of men throughout the twentieth century.[41] Therefore, it is unsurprising that, even though Mayo villages had traditionally relied on reciprocal gender roles in which men and women carried out specific duties that were each viewed as equally vital to a village's physical and cultural survival, only men wrote petitions to the state on behalf of the ejido. Their voices unavoidably dominate official, state-centered primary sources. However, while the male-led ejido system kept official power out of the hands of women, this did not prevent the latter from maintaining an influential voice in community decisions. In oral histories, women appear again and again as both figures of respect and repositories of knowledge. In response to both specific and indirect questions about the role of gender dynamics in twentieth century Mayo history, both female and male interview subjects generally downplayed gender's centrality, instead emphasizing their efforts to form a united front against a hostile world.[42]

No matter if it was Benjamin Johnston or a six-man ejidal committee, whoever solicited irrigation concessions from the state controlled their corner of the Fuerte valley in the twentieth century. But by the 1950s Johnston was long gone, and so too was the era of ejidal political strength. Through the 1940s government interest in small-scale, subsistence agriculture waned and the state's developmentalist plans took access to canals and pumps out of the hands of most Mayo villages.[43] Once again large landowners monopolized the use of river water as state functionaries flouted the spirit of the progressive 1917 Constitution and the 1926 Federal Law of Irrigation, which ensured all Mexicans equal access to land and water. The elimination of access to canals and pumps vitiated the productivity of Mayo farmers' lands, traumatizing their communities and, at times, even threatened their religious identity. Still, today Mayo people remain as vibrant and resilient as ever. How can we account for the durability of Mayo identity? In a few words, hydraulic social mobilization. Irrigation construction, as we will see, initially hurt Mayo communities, but they did not fold in the face of the challenge. Rather, they rose up and turned the very weapons used against them into tools to ensure their survival. *Strength from the Waters* is a story of how and why that came to be.

Structure and Organization

This work consists of five chronologically and thematically arranged chapters. Chapter 1 starts by analyzing how Mayo people have forged their identity via the Fuerte River throughout history. It then explains the process of Mayo ethnogenesis that culminated in Felipe Bachomo's 1913 revolt, the failure of which forced Mayo leaders to seek different mobilization strategies in the 1920s. Some Mayo farmers took advantage of postrevolutionary legislation, such as the 1926 Federal Law of Irrigation, to maintain access to the Fuerte River. Using the township of Los Goros as a window into this process, chapter 1 investigates how Indigenous villagers altered their relations with water providers, the state, and the socio-natural landscape from 1927 to 1942 so that irrigation infrastructure might protect their communities, land, farming practices, and riverine religious rituals.

Chapter 2 analyzes how, in order to mobilize the nascent strength of the region, the federal government formed the Sociedad de Interés Colectivo Agrícola Ejidal (Agricultural Society of the Collective Ejidal Interest, SICAE)—a state-backed sugarcane cooperative—to dole out irrigation concessions. This entity would impact the social, political, ecological, and ethnic dynamics of Fuerte valley villages from 1944 to 1958. Not all Mayo farmers were members of the cooperative, and those who were became pitted against those who were not. Focusing on the experience of select villages from 1944 to 1958, this chapter explores this conflict and how Mayo nonmembers defended their lands and maintained access to irrigation water by aligning with outside labor and campesino organizations. This feud would have a powerful influence over local water development strategies and be a cultural wound that took the Mayo people decades to heal. This chapter also serves as an imperative transition between the postrevolutionary era of the first chapter and the postwar era discussed in the rest of the book. The shift in hydraulic social mobilization tactics that Mayo farmers engaged during this period (1940s and 1950s) informed their approaches to the state, Yoris, and hydraulic infrastructure as discussed in the last three chapters.

Chapter 3 explains how the combination of the SICAE's control of the Fuerte River and large landowners' emerging political power in the mid-1940s to mid-1950s compelled Mayo communities to creatively draw from ancient wisdom and make what was once old into something new and vibrant. As the state diverted river water to private farms, Mayo villages lost hope with an obviously biased government and had to look to the skies. When rain did not come as regularly or in the quantities they needed, many Mayo leaders laid blame on private farms' recent clearing of natural vegetation. Rather than resigning to a difficult situation, they revived and increased their reliance on ancient, traditional rituals like the rain-requesting ceremony known as Yuco Conti.

Chapter 4 analyzes how a development-minded state encouraged not only large Yori landowners' growing hydraulic power but their domination over the physical and cultural landscape of the Fuerte valley. Most notably, these landowners became empowered to interfere with the Mayo connection to the Fuerte River, changing how Mayo villages conducted such riverine rituals as the important San Juan ceremony—a celebration that bound native villagers to both the river and each other. The grotesque irony was that Mayo people served as the primary labor force in canal construction from the mid-1940s through the early 1960s even though these very structures constrained their autonomy, dispossessed them from their land, and led to an even greater concentration of Yori power. To contextualize this shift in regional power dynamics, the chapter compares Mayo hydraulic social mobilization in the Fuerte valley with that in the nearby Mayo valley, and how both regions responded to an Indigenous millenarian religious movement that erupted in these pivotal years.

Chapter 5 charts how, during the 1950s and 1960s, Fuerte valley Indigenous farmers had to, once again, adapt to new technology to maintain access to water. While the Mexican state attempted to assert a more politically centralized developmentalist approach, federal agencies such as the Fuerte River Commission (CRF) collaborated with large landowners to construct canals and massive hydroelectric dams, such as the Miguel Hidalgo Dam, on the Fuerte River. Partly due to the sheer scale of capital now invested in hydraulic infrastructure along the river and partly due to impact of decades of political and economic marginalization, Mayo villages in this period were unable to mobilize effectively. The creative, shifting strategies that had served them with varying effectiveness for the last half century fell flat. During this nadir in Mayo history, when their efforts at hydraulic social mobilization most clearly failed, popular Mayo attitudes and relationships with the local ecosystems—the Fuerte River in particular—began to shift and, according to Mayo elders, deteriorate. During this dark chapter of Mayo history, a generation of Mayo came of age who had never known or experienced the river in its full majesty. Rather, for some, the Fuerte River had only ever been a polluted, anemic trickle made to serve the interests of Yoris at the expense of Yoremes that hardly warranted reverence.

The epilogue provides a broad overview of what changed for Mayo people from the mid-1920s to 1970, particularly from the perspective of their relationship with the Fuerte River. It also offers a brief analysis of post-1970s Mayo hydraulic social mobilization tactics. Even in the depths of Mayo despondency in the late 1960s, the Mayo people never gave up. In the years since, new challenges have arisen but so too have new opportunities. For instance, one of the current challenges of maintaining Mayo identity is the Yori appropriation of Indigenous cultural practices, a phenomenon which has led to two opposing reactions among Mayo people. Some Mayo villages view this cultural appropriation as positive because the overall growth of Indigenous religious practices will prevent them from disappearing, while others believe that allowing Yoris to participate at all dilutes Mayo identity.

Would Antonio Bacosegua, the Mayo farmer to whom God appeared in 1957, have been satisfied to see what had become of the Fuerte valley six decades later? On the one hand, no divine flood came and washed away the inequities so prevalent in the Fuerte valley. Even today, the poor remain poor and those favored by the state remain privileged. But on the other hand, Basosegua never prophesied an absolute apocalypse. Rather, when God spoke to him, it was a call to renew Mayo people's connection to that which was sacred, divine, and timeless. It was a call to find meaning in the community. In this respect, Mayo people did rally to that call in the mid-twentieth century and struggled, against intimidating odds, to reaffirm and find meaning in their connection to their river. Their historic battle for economic and cultural autonomy teaches us what can be accomplished when humans stop treating water solely as a commodity to be hoarded or maximized. In the ongoing, global struggle for water justice, activists can learn from Mayo history the advantages of approaching bodies of water as active historical agents deserving of respect.

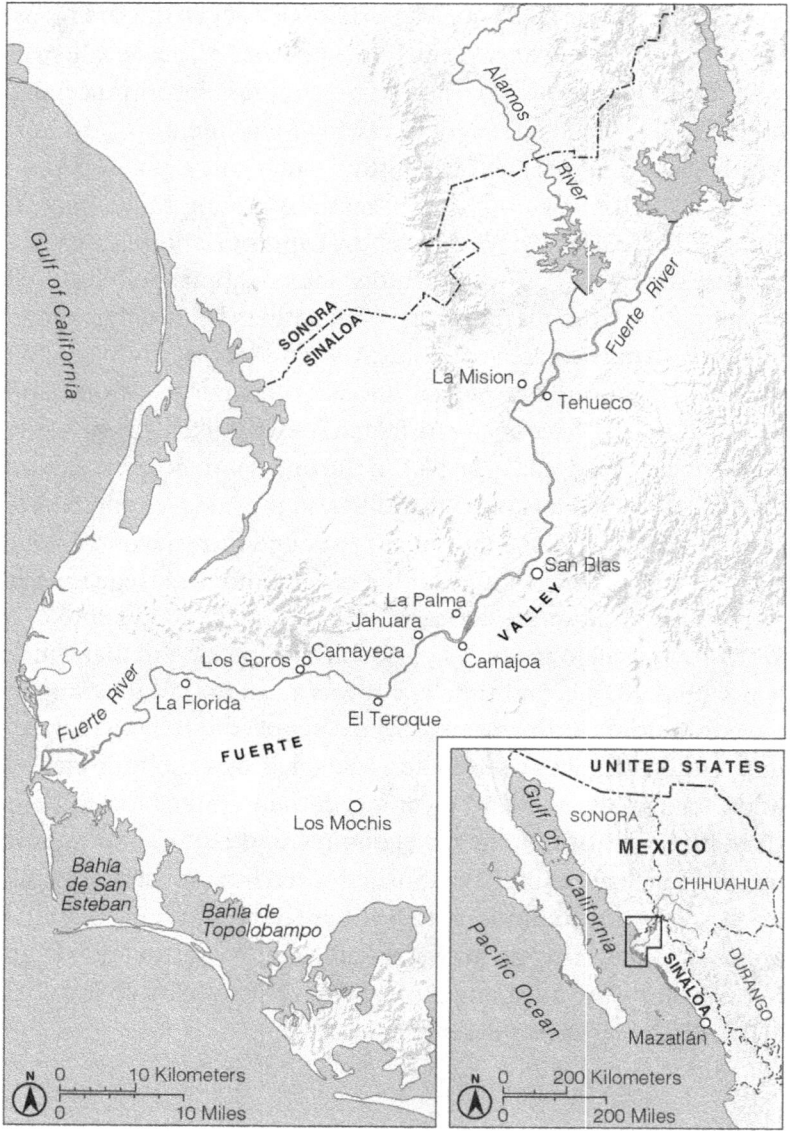

1. Fuerte River and Fuerte valley Mayo villages.
Mapped by Pease Press Cartography.

ONE

Their Technology, Our Way

Los Goros and Fuerte River Infrastructure, 1927 to 1942

On May 13, 1931, leaders from the Mayo town of Los Goros, along with their neighbors from Camayeca, petitioned Mexico's Secretaría de Agricultura y Fomento (Ministry of Agriculture and Development, SAYF) for the right to irrigate their corn, bean, and squash crops from the pump of a non-Mayo neighbor.[1] There was nothing new in Mayo farmers petitioning the state. For years the farmers of Los Goros had applied for water concessions from the government, and for years the state typically turned them down. Los Goros's only other choice was to seek out private agreements with individuals or companies who already had a concession. While these were far more available, private agreements ran the gamut from mutually beneficial to brutally burdensome depending upon the situation. For a small, Indigenous community, burdensome agreements were more common than beneficial ones and exploitation was always a persistent problem. But by 1931 matters had changed. The Los Goros leaders were optimistic that the SAYF would approve their petition, for five years earlier the federal government passed legislation that seemed to promise that the agency would be more generous with water concessions to a broader segment of society. The new legislation—the Law of Irrigation with Federal Waters of 1926—granted smallholders irrigation rights and curbed the power of large, powerful corporations like the United Sugar Companies. More importantly, the law paved the way for Mayo villages like Los Goros and Camayeca to obtain water rights when they became ejidos in the late 1930s.[2] Beginning in 1926 and extending through the early 1940s, dozens of Mayo villages and individuals became empowered to formally apply for recognition of their water rights and sought permission to use new water pumps, build concrete-lined canals, and establish working relations with other small farmers and larger corporations, all to continue their subsistence agriculture.

That it was Los Goros submitting this petition is not in the least surprising. Indeed, in the period between the mid-1920s through the early 1940s—if the archival record is any indication—this village was perhaps the most active in the Fuerte valley in attempting and succeeding to secure water access. Often, as in the case of the 1931 petition, that meant soliciting help from federal agencies, but nearly as often it could mean negotiating agreements—sometimes even informal understandings—with agricultural corporations or individuals with irrigation access and hydraulic capital. Yet there was nothing about this activism and reliance on water that was unique to Los Goros. If the village was exceptional, it was only because it was more willing and ready than other Indigenous communities to adapt and move on, allowing it to try a variety of strategies more frequently and leave a longer archival record.[3] Collectively, the hundreds of documents that Los Goros's relentless hydraulic social mobilization efforts left behind reveal this village's resourcefulness in their efforts to secure water access. They present us with an opportunity to dive in deep and explore the shifting and evolving nature of Mayo strategies as community leaders and members experimented and tested new agencies and laws that were—at the very least supposedly—intended to help them. This chapter uses Los Goros as a case study to investigate the petitions process from 1927 to 1942, a period in which Fuerte valley Mayo villages adapted and changed in an effort to maintain their Indigenous identity.

Water was key to keeping northern Sinaloan Indigenous communities together and their identity strong. The inhabitants of Los Goros and other Mayo villages sought water not just to assure a bountiful harvest but as a way to deepen their legal claim to the title of their land.[4] Moreover, having control over ejidal lands made it easier for Mayo farmers to maintain access to abutting forests, pastures, and—by far, most importantly—river banks where they performed religious rituals that both solidified their social relationship and centered their culture.[5] Like blood is to the body, water was—and remains—to the Mayo peoples' concept of land and themselves. Vital for Mayo people, water was both practical and spiritual. Without it not only would their crops die but also the ceremonies, rituals, and practices that manifested their culture.

Mayo Reciprocity, Spirituality, and Connection to the Fuerte River

Located on a stretch of the Fuerte River—or río Zuaque as the Mayo refer to it—not far from where the Fuerte valley begins to open up and reach out to the Gulf of California, Los Goros resides where it is for reasons that extend far beyond Mexico's colonial past. As Mexican ethnologist Hugo López explains, "The spatial structure and policy of the old villages derive from their relation to the Fuerte River, it appears this way especially, because of the impact of agricultural development in the fertile plains."[6] According to Indigenous oral tradition, the term *Mayo* derives from the Cáhita word *mayombo*, which means "the people of the river-banks."[7] Mayo communities created and maintained settlements on strategic locations along the banks of the Fuerte River, places where they could reliably irrigate their crops with its annual over-flow. The yearly floods delivered not just water but nutrients for the soil and were so reliable that the Mayo people developed an interdependence with the river, anointing themselves its protector.[8]

In the Mayo world, the river nurtured them and they, in turn, nurtured it. For centuries the river provided drinking water, irrigation for crops, raw materials for religious ceremonies, and fish to eat. In exchange for its gifts, the Mayo people acted as the river's guardians, performing religious rituals in its honor. This approach of giving back to the river, rather than commodifying it as a mere resource, would be an important distinction between Mayo people and the Yori inhabitants of the Fuerte valley.[9] Since the large-scale influx of the Yoris in the late nineteenth century, Mayo people have always taken great pride in their ability to communicate and coexist with the Fuerte River while upbraiding Yoris for abusing the river to advance "selfish" strategies of profit.

The differences between how Yoremes and Yoris approach the Fuerte River extend beyond how they physically interact with it and into how they perceive it. Mayo elders characterize the relationship between the river and the Mayo people in quasi anthropomorphic terms so intense and loving that the river, at times, appears to become almost a spouse.[10] As Mayo elder Daniel Galaviz of Camajoa explains, "The river is alive; breathing, thinking, reacting, and serving all living creatures. The relationship is reciprocal and ancestral, a vital component to our history. Water provides life for Yoremes, but we serve the river. It is a blessing, so we pay homage through rituals for all the river has done for us."[11] This Indigenous reciprocity with river systems is not unique to the Mayo people, but their approach in using new laws and irrigation technologies in the mid-twentieth century to protect this connection merits further inquiry into this relationship.[12]

River water acted as the lifeblood of the Mayo villagers who, in turn, revered the river not just for what it offered but also out of fear of what disrespect would bring. Mayo people have long believed that local waterways were ruled and protected by a god known as the "old water woman," who would kill them if they did not ask her permission to extract fish or other resources.[13] Mayo people still today take great care to pay homage to her and to the river itself. The river's duality as both provider and destroyer have compelled Mayo people to protect, respect, and communicate with the Fuerte River.

The river had other human characteristics as well, including wisdom. Mayo elder Librado Cuadros of La Palma explains, "The Fuerte River is the river of knowledge because Yoremes extract information from it, requesting it through ceremonial singing and dancing. We have to give back if we are to receive."[14] The river could be a repository of Mayo experience and even oracle of sorts. As Narciso Bachomo and Carlos Salcedo, elders and teachers of the Mayo language, add, "The word *Zuaque* comes from the Mayo word *Zua*, meaning reasoning and intelligence. Yoremes concentrate on reasoning, that is our ethnicity. Then the whites changed the name to Fuerte River, but it made no difference. The natural connection of Yoremes to the river remains today."[15] The Mayo people alone appreciated that the river, like them, had the ability to reason and offered enlightenment for those willing to listen.

For Mayo people, the Fuerte River has never been a thing to be used but a living presence to be respected and honored. Indeed, Mayo cultural practices—particularly their relationship to the Fuerte River—distinguished them from the dominant Mexican society.[16] Many scholars point to language as the critical divide between Mayo people and their Spanish-speaking *mestizo* neighbors, but anthropologist N. Ross Crumrine goes further and argues that Mayo people saw themselves not merely as a separate ethnicity with a unique language but as people who lived with and within the world differently. While mestizos believed they had attained a mastery over nature that entitled them to manipulate and hoard resources, the Mayo people saw themselves as integral to but still merely one part of the natural world, or Juyya Annia. They were not the "owners" of the river, its fertile banks, or the animals living there.[17] This distinction is not trivial. Nothing in the Juyya Annia, especially not water, could be reduced to a commodity or an input for human ends.[18] All aspects of the river, including what modern readers would identify as its larger ecological system, were parts of a larger, holistic whole, each imbued with a spiritual essence that should be—indeed, the Mayo people argued, had to be—respected.

When Jesuits introduced Catholicism in the Fuerte valley in the sixteenth century, they found Juyya Annia too deeply rooted to be pushed aside. Instead, they co-opted it, weaving the veneration of saints into existing Indigenous traditions, festivals, and beliefs, especially those who celebrated Juyya Annia on the banks or in the waters of the Fuerte River.[19] Even today, this heady mix of Mayo ancestral practices and traditional Catholicism is a major constitutive element of Mayo identity, and in Yoreme cosmology religion, society, culture, and ethnicity are different aspects of the same reality.[20] As Mexican anthropologist Gabriel Uriarte writes, Juyya Annia is "constantly used in indigenous conversation, [in discussing] both matters of everyday life and their deepest religious cosmology. Today Catholicism and Juyya Annia are the perfect combination in the Mayo Indian faith."[21] Even in ostensibly Catholic religious ceremonies, performers invoke nature by dressing as deer dancers who mimic the animal's movements. In these rituals, as in the Indigenous world, the entirety of nature—flowers, deer, and birds—all sing in unison.[22] Every living thing is respected within this cosmology and, at its center, the Fuerte River flows.

Even in everyday practices, Mayo people demonstrate that all living things are vital to a functioning ecosystem. Uriarte explains that the Indigenous people of the Fuerte valley are "one with their surroundings, respecting other forms of life, considering that the individual is only part of a cycle, where everyone has their place, and where everything depends on each other for survival."[23] For instance, according to several elders, similar to how they ask old water woman's permission to extract fish, when most Mayo people cut lumber, they explain their actions to the tree, ask its permission, and leave enough wood so that it can survive.[24] The sanctity of nature is not an abstraction for the Mayo people, nor is the vitality of nature measured by how well it serves human needs. Indigenous inhabitants of northern Sinaloa treat each part of the world around them with the same respect and decency they show each other because they themselves are but one more piece of Juyya Annia.

Mayo Adaptation and Revolt

Mayo social structure was not a static, pristine order that had stayed perfectly intact since before conquest but rather more a flexible set of historical relationships that had united the Indigenous communities of the Fuerte valley during challenging times.[25] The available evidence suggests that for centuries the Fuerte valley has been inhabited by separate, decentralized Indigenous groups who bonded over shared languages and cultural practices rather than a timeless, monolithic notion of Mayo identity.[26] Although the valley was generally diverse and the groups who lived there were autonomous and intensely local, Juyya Annia was never an easy place to live. It posed challenges that Indigenous people had to confront, overcome, or adapt to, and moments of crisis could bring together villages in the valley and throughout the broader region.[27] None of the challenges Fuerte valley Indigenous communities faced, however, compared to the continuous stream of adversity beginning in the sixteenth century when Spanish armies arrived. Over the course of several hundred years, the stress and crisis caused by colonization united these Indigenous groups and facilitated a Mayo ethnogenesis—the process by which new ethnic identities emerge—and a relatively homogenous culture by the 1920s. Rather than having a centrifugal effect upon Indigenous communities— pulling them apart and folding them into Yori society—Spanish arrival and colonization had a centripetal effect and forced them to find common cause and embrace a larger pan-Mayo identity.[28]

Why did colonization help forge a vibrant Mayo identity by the early twentieth century when the same dynamics in other Indigenous populations led to genocide and ethnocide? One simple reason is that the region's arid environment and rugged natural landscape hindered large-scale development, limiting the number of Yoris in the Fuerte valley. Since 1533 there had been a small Spanish presence in the valley, spurring on the consolidation of Mayo identity, but it was not until late in the nineteenth century that Yoris came flooding into the region, looking greedily upon the natural resources and lands of Indigenous villages and rapidly accelerating Mayo ethnogenesis. The relative suddenness and size with which this wave arrived had a powerful effect on the Mayo people of the Fuerte valley, forcing them to embrace commonalities and forge a more cohesive group to combat the inevitable challenges of keeping their land, guarding their river, and protecting their cultural identity. While the Indigenous population's embrace of a Yoreme identity was, initially, more a defensive act of self-preservation than a celebration of commonalities, in the first years of the twentieth century, Fuerte valley Mayo villagers went on the offensive.[29]

In 1913 a Mayo general named Felipe Bachomo led thousands of Mayo villagers in an uprising to regain usurped ancestral lands. Bachomo had gained distinction during the first phase of the Mexican Revolution by helping Francisco Madero and other revolutionaries overthrow Porfirio Díaz. After returning home to the Fuerte valley with other Mayo soldiers, he came to find that more Indigenous lands had been usurped by outsiders while they were away. He directed his revolt against the *caciques* (local political bosses) and *hacendados* (owners of estates and plantations) of the Fuerte valley who had claimed thousands of acres of Mayo lands by force. He aimed to recover Indigenous lands, ensure the freedom of all native people, and make use of that autonomy to carry out ceremonies and other cultural practices essential to Mayo culture.[30] This revolt therefore went beyond merely land and assets and, at its heart, fought for the existence of Indigenous identity.[31] Indigenous people responded to the call and Bachomo united roughly six thousand Fuerte valley Mayo peasants from such mixed towns as Mochicahui and San Miguel, and Mayo villages like Tehueco, Pochotal, Camajoa, Los Goros, La Palma, and Camayeca into a regionally dominant fighting force.[32]

Bachomo and his followers had one foot in the past but—as Mayo people had done and would continue to do throughout the twentieth century—also kept one shrewdly in the present. They fought to keep their ancestral lands and customs and, according to oral sources, relied on their ancestors' ancient wisdom, using petroglyphs scattered throughout the countryside to tell them where they could find water running underground.[33] Familiar with the local topography and environment, they knew where to attack the forces that the hacendados and caciques sent after them and how to find the hidden fords of the Fuerte River when they needed to cross and flee.[34] They also took advantage of the fact that in many areas, heavy vegetation reduced visibility to only a few dozen yards.[35] Even though large cavalries pursued and harassed them, Bachomo's troops were never crushed in the Fuerte valley.

Yet Bachomo lived in twentieth-century Mexico and was the leader of a marginalized people who had to make difficult compromises in order to achieve larger goals. For example, Bachomo's forces needed modern weapons to take back their fields and sacred sites, but they were in short supply. However, there was one local power broker who offered them: Benjamin Francis Johnston, the owner of the United Sugar Companies and the largest landowner in the region. Bachomo negotiated a secret pact with Johnston—who had, in the decades prior, usurped their lands—in which Johnston provided the rebels with modern rifles necessary to carry out their revolt against the other Yori landowners, but in return he demanded the Indigenous army leave his sugarcane haciendas untouched.[36] While these weapons proved vital to Bachomo's success, the agreement to leave Johnston's properties alone limited the number of ancestral lands they could recover.

Though the vast majority of Bachomo's troops did not follow him when he aligned his regional, Mayo-centered revolt with Francisco "Pancho" Villa's Conventionalists in 1915, Bachomo had been a catalyst in the nearly three years he was active in the Fuerte valley, taking already emergent elements of a Mayo identity and forging them into something that Indigenous people up and down the valley could—and did—embrace. Certainly, a large part of this shared identity came from having a common enemy in powerful Yori landowners, but there was more. Bachomo's revolt was a pivotal moment in Mayo ethnogenesis, when the Indigenous people of the Fuerte valley saw themselves as part of a broader Mayo community rather than as members of local, insular villages. Ethnic identity is a social phenomenon that is both fluid and contingent on social interaction, and there are few social interactions as supportive of a shared identity as bonding together and risking your life against a common foe.[37] While it was ultimately unsuccessful, Bachomo's revolt laid the foundation of cultural unity and shared grievance on which the Mayo people would build their first hydraulic social mobilization tactics in the 1920s.[38]

With Bachomo's defeat and death in 1916, the opportunity for an immediate, violent overthrow of the social and economic structure of the valley passed and from then on Indigenous farmers approached the issue of water and land with caution. Powerful landowners remained in the valley, many of whom had been targeted by Bachomo and looked to return the favor by cutting off Mayo farmers' access to water so that they might take their land. Unable to accomplish widespread social change through military might, Indigenous communities had to settle for the victories they had secured, such as the recovery of some of their ancestral lands from Yori usurpers and the ability to keep their cultural practices intact. But out of the chaos and bloodshed of the revolution— Bachomo's revolt being just one small episode—came glimmers of hope, none so bright as the 1917 Constitution, which promised land and water redistribution. However, that glimmer was faint in the Fuerte valley, blocked by smaller farmers' largest obstacle: corporate farms.

Sugarcane Irrigation and Twentieth-Century Water Legislation

Mayo farmers' ability to access irrigation water in the mid-1920s represented a turning point in the hydraulic history of the Fuerte valley, where since the late nineteenth century large corporations like United Sugar had monopolized river water. For a quarter century after 1901, the United Sugar Companies (USCOS), a massive conglomerate of subsidiaries owned by Benjamin Francis Johnston, operated as though the Fuerte valley were its private fiefdom. In 1901, as part of an effort to prioritize foreign investment, President Porfirio Díaz (1876–1911) granted one of Johnston's subsidiaries, Sinaloa Sugar Companies, a concession for use of the water of the Fuerte River.[39] By the end of the Mexican Revolution, Johnston had gained control of most of the Fuerte River's waters to irrigate his sugarcane plantations and stood poised to consolidate his power over not just the region's agricultural economy but its politics too. While some of the USCOS's sugar fulfilled local demands or went into making products such as alcoholic beverages, most was intended for export, primarily to the United States.

By the mid-1920s, Johnston's conglomerate owned nearly fifty sugarcane-producing plantations and ranchos in the Fuerte valley, totaling over four hundred thousand acres.[40] One of the companies under the United Sugar umbrella was the Compañía Explotadora de las Aguas del Río Fuerte, or the Water Utilization Company of the Fuerte River, which acted as the irrigation arm of USCOS. In 1917 Compañía Explotadora alone used 252 million cubic meters of water from the Fuerte River to irrigate USCOS sugar plantations, for which it paid the government a sum of just over twelve thousand Mexican pesos ($US615).[41] This concession was enormous even by today's standards, and cost Johnston a pittance considering that in 1924 USCOS properties were appraised at $US17 million.[42] Even scarier for the small farmers around Johnston was that while nearly all of USCOS's four hundred thousand acres were fully irrigated, as of 1924 not all of the river's flow had been utilized yet. As USCOS engineers realized they could syphon off much more of the river they would undoubtedly look for more land. Johnston could only do this because his political power allowed United Sugar to dominate the Fuerte River and compelled the federal government to deny access to many obviously frustrated and angry small farmers.

The political favoritism the federal government showered on United Sugar created conflict from the start. In 1924 the corporation claimed that "the diversion of the flowing waters of the Fuerte River into the canal system of the United Sugar Companies has been continuous and undisputed for years."[43] But, as evidenced by their petitions to the government, farmers in the valley had disputed United Sugar diversions since 1901—the very year Díaz first bestowed Johnston with a water concession. Small farmers were not the only ones crying foul. In the closing months of 1920 large estate owner José Zakany wrote a letter to the SAYF complaining that the new irrigation concession of seven cubic meters made to Rafael Ibarra and Company (a United Sugar subsidiary located upriver from his land) basically nullified his own concession. Combined with the concessions the government had previously granted United Sugar subsidiaries Compañía Explotadora and El Aguila Company—which together totaled thirteen cubic meters a second—the new Rafael Ibarra concession essentially eliminated all available water in the river.[44]

The framers of the 1917 Constitution had included language in the document intended to end such sweetheart deals, but in the early 1920s, when Zakany wrote his petition, all it took was a letter from a United Sugar Companies lawyer to kill any new party's proposed concession.[45] Government partiality toward large corporations lasted until the National Irrigation Law of 1926 finally mandated the original spirit of the progressive 1917 Constitution. Created in order to weaken large landowners' power over land, politics, and natural resources—particularly in the northwest—the law nationalized private irrigation systems, legislated construction of additional hydraulic infrastructure, and established the Comisión Nacional de Irrigación (National Irrigation Commission, CNI), which meant that, in principle, state functionaries would consider all petitions for irrigation concessions equally.[46] These changes made it easier for new parties, particularly smallholders and companies not belonging to United Sugar, to gain access to river water in the Fuerte valley.

As part of his overall strategy to create a Mexican agrarian middle class, President Plutarco Elías Calles (1924–28) intended the irrigation law to fashion an infrastructure and distribution of water modeled after California—notably, a style of agriculture that became prominent in the president's home state of Sonora.[47] Environmental historian Mikael Wolfe points out that part of President Calles's motivation was to simultaneously avoid another revolution and spur economic development, believing that "technology would bring social liberation to the agrarian masses without the government having to radically alter existing land-tenure patterns."[48] In the meantime, increasing water availability seemed like a relatively cheap and easy way of mollifying Mexican people until the adoption and use of technology could bring real change. The president, however, miscalculated and change did not come quickly enough.[49] A decade later his successors, namely Lázaro Cárdenas, would go further and attempt to make wide-scale land reform the answer to the problem of rural poverty.

At the time, however, the irrigation law seemed to promise real change in the Fuerte valley. Previously, United Sugar irrigated their massive tracts of land with by far the largest water concessions from the Fuerte River, but in the very first year of the law, new companies and individuals started to attain irrigation rights. In 1926 alone, United Sugar opposed twenty-two new irrigation concessions but could not suppress any.[50] Many of the entities were first-time recipients and did not have the resources or capacity to use all of their concession. In order to profit from them, they resold portions of their water to small farmers like those from Los Goros.

With the metaphorical spigot to the Fuerte River now open to them for the first time in decades, how, or if, Indigenous villages secured access to water via irrigation infrastructure like dams, pumps, and canals was a decision made case by case. The answer usually depended on the kinds of resources they had available. Many simply made arrangements with those who had been granted concessions too great for their needs. This made sense as it did not require these smaller farmers to invest in irrigation technology or infrastructure themselves. Others followed a straightforward path and petitioned for their own, independent concessions— with mixed results. Still other Mayo communities took their cue from powerful adversaries like Johnston and tried to curry favoritism with government functionaries. No matter what strategy they employed, the 1926 irrigation act represented a new phase of history for the Mayo people. This was the first significant reversal of three hundred years of government oppression and the first time in modern Mexican history that Mayo farmers had the opportunity to be modern agriculturalists. From here on out, the question of whether Mayo farmers would remain on their ancestral lands and keep in contact with their sacred river would come down to whether they had access to water.

The Shifting Strategies of Margarito Aguilar

Despite the fact that diversity characterizes how Fuerte valley Mayo villages reacted to the 1926 irrigation law, most at least tried, in some fashion, to petition the Mexican state for water rights. Among the petitions various Indigenous communities filed with the Mexican federal government between 1927 and 1942, Los Goros exemplified the savviness Mayo leaders demonstrated in capturing the newly available legal and hydraulic infrastructure of the postrev-olutionary period. The village always had a close relationship to the Fuerte River, as the word *Goros* roughly translates to "place of white herons." It is a simplification of the Mayo word *corohue* or *coroche*, meaning "water birds."[51] While white herons may be most famous for their stillness, the villagers of Los Goros were anything but. Beginning with news of the 1926 irrigation law, they carried on a feverish pace of petitioning, always searching for a sympa-thetic ear who would expand their irrigation access.

In the late 1920s there were few in Los Goros more engaged—entrepreneurial even—than Margarito Aguilar. A small-holding Mayo farmer, his lands were not significantly different than many other autonomous, private farmers in the area, but Aguilar had a keenness that belied his lack of formal schooling.[52] Through the latter years of the 1920s Aguilar learned a great deal about secur-ing water and land rights for himself and his entire village, an education that would serve him well a half-decade later when he became the committee executive of his ejido. He brought a steady hand as Los Goros navigated the waters and politics of the post-revolutionary state.

Aguilar first appears in official state records after he attempted to attain water rights to irrigate his small property. On January 28, 1927, Aguilar submitted a petition to the Ministry of Agri-culture and Development (SAYF) asking to draw 150,000 annual cubic meters of the calm waters of the Fuerte River using a pump owned by Lorenzo Valdés and Company, an agricultural corpo-ration.[53] Aguilar was not alone that year, as several other small farmers in the Fuerte valley looked to take advantage of the 1926 Law of Irrigation with Federal Waters, but he has the distinction of being the first recorded Mayo farmer to petition for such rights. The request was suspicious, however, as the amount far exceeded the irrigation needs of a small farmer. It turned out that Aguilar sought to procure this concession for Valdés and Company, who intended to resell this water to small farmers, including Aguilar.

At this point, Aguilar's only chance to physically withdraw water was through this large corporation, so he was willing to fabricate his intentions. He knew the state wanted to help small farmers like him and that it shied away from granting huge concessions for large corporations like Lorenzo Valdés's, so he and his brothers acted as the recipients of the irrigation water while Valdés and Company provided the capital and know-how. At first glance this might seem a strange union, but the reality was that though the 1926 irrigation law had opened up concessions for all farmers in principle, only those with the financial capital to purchase and maintain expensive water pumps could actually draw water from the Fuerte River.[54] At the same time, under the new law corporations such as Valdés and Company needed additional irrigation but were less likely than small farmers such as Aguilar to get it. None of this fooled the SAYF, who responded to Aguilar's petition four months later, telling him that it would not approve his request and recommending that he and other farmers form a cooperative and reapply for rights to the rough but easier to obtain waters of the Fuerte River.[55] The Ministry also suggested that to prevent exploitation, the petitioners should disassociate themselves from Valdés and Company which was rumored to charge 40 percent of farmer's harvests in exchange for irrigation water.[56]

Aguilar heeded the advice and responded that November with another, more modest, petition to the SAYF, this time asking for the right to utilize irrigation water from the rough waters of the Fuerte River. Yet he made clear he still intended to work with Valdés and Company: "We have formed a cooperative society with Valdés and Company, and other small farmers. Our plots barely support our families, we cannot afford to purchase a pump or maintain its upkeep. The company does not charge 40 percent of farmer's harvests for water. We only pay 25 percent."[57] Here, in a few simple words, lay the paradox of the 1917 Constitution and the 1926 irrigation law, both of which intended to help end rural poverty. Water was undoubtedly more available, but it was far from free. For farmers like the Aguilar bothers, it had to be maddeningly frustrating that the river was so close and yet, from the perspective of their fields, so far away.[58] And though 25 percent of a crop's yield was far from the extortionist 40 percent the SAYF feared, it was still steep enough to ensure that small farmers would only ever just get by.

Though the frustration over limited options in the Fuerte valley undoubtedly came from Aguilar, it is likely that someone else, possibly a representative of Lorenzo Valdés, wrote the letter. The knowledge of technical details regarding water contracts in the letter far exceeds most petitions written by someone from the general public. The legalistic tone of the letter is also suspicious, for Aguilar addressed each and every concern that the SAYF raised previously. For instance, the Ministry had suggested that the small farmers form a cooperative, and he responded by saying that their arrangement with Valdés and Company constituted a cooperative.[59] Regardless of who authored the letter, it clearly had Aguilar's backing, for at that moment financially strapped farmers and villages had no choice but to rely on corporations like Valdés and Company for irrigation water.

The example of the Aguilar brothers and Valdés and Company demonstrates that Mayo communities and individuals had no compunction about exploiting loopholes in the system to take their destiny into their own hands. It also warns against generalizing too much about Yori-Yoreme opposition. While Valdés and Company essentially used Aguilar as a proxy in order to gain irrigation benefits, it treated him—and other Mayo farmers—far better than other companies.[60] It dealt with the Aguilar brothers ethically and offered them an alternative to wage labor, proving that within the Fuerte valley—though there were certainly some despotic, highhanded corporate practices—there were others based on cooperation and mutual benefit.

After the SAYF denied the Mayo farmers' second petition, Valdés and Company admitted that it had previously sold water to farmers such as Aguilar illegally and then attempted to establish full water rights in its own name.[61] This admission, along with supplemental documents, show that despite the implementation of the 1926 irrigation law—specifically designed to open up new water concessions for smallholders and villages—water was not going to those who needed it most. Though corporations were no longer favored by the state and even small farmers now enjoyed equality of opportunity, this did not translate into equality of outcome. To achieve that required actual investment in equipment and capital that Mayo communities and individuals did not have and state agencies such as the CNI or the SAYF were unwilling to undertake.

Instead, Indigenous farmers and entire villages relied on second parties with irrigation concessions—often, as was the case with the Aguilar brothers, large corporations—to sell them water in the 1920s and 1930s. Sometimes the relations between Mayo famers and Yori water providers were amicable and mutually beneficial. Margarito Aguilar's efforts in 1927 were the first documented examples of Fuerte valley Mayo farmers attempting to legally secure the use of modern irrigation infrastructure, yet the documents also reveal the ease by which Aguilar had previously purchased water illegally—undoubtedly an action that other Indigenous farmers had taken. The 1926 irrigation law ended up creating strange bedfellows, but for Mayo farmers like the Aguilars this was of little importance. If they had to buy water illegally or partner with a Yori-led corporation that had done them no favors before 1926 and intended to exploit the Fuerte River as a natural resource, they would. In the end what mattered was feeding their families, keeping a hold on the land their people had lived on for generations, and being near the river that centered their world. If the Mexican government was only offering them partial remedies, they were creative and savvy enough to find the rest on their own.

Los Goros and Camayeca's More Cohesive Approach to Irrigation Infrastructure

Since the first appearance of the Spanish, Mayo life had been marked by fluidity and strategic adaptation, and the postrevolutionary period was no different. If partnerships between private parties, like those between the Aguilar brothers and Lorenzo Valdés and Company, did not work, they would have to try other approaches. Sometime in the early 1930s the Mayo farmers of Los Goros struck upon an idea: If they could not secure water concessions as individual farmers, then perhaps they would have more luck portray-

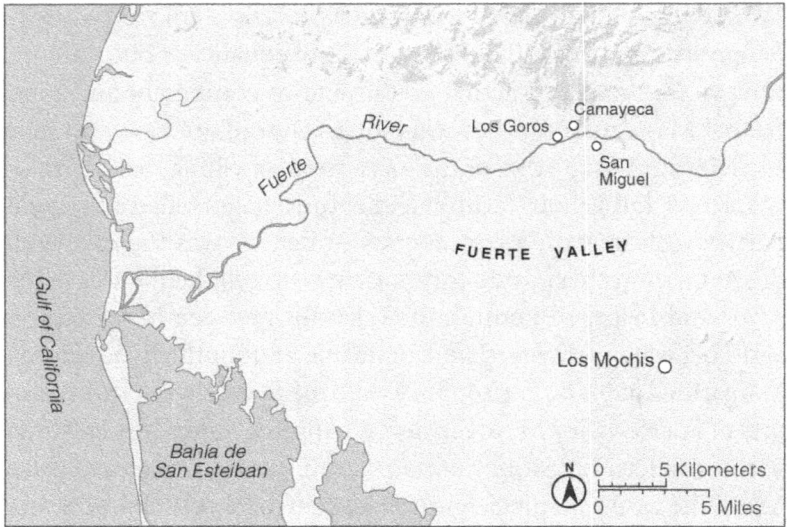

2. Los Goros and Camayeca on the Fuerte River.
Mapped by Pease Press Cartography.

ing themselves as a community whose origins stretched back to before modern, large-scale agriculture even appeared in the region. Their greatest asset might not be that they were hardworking, small farmers in a region dominated by large agricultural companies (which they were), but that they were an Indigenous community. If being native to the land was an asset the government sought to promote, then perhaps the recognition that their corner of the valley was primarily Indigenous would make the government more likely to listen to their petition.

In May 1931 the self-defined *indígenas* (Indigenous) agrarian leaders from Los Goros and Camayeca sent a petition to the SAYF. They claimed to be the owners of eighteen lots of land they inherited from their grandparents, but their land titles, originally authorized by President Benito Juárez (1858–72), had purportedly disappeared in the chaos of the Mexican Revolution. Their holdings amounted to roughly 150 hectares, of which 140 were fit for cultivation, but they needed water. They collectively asked the SAYF not to grant them a concession but instead to extend one to their Yori neigh-

bors. Lacking the capital to invest in their own hydraulic infrastructure, the leaders explained they had agreed to pay 20 percent
of their annual harvest to a small, Yori farmer, Juan Kelly (Kellis
in the initial petition), in exchange for use of his water pump.[62] If
the SAYF would grant a sufficient concession to Kelly, the leaders
declared, they could use his ten-inch water pump to draw water,
irrigate their crops year-round, and end their reliance on incon-
sistent rainfall.[63]

It is no coincidence that the two communities referred to themselves as indígenas throughout the entire petition process. If Kelly
came to the deal with a pump that Mayo farmers needed, the communities came to the deal with the political capital he needed. Kelly
had unsuccessfully petitioned the SAYF for a water concession just
a year before, but by the early 1930s indigenismo was beginning to
gather steam in Mexico.[64] As historian Christopher Boyer defines
it, postrevolutionary indigenismo was "a political and intellectual
movement suggesting that native culture had an intrinsic value
and that the state bore a responsibility to lift Indian communities
out of poverty."[65] As attuned to the shifting winds of power as their
Mayo forebears, the farmers of Los Goros and Camayeca understood the utility in classifying themselves as indígenas. Not only
could they use it as leverage to secure irrigation access but, given
that their titles were lost, if the state responded positively to their
petition, it could only help them further secure their land claim.

Yet, as the official documents make evident, the leaders of Los
Goros and Camayeca were somewhat unique in the way they
referred to themselves as indígenas. The tendency to self-represent
as Indigenous was not very common in this region and time period.
Before the first stirrings of indigenismo, the Mayo people of the
Fuerte valley were just that: Mayo. Their world was still largely
bound by the valley, and their connection to other Indigenous
groups across the country, while recognized, remained largely an
abstraction. Indeed, the term indígena hardly arose before the early
1930s in northern Sinaloa. Tellingly, it did not last long. The notion
of indigenismo never fully caught on in the Fuerte valley; the federal government never recognized Mayo rights to land and water

based on ethnic homogeneity in the early to mid-twentieth century. As it became clear that indigenismo would do them no favors, Mayo petitions dropped references to being indígena. Yet when they thought it might help, Mayo leaders happily embraced it.[66]

Ironically, though Aguilar and the other Mayo leaders thought they might exploit indigenismo, obscuring their indígena status actually served them better on occasion. On May 13, the same day they sent their petition to the SAyF, they mailed a copy to Mexican president Pascual Ortiz Rubio. Accompanying the letter, still addressed to the SAyF, was a summary of the petition written on letterhead from the Federación de Agrupaciones Agrarias del Río Fuerte (Federation of Farmer Groups of the Fuerte River). They did not, however, identify themselves as indígenas in the summary, as they had in the accompanying petition to the SAyF.[67] The correspondence apparently made an impression on Mexico's president, who thought that a small community of ethnically ambiguous farmers had devised a solution out of their own poverty. His secretary penned a letter directly to the SAyF ten days later urging their office to resolve this manner using terms of "strict justice."[68] While Ortiz Rubio did not demand the SAyF grant the concession, his interest in the situation clearly signaled that he was putting his influence behind the community's cause. While the SAyF did not award Los Goros a concession based on this petition, a letter from the president's office was no small matter. It meant that the wheels of Mexican bureaucracy would turn much faster in the case of Los Goros's petitions, giving their leaders the confidence to try new tactics.

For the owners of the eighteen individual plots cited in the petition it would be a victory just to have their names appear as part of established communities in official government documents. Families and companies that owned large amounts of land during the Díaz regime (1876–1910) found it much easier to expropriate the lands of individual smallholders with undocumented or dubious titles than it was to confiscate the property of communities recognized by the federal government.[69] There was at least one more angle to securing the concession. Not only did individual landowners secure official recognition but so too did the villages of Los Goros and Camayeca. Although both communities had existed since before the arrival of the Spanish, they had not officially existed in the eyes of the Mexican government. Now that they did, leaders in both likely hoped that the federal government would be more willing to grant them an ejido. At the same time that he was leading a push for water rights, Aguilar was petitioning for Los Goros to receive a *dotación* (communal land grant), which, at this time, would have given the village another avenue to pursue further water concessions. Aguilar and other village leaders hoped that the Mexican state would grant at least one, if not both, requests.

After the president sent his directive, the SAYF mailed another letter to Aguilar on May 26 explaining a miscommunication between the agency, Kelly, and the villages. This letter, which constituted the state's continued response to the village's request, stated that Kelly only needed to file a new petition in order to receive a concession. It appears that Aguilar never passed this information to Kelly and it remains a mystery why. Both Los Goros and Camayeca had previously given Kelly written permission to take irrigation waters from the Fuerte River on their behalf. All Kelly had to do was resubmit his original request from December 1930 and attach the letter of approval from the two communities' leaders. No doubt surprised, the SAYF soon received their letter in a return-to-sender envelope. Whether the villagers of Los Goros never saw the letter addressed to Aguilar or chose to ignore it is unclear.[70]

The evidence points to Aguilar pursuing his own route to a better deal and squeezing Kelly out of negotiations with state functionaries. Perhaps Mayo leaders felt that a presidential order would expedite their request and grant them water directly. Having rights to draw water straight from the Fuerte River would have allowed Mayo leaders to turn to whichever pump provider was willing to give them the best deal, ending their reliance on Kelly. They could use this concession to leverage a more advantageous deal for the use of Kelly's pump. The fact that all of Los Goros's petitions from that point did not include Kelly's name strongly indicates that this was their intent. If so, Aguilar and other Mayo leaders were shrewd as well as tenacious. Throughout this process Indigenous leaders continued to present petitions, with each successive correspondence exploring new language and terms that they hoped would give them the best opportunity to legally receive access to a water concession.

On August 30, 1931, Los Goros's leaders submitted the last in their series of petitions. It represented an astute effort to appeal to postrevolutionary state functionaries in order to attain land and water concessions. The new petition, sent directly to President Ortiz Rubio, was very similar to the original submitted in May but with notable changes. This letter asked directly for a water concession and completely omitted Kelly's name. The letterhead now announced the village's membership in a new group, the Comité Particular Ejecutivo Agrario de Los Goros y Camayeca (Executive Agrarian Committee), suggesting that the communities' leaders had complied with land reform legislation to create an ejido.[71] They had also apparently become members of the Federación Sindicalista de Obreros y Campesinos de la Zona Norte del Estado de Sinaloa (Trade Union Federation of Workers and Peasants of Northern Sinaloa).[72] Inclusion in this union was most likely an attempt to show the state that they were willing to align with non-Indigenous Mexican campesinos and that they embraced the idea that strong unions would shape Mexico's future. Earlier that year the federal government helped empower labor unions by passing the Ley Federal de Trabajo or Federal Labor Law, which established boards of conciliation and arbitration made up of representatives of the government, employers, and labor unions.[73] Much like how they imagined they might curry favor by invoking the language of indigenismo earlier on, the leaders of Los Goros now tested the political winds and determined that the current administration favored unions and so then they would too. Whatever kind of ideal farmer the federal government desired they would become if only to remain secure in their homes and lands.

By August, after several iterations of correspondence, leaders of

Los Goros and Camayeca seemed willing to use various rhetorical strategies to gain formal access to land and water. They no longer announced their indígena status but quietly explained that since their grandparents and parents were Indigenous (allowing them to tactfully avoid stating outright that they were too), they had occupied the lands of Los Goros and Camayeca—the same lots where they currently resided—since time immemorial and that "all of the occupants of our lands . . . want irrigation to improve our harvest yields. We understand that before we can request a water concession, we first need to validate ownership of our land, because we lack formal titles."[74] But despite their willingness to align with primarily Yori campesino groups and use the state's land reform process, their inability to produce land titles proved the determining factor in being denied irrigation concessions.[75] While Article 27 of the 1917 Constitution encouraged communities to apply for a land dotación—which, if granted, ensured an ejido—the majority of these requests were rejected until the mid-1930s.[76] The state ultimately denied both Los Goros's ejidal request and the petition for a water concession in 1931.

From a historical perspective, losing a potential water concession was less momentous than the fact that in the early 1930s the farmers of Los Goros and Camayeca were willing to collaborate with Yori farmers like Juan Kelly. No longer were all Yoris viewed as enemies bent on destroying their culture and stealing their land. When asked specifically about these early 1930s petitions, Alejandro Inzunza provided a story that confirmed the value of unity across ethnic boundaries. He claimed, "Kelly came to our village to congratulate us when we got water rights. He was a nice man with a great smile."[77] Old enough to remember Kelly, Inzunza's brief recollection hints at a historical reality not captured in the SAYF's archives. First, the two villages eventually secured water in the period but not through the SAYF, suggesting that they, along with Kelly, worked through more informal, even illegal, channels. Second, this historical memory demonstrates the enduring importance of water within Mayo knowledge both then and now. Third, during the afterglow of the revolution, that a Yori farmer like Kelly could come and congratulate his Mayo neighbors on their success suggests that they were not just friendly but may have recognized themselves as confederates who were largely in the same position in regards to the government.[78] This is a good example of the Yori-Yoreme collaboration that was somewhat common in the postrevolutionary era but—while still existing—became less frequent in the postwar period as historical antagonisms returned.[79]

By the 1930s some Mayo leaders began to understand an important lesson of the postrevolutionary period: though armed revolt was no longer an option, the state offered at least minimal opportunities. Aguilar's efforts, after all, only failed on the technicality of missing land titles, and the legal system of petitions could provide access to new irrigation infrastructure and technology. Alejandro Inzunza recalled, "Our leaders understood the legal system, and used it to defend our rights."[80] As these petitions attest, the leaders of Los Goros adapted quite well to the postrevolutionary state's legal system. But they were not alone. Several other Mayo communities in the Fuerte valley, including Bamoa and La Palma, also petitioned the Mexican state for access to water rights.[81]

Still, barriers existed for Mayo villages, ones the state was unable or unwilling to do much about. In addition to the legal issue of a lack of property titles, there was still the high cost of pumps and other hydraulic infrastructure. While Mayo farmers of Los Goros were not officially able to secure irrigation concessions by this point, they nevertheless had water. However, because how they accessed the water was likely illegal and hidden from the government, later documents are unclear about whether leaders of Los Goros reached an agreement with another party or used Kelly's pumps.[82] Had they elected for the latter this meant that despite their predilection for using the petitions system already set in place, they were not above continuing to circumvent established legal channels and would tack against any wind as they navigated obstacles in order to protect their harvests and, ultimately, their identity.[83]

As would be the case for the rest of the century, setbacks did not stop Mayo leaders, but in the unique political climate of the postrevolutionary years they were particularly tenacious. For example, on March 14, 1932, a little more than six months after his last, unsuccessful petition for land and water rights, Margarito Aguilar was back to writing the sAYF. In this new correspondence, he complained about the Lorenzo Valdés and Company's Canal de Avenidas. Just a few short years before the company had been an ally of Aguilar—he had said it was a friend to small farmers—but now it was a nuisance. A canal the company had built long ago ran right through the property of Los Goros and Camayeca but, Aguilar alleged, had been out of service since December 1925, when Valdés and Company began using a pump to draw water from the Fuerte River. Citing the 1930 Law of Waters of National Property, Aguilar requested the sAYF cancel the company's right to use the canal so that it could be demolished.[84] Article 34 of the new law addressed the revocation of water concessions, and state in its very first paragraph that a water concession could be revoked if it had not been in use for a period of three consecutive years.[85] Believing he was well within his rights to do so, Aguilar asked on behalf of both villages for the government to grant his request.

Having waited five months with no response, Aguilar sent a more detailed follow-up letter to the sAYF in August 1932. He stated that in July, leaders of the two villages informed local officials of their intent to demolish the Canal de Avenidas and reclaim community member lands. In an apparent attempt to defend the interests of the corporation over the Indigenous villages, the Municipal Commissioner of Cachoana stepped in and thwarted these plans. Aguilar, in turn, went over the commissioner's head to the sAYF, repeating his earlier request that the agency allow villagers to demolish the canal and recover their properties.[86]

What had happened in the five years since Aguilar had celebrated the role Lorenzo Valdés and Company played in the Fuerte valley? There is no record of any sharp animosity arising from either side. The fact was that Lorenzo Valdés and Company had once been a partner, but that moment had passed. Leaders like Aguilar had to prioritize what was best for their community and sometimes did so out of sheer determination to overcome all obstacles. With water secure from another source—likely a better albeit illegal arrangement with Kelly—Aguilar could turn back to the perennial problem of reclaiming land that had been stolen earlier when the government neglected Mayo people's interests.

Whether through impatience or concern that his previous arguments were not compelling enough, ten days later Aguilar sent a third petition riddled with vague inaccuracies. In addition to stressing that the canal was located on ejidal lands when it was not, Aguilar now explicitly pointed out that because of its location it would fall under the jurisdiction of the SAYF. Aguilar also falsely claimed that the SAYF dictated an agreement a few months earlier in April in which the temporary water permit assigned to Valdés and Company was declared null and void.[87] Based on the supporting materials, it is unlikely that the SAYF actually rescinded Valdés and Company's water rights, so it is curious that Aguilar would make such an assertion when the SAYF could just check their records and verify that this was false. The simplest explanation was that he was bluffing. A shrewd leader who was willing to bend the rules and even lie to secure the safety and success of his village, Aguilar might have been banking on the incompetency of the agency and hoping that he might sway a receptive state functionary to entertain or even endorse his claims about the canal. Or, if not, he might have been turning the problem of no land titles to his advantage. With no clear title, there were often no clear boundaries between properties, and it might be the case that some state functionaries would be at least mildly receptive to his requests.[88] No record exists of the SAYF's final verdict in the matter, but even if Aguilar lost, it is doubtful that he gave up.

Using the Land to Secure the Water

From the perspective of Mayo people, the land of the Fuerte valley and the water of the Fuerte River were, from the first evidence we have, interconnected. One existed only in the presence of the other with Mayo villages such as Los Goros there to safeguard both. It is no wonder then, that Mayo leaders took full advantage of the sympathetic political climate after the revolution to secure both simultaneously. Along with the petitions they sent for water,

Los Goros also submitted several to the SAYF asking for land. The first of these was in July 1931, in which these leaders requested a land dotación that would have ceded an ejido (communal land tract) to the village.[89] In a rhetorical tone commonly used by other communities seeking the same land rights, the Los Goros ejidal petition argued that the purpose of the postrevolutionary government should be to fulfill the promises of the revolution. Such promises, according to Aguilar and the other Mayo leaders, consisted of returning land and water rights to those who had been cheated out of them in the past.[90]

By 1934 Los Goros found an ally who eventually helped them attain tenuous access to land and irrigation water. Scholars have written extensively about President Lázaro Cárdenas's (1934–40) progressive policies, showing what he accomplished as well as the shortcomings of his penchant for increased state control, and this was no less true in the Fuerte valley.[91] For instance, the 1934 Agrarian Code allowed the state to redefine "public interest" to include water redistribution.[92] Cárdenas used these powers to cede water and land to communities like Los Goros in the form of an ejido. This was a temporary victory for several Mayo villagers, as such strong governmental control also permitted future state functionaries (many of whom would not be as sympathetic to ejidal interests, particularly after Cárdenas left office in 1940) to intervene more directly in the management of land and water within such communities.[93]

It took six more years and at least five additional ejidal petitions, but on July 21, 1937, a presidential resolution granted Los Goros a dotación that came with something as valuable as (and perhaps even more valuable than) the land: a significant amount of irrigation water.[94] A total of 870 of the 1,480 hectares that the government granted Los Goros had been previously irrigated by pumps. While this was a substantial irrigation concession compared to what other ejidos in the region received, the dotación did not include the expensive pumps needed to draw water from the river.[95] This meant that the new ejido would have to make a deal with another, more well-off farmer who had a pump and who, in turn, would demand a portion of their crops. So, while the federal government may have thought it was being generous in its granting of both land and water rights to Los Goros, leaders in the village knew otherwise. Further, they were aware in a way the government apparently was not that victories were fleeting, relationships with irrigation providers tenuous (and typically exploitive), and water rights for Indigenous farmers could be reduced at any time. So they pressed on, continuing to petition the federal government for additional land and water access.

Their efforts paid off a year later, but only to an extent. On September 21, 1938, the Mexican state awarded Los Goros an *ampliación* (land extension) of 1,103 hectares, but this time only 116 hectares had secured irrigation, enough to serve the needs of a mere 68 ejidatarios. The limited amount of irrigated land (around 10 percent of the total) suggests that state officials were appeasing this tenacious village. The concession gave the politically active village of Los Goros just enough to keep it aligned with the state while not sacrificing too much water at the expense of local businesses and Yori landowners along the river.[96]

The land distributed to the Los Goros ejido through dotación and ampliación was located next to the Mayo small property owners of the same community. This geographic proximity had two important consequences.[97] First, it extended the ejido's implicit authority far beyond its formal, legal boundaries. Because some small property owners like Aguilar were also part of the ejido, the Los Goros community, for all purposes, included these private lands too. Second, large swaths of the dotación included sacred sites and having communal access to them again kept their community united. Most of Los Goros's ejidal plots came from land that had been confiscated by large landowners. Yet though their holdings had been reduced, the Mayo farmers who had been cheated had not strayed far—many of these farmers had holdings that butted right against the confiscated lands. When the government returned land to them in the form of dotación and ampliación they went right back to using it to procure materials necessary to carry out rituals and as ritual spaces.[98] With ejidal title in hand, none of their neighbors—not a larger landholder, not a corporation—could deny the villagers the access that had been denied them for over a generation.

A particularly ingenious demonstration of hydraulic social mobilization, the dotación and ampliación requests were always first and foremost about securing water rights. In that sense these Mayo farmers were not much different from their Yori neighbors. But the purposes these farmers intended to use the water for could not have been more different. Agricultural ecologist Gary Paul Nabhan asserts that how much concern cultures show for the ecological integrity of food producing plants is reflective of the spiritual life of that culture.[99] In this sense, Mayo spiritual life was very much alive and well, for while Mayo farmers—like their Yori neighbors—adopted modern irrigation infrastructure into their farming, their goals differed drastically. Mayo people's spiritual connection to the land and water preserved their identity, so by protecting the land and water they protected their Indigenous identity.

Access to the river shore proved beneficial for Los Goros as a community on both sacred and profane levels. It ensured villagers could perform religious ceremonies along the river and collect the raw materials necessary to conduct sacred rituals. In a secular sense, having control of the river front meant that companies and Yori individuals would legally need to ask these Indigenous smallholders for permission to build irrigation infrastructure on their land. Granted, some of these Mayo ejidatarios, such as the Aguilar brothers, also owned private property and had years of experience dealing with water providers and negotiating with both Yoris and the Mexican state for the use of canals, pumps, and aqueducts. This experience allowed Los Goros farmers to understand the intricacies of irrigation technologies, making it easier to accept them into their practices when they became ejidatarios.

All of the small property owners and ejidatarios of Los Goros were Mayo, but not all small property owners were ejidatarios and, therefore, not all were guaranteed water. Unlike the ejidatarios of Los Goros, small property owners in the village had to secure their own water rights, and in January 1938 they collectively signed an agreement with a Yori farmer named Cecilio Román to receive water from his pump in Camayeca in exchange for 20 percent of their harvest. These smallholders then wrote a letter in the same month asking the SAYF for permission to execute this deal and receive irrigation water from Román's pump. The petition explained that they were forty-two farmers who had been in possession of their land for more than thirty years and whose holdings ranged from one hectare to eight hectares.[100]

Yet the largest landowner of the group was none other than Margarito Aguilar, who held 8.2 hectares and was also an ejidatario.[101] As he had water rights already through the ejido, Aguilar's presence among the forty-two farmers demands explanation. One reason may be that it fell to leaders like him to keep the peace in the village while benefiting himself. He was one of the larger smallholders and a village leader, but his efforts to improve prospects for Los Goros invariably improved his own as well. His leadership in petitioning for an ejido benefitted everyone in the village, especially landless villagers, but it also meant that he too received a portion of irrigated ejidal land. Likewise, when the smallholders whose lands would not receive ejido irrigation sought redress, Aguilar crafted a deal that secured them—and his non-ejido lands—irrigation. His self-interest and benevolence appear to have never tripped the other up.[102]

Irrigation Infrastructure as Indigenous Heritage

As the 1930s moved into the 1940s many things changed in Mexico, but in the Fuerte valley at least one thing did not: irrigation agreements remained fickle, fragile things. Four years after he had collaborated with Mayo farmers, Cecilio Román pivoted and found a better partner. In October 1942 he joined with Juan and Rosario Valdés in founding the Compañia Irrigadora del Río del Fuerte (Irrigation Company of the Fuerte River). This water distribution company intended to widen a canal that the villagers of Los Goros had originally constructed in the 1930s on Mayo private properties.[103]

Company administrators soon realized that since the canal was located on the property of some of the smallholders of Los Goros they would need these Mayo farmers' permission to broaden it, and they initially offered to meet with the village's leaders in order to discuss an arrangement.[104] However, likely emboldened by local politicians who were willing to bend rules in its favor, the company reneged on the offer to meet and informed the villagers that it did not need their permission; it would simply expropriate their lands and proceed with construction. Such blatant disregard for Indigenous rights had never completely ended, even during this era of increased campesino rights, but the company's dismissal of the Mayo farmers signaled the end of benevolent policies of the 1930s. As the 1940s opened, it was subtly becoming clear that a golden era had passed; what would take its place was not, as yet, obvious. The leaders of Los Goros were disappointed by the company's refusal to even negotiate, but they had to have been completely disheartened by the response from the office of the municipal president. When they traveled to Los Mochis to discuss the matter with him, the president's lawyer simply threatened to expropriate their lands. That he also went on to say the municipal president's office was ready to provide "help" in a completely fair and legal manner was no consolation. The Los Goros farmers could read the writing on the wall.[105]

These Mayo leaders returned to their homes and penned a letter to the sayf complaining about the treatment they had suffered and stating that they would not let the irrigation company abuse their properties in order to gain more space for the canal. "We are in no way intransigent," they informed the sayf, "but we are being forced into signing a one-sided contract that would hurt our interests as small property owners, and leave us in a state of destitution."[106] The very place—the municipal president's office—where the Indigenous smallholders sought confirmation that they were integral members of the future of postrevolutionary society was where they were rudely reminded that some local officials still viewed them as second-class citizens and, at worst, as savage Indians.

In addition to complaints about the abuses and corruption of local officials, the letter to the SAYF included a revealing phrase, one that hints at shifting Mayo attitudes to physical hydraulic infrastructure and how it was becoming not merely an incidental tool to preserve their identity and world but a part of their culture. The letter stated, "We are in the best disposition to sign a contract. We also need to take into account the special circumstances of first, having built the canal ourselves, and second, our desire to guarantee our *patrimonio*."[107] This term, patrimonio (patrimony), is a fascinating choice of words. On one level, it referred to property and, as the canal ran through their land and they had constructed it, it was theirs. Yet patrimonio's other meaning—heritage or legacy—applied equally. The canal helped increase the surface area under cultivation, allowing them to keep their community productive and intact. It had become an artery running through the village and was inseparable from their hopes that their children would carry on Mayo traditions and safeguard their village's identity. The canal was more than a useful interloper crossing the village; the canal was part of the village.

The canal's status in the community did not reach the esteemed levels of the forests or river, since Mayo people believed that these were living, breathing entities that they had developed relationships with over several centuries, yet the canal was more than a mere ditch bringing in an agricultural input. While the villagers of Los Goros, like their Yori neighbors, used the canal to produce crops for subsistence purposes, the canal also allowed them to maintain a spiritual and cultural connection to the Fuerte River. In so doing, it had become part of their Mayo heritage. Mayo cultural resiliency lay in its adaptability and flexibility, and while no one would have mistaken a canal running past their village for the actual Fuerte River, for the Mayo people of Los Goros the difference between the two was one of degrees and not categorical.[108]

Cecilio Román and the Valdezes never bothered themselves with how Mayo people used or appreciated the canal. For them, it was an opportunity to expand their personal wealth, and they knew, despite the grand statements being made at the federal level, they could rely on local authorities turning not just a blind eye to their illegal actions but, in this case, actively facilitating them. Indeed, buying and selling the Fuerte River's water was always a murky business, but this went further than typical. Internal SAYF memos suggest that there was no record of Román or this irrigation company ever having water rights or the permission to carry out hydraulic construction plans, but even though they did not possess permits to commence construction, local politicians still allowed these Yori developers to proceed.[109] While the nation claimed it was moving forward from past injustices, legislation could not end the legacy of greed and mistreatment of Indigenous communities that carried on throughout Mexico.

After a flurry of internal SAYF memos, no further documents reveal what steps the agency took, if any, to stop Román and the irrigation company from pursuing their illegal actions. In December 1942 the small property owners of Los Goros sent a follow-up letter to the SAYF saying that they had not received a response to their previous complaint. They added that they were indígenas who owned their land since time immemorial and stated, "Hopefully our written acknowledgment will resolve this matter. We do not want our rights violated by the ambitious profits sought by this company that is protected by powerful influences, in order to carry out their sinister purposes in relation to their pretension."[110] This was the last complaint Los Goros farmers sent to the SAYF, suggesting that the agency put a halt to the development plans. But they certainly did not do so because the authors identified as indígenas. The time when that identity curried political favor had long passed and never had much impact in the Fuerte valley. Their being Indigenous was likely incidental to the SAYF. Rather, what is more notable about the episode is that this would be one of the last times the agency prioritized the water rights of small farmers (especially Mayo smallholders) in the 1940s.[111] While some government functionaries may still have cared about equity across ethnic lines, at the very least they were willing to adhere to the law. From this moment on, the agency would either engage in bureaucratic battles with other agencies in the region, or, with disturbing regularity, bend the law to suit the needs of corporations, large farmers, or cooperatives.

Conclusion

The history of Los Goros demonstrates how one Mayo village used all the tools at its disposal to confront obstacles. While not all Mayo villages engaged with the state, corporations, and individuals as actively as Los Goros, archival evidence reveals that other communities followed similar strategies. Los Goros therefore serves as an apt case study that reveals how Indigenous leaders had to perpetually change tactics to keep up with the ever-shifting political and economic realities around them. The strategies that the smallholders and ejidatarios of Los Goros used to gain access to irrigation infrastructure shows that Mayo villagers were as adaptable in the early twentieth century as they had been for the previous four hundred years. Margarito Aguilar was just one more in a long line of Mayo leaders searching, scheming, and wrangling to get for his community what it needed. He and other Mayo leaders were ready to do whatever it took and make deals with whomever was available in order to keep the Fuerte River flowing through their lives.

Mayo petitions for water and land rights did not differ drastically from those submitted by Yori campesinos seeking similar privileges, yet the nascent Yori communities—and ejidos created by state functionaries lumping campesinos together—did not have the same historical and symbolic ties to land and water as Indigenous villages. Mayo villagers even bestowed a degree of reverence upon irrigation technologies because they had become crucial to community survival. There is no parallel to this in the culture of their Yori neighbors. For many Yori farmers in the Fuerte valley, the region was just one of many in Mexico that was attractive because it promised profit. That was not the case for the Mayo people of villages like Los Goros.[112] For them, this land was the only place in the world where they belonged, and they would do whatever it took to stay next to the river that centered their culture.

People like Margarito Aguilar and his brothers made sure this happened; he formed and dropped alliances in accordance with how well they achieved the goal of remaining. He demanded the attention of government agencies when he needed it but did not hesitate to sneak around official rules at opportune moments. In short, the bond that he and his fellow Yoremes shared with the river was stronger than any government decree or contract with a Yori. In this sense, he was one more in a series of effective Mayo leaders that stretched back before European history began in the Fuerte valley. He did not capture the fame or notoriety of the rebel leader Felipe Bachomo, but like many other Mayo leaders before him, Aguilar's work was crucial to his community and its efforts to survive and maintain their vigilance over the river.

We know nothing of Margarito Aguilar's formal education, but he clearly learned a timeless lesson: Mayo identity, like the Fuerte River, flowed and changed and yet always remained. A great deal of Aguilar's success was tied to the historical moment in which he lived. From 1927 to roughly 1942 Mayo farmers enjoyed a period of stability and relative prosperity, and it was in some measure because, for the first time since the Spanish arrived, they enjoyed a degree of fairness. The government crafted laws that promised equal and honest treatment and authorities actually enforced them. But this golden moment would not last even a generation. Beginning in the early 1940s, access to the legal system and irrigation became increasingly difficult for Mayo farmers to attain, signaling a transition into a new era in which they would have less control over their water resources.

Between 1941 and 1943 Mexico invested 10 percent of its federal expenditures into irrigation projects—an unprecedented sum globally.[113] In return, the federal government expected a return on this investment and therefore prioritized large scale agriculture over subsistence farming. In the Fuerte valley older patterns of abuse that had been common a generation or more before started to reassert themselves as Yoris conspired with indifferent and even hostile local and federal agencies to defraud and pressure Mayo people into second-class citizenship. As this new, difficult era unfolded, the villagers of Los Goros would look back at the years after the revolution with longing, hoping that what had worked then might still, somehow, work again.

TWO

Sweetness and Water Power

The SICAE Sugarcane Cooperative and
Mayo Struggles for Water, 1944 to 1958

E arly in 1956 a group of Indigenous farmers stealthily made their way through acres of thick sugarcane fields surrounding El Teroque. They avoided detection from their adversaries: fellow Mayo ejidatarios who they had shared the village with for generations. After years of efforts, they concluded that they had exhausted every peaceful, legal avenue to reclaim the land and irrigation infrastructure that had been taken from them by their "white" neighbors. So on this morning they armed themselves and set out to rectify these wrongs. Their objective was to sneak out and capture the village pump that drew water from the Fuerte River, the artery of El Teroque's profitable sugarcane operation. After traveling a short distance, they soon had their first victory in years. Within a day this group accomplished what they could not for over nearly two decades: regaining access to water rights and over six hundred hectares of irrigated land that was key to both their identity and political power in their village.[1]

An ejido, one of many communal land parcels that President Lázaro Cárdenas (1934–40) granted predominately to landless farmers, was created at El Teroque in 1938. In that same year, however, the federal government created a state-backed sugarcane cooperative, the Sociedad de Interés Colectivo Agrícola Ejidal (Agricultural Society of the Collective Ejidal Interest, SICAE) that would complicate the lives of everyone living in El Teroque. The cooperative was supposed to help ejidatarios by paying them a fair wage to produce sugarcane—a crop requiring large amounts of water—full time. Though Cárdenas hoped for the majority of the ejidatarios in the Fuerte valley to join, a limited water supply forced the SICAE to accept only about five thousand members, who became known as "collectivists." This meant that there were now two groups of ejidatarios in both El Teroque and the Fuerte valley generally: those connected to the SICAE and those not.

In El Teroque the SICAE recruited only 120 fortunate and well-connected Mayo farmers to the collective, and with the SICAE's support, over the course of eighteen years this select group transformed landholding patterns in the village. When the ejido began, officials had distributed plots equally among the slightly more than 200 ejidatarios, but in time the SICAE's collectivists gained control over the ejido's irrigation resources and 2,300 hectares of its land as well. Meanwhile, the remaining 104 members of the community (also Mayo villagers who came to be known as individualists) left out were reduced to cultivating a mere 200 unirrigated hectares. SICAE officials propagated labels connoting selfishness, such as the term "individualists," to create political cover for the Mayo collectivists who supported the cooperative and to denigrate those who were left out.[2] Though Cárdenas had sought, in 1938, to better the lives of ejidatarios generally, he created an institution that drew a line through communities and showered benevolence on some but drove others to ruin.[3]

At stake in El Teroque were not just the thirty thousand tons of valuable sugarcane the contested property produced but also, more importantly, the fate of irrigation resources at the ejido. The individualists' decision to reclaim access to water by force underscores how crucial hydraulic resource control was to Indigenous autonomy.[4] It wasn't just that the individualists had been cheated out of ejido land, for whether they had a mere two hundred hectares or one thousand, none of it was worth much without water. That meant the nonaffiliated ejidatarios of El Teroque could either rely on rainwater, struggle for irrigation rights, or both. El Teroque individualists were not alone in their fight; wherever the SICAE came to power in an ejido they also gained control over its water and limited the Mayo individualists' connection to a river central to their subsistence, identity, and religious ceremonies.

Collectivists maintained an advantage over other ejidatarios by honoring an implicit agreement: in return for access to irrigation and suitable wages to harvest sugarcane, cooperative members would seize individualists' properties at the behest of the SICAE.[5] There was an ethnic component behind this divisiveness, highlighted by a phenomenon in which Yori administrators and privileged Indigenous collaborators used their power as members of a state-backed organization to impinge on other Indigenous peoples' natural resources.[6] Encroachment appears to have been specific to the unique circumstances in each ejido, but in the Fuerte valley there were generally three fronts upon which collectivists encircled individualists. First, collectivists began by planting their own sugarcane crops on fallow, communal sections. Second, the SICAE shrewdly made sure to extend cooperative membership to enough collectivists so that they would have, at the least, a slight majority in every ejido. And finally, collectivists took advantage of their numbers and operated as a political bloc in ejidal meetings. When communal land was taken or the boundary between communal land held by an individualist ejidatario was contested, the collectivists acted and voted to ensure that the collectivists' interests were always secure and individualist complaints ignored.

Once they held a firm grasp on ejidal power, collectivist leaders gradually stripped individualists of the majority of their acreage and reassigned it to collectivists. Clinging to small plots with no access to irrigation, individualist farmers struggled to both eke out a living and keep enough land under cultivation to prevent collectivists from taking their entire holding.[7] This struggle created village disharmony and forced individualists to challenge the SICAE and its local representatives, the ejidal leaders.[8] But this was no simple matter for the ejidal leadership, though loyal to the SICAE, was also part of the Mayo community. By contesting collectivist leadership, individualist Mayo farmers raised two difficult questions: Who should have access to the Fuerte River and its fertile banks? And how should Mayo farmers define their connection and responsibility toward each other?

Postrevolutionary functionaries had hoped ejidatarios would support the populist organization in exchange for gainful employment. However, by allowing only some ejidatarios to use the limited water from the Fuerte River to grow cash crops like sugarcane, the SICAE ensured a resource war. By creating a privileged collectivist group within ejidos and then actively supplying that group at the expense of individualists, the SICAE revealed itself as a clientelist organization that manufactured and then exacerbated rifts in Mayo villages. But the irony of the SICAE does not stop there. This story illustrates how a collective—allegedly created to mobilize ejidatarios—would become as commercial, profit-driven, and export-oriented in the 1940s as any of the large Yori farms had been in the decades before (and the ones that would come after). Like those Yori farms, the SICAE could be ruthless to the ejidal farmers—many of whom were Mayo—in the Fuerte valley.[9]

The SICAE would never be content until it dominated the arable land and ran enormous economies of scale through its collectivist members. Individualist Mayo farmers responded to this threat by joining campesino advocacy groups, petitioning the government, and modifying the natural landscape, but none of these tactics were as aggressive as those used by their peers in El Teroque.[10] This chapter, along with the following three, challenge Mexicanist scholarship on campesino political and social movements in the post-Cárdenas mid-twentieth century that has overlooked the importance of hydraulic social mobilization—especially its more extreme, physically aggressive forms.[11] By periodizing the evolution of Mayo farmers' hydraulic social mobilization tactics, these chapters highlight the diversity and evolution of Mayo strategies in the postwar era. The time period discussed in this chapter—stretching from the mid-1940s to the late 1950s—constitutes a bridge between the relatively benign postrevolutionary era of the first chapter and the far more difficult postwar developmentalist era discussed in the rest of the book.

The Idealistic Origins of a Collective of Ejidos

The SICAE-affiliated ejidos employed a new strategy of cooperative agricultural production that sprouted up throughout Mexico in the 1930s. Mexican economist Salomón Eckstein describes collective ejidos as ejidal societies of cooperative production.[12] Previously, ejidos remained collections of small, independent farmers who were poor enough to warrant special protection and support by the state but whose approach to agricultural markets were not different than that of any other small, subsistence farmer. Beginning in the late 1930s, ejido collectives changed that by uniting ejidatarios under umbrella organizations—such as the SICAE—that paid them fair wages in exchange for working communally to produce important cash crops on their ejidal lots. The most famous collective system at the time was in the Soviet Union, where officials collectivized land, but cooperative production in Mexico much more varied in practice.[13] The practice of communally harvesting various high-value crops throughout Mexico garnered significant attention from the media, politicians, and academics, as Mexico embraced cooperative production on a scale far greater than anywhere else in the Western Hemisphere in the twentieth century.[14]

Cárdenas, Mexico's most left-leaning president, pushed for the growth of collective ejidos. Such ejidos perfectly exemplified a Cardenista project in that their level of support depended on how much Mexicans believed they harmed or helped their interests. As historian Alan Knight suggests, "Both supporters and opponents saw the regime as attempting radical new initiatives that they loved or loathed according to taste."[15] Cárdenas ideally wanted to use state resources to create alliances that empowered campesinos to challenge existing power structures like large-scale agribusiness and corrupt politicians providing unfair advantages to such endeavors. Yet he was also a politician and not above leaning on traditions of Mexican clientelism by granting economic opportunity to cooperative members in exchange for political patronage.[16]

Cárdenas believed that collective ejidos would garner campesino political support, boost the economy, and fulfill the 1917 Constitution's mandate to utilize lands and waters more efficiently. Environmental historians Emily Wakild and Christopher Boyer describe Cárdenas's vision as "development-minded social landscaping, that is, a holistic political project intended to manage rural society and nature together to rationalize the countryside."[17] With the help of bureaucrats, Cárdenas established approximately seven hundred to eight hundred collective ejidos in the most fertile regions of Mexico to implement his grand vision.[18] Collective ejidos represented a Cardenista experimental program that accessed natural resources to support campesinos but with limits and requirements dictated by the state that intended to minimize their potential for economic failure—what Boyer defines as "regimented empowerment."[19] Given that much of the opposition to Cárdenas's left-leaning reforms focused on the massive federal expenditure involved, he was reluctant to grant cooperative members independent control over agricultural regions like the Fuerte valley, the output of which remained pivotal to the growth of the national economy.[20]

In 1937, just prior to the birth of most Fuerte valley ejidos, the Federal Agrarian Code changed an ejidal policy that, in the view of Cardenistas, encouraged ejidatarios to produce cash crops yet, in the eyes of many cooperative members, revealed the state's priority to control them. Article 139 of the revised Agrarian Code mandated that ejidatarios had to harvest all capital-intensive crops collectively, meaning they would have to become cooperative members in order to produce such crops. Even indirectly, the state maneuvered to ensure the cooperative members' subservience. Article 148 stated that the Departamento Agrario (Agrarian Department) and the Banco Nacional de Crédito Ejidal (National Bank of Ejidal Credit) were to direct and oversee ejidos and credit societies.[21] The Cárdenas administration instructed these state agencies to offer cooperative members loans and technical support that was supposed to be available to ejidatarios generally but was harder for nonmembers to come by. State functionaries were also put in charge of ensuring that collective administrators paid members both regular salaries and a portion of the profits.[22]

While collective members received better economic opportunities than other ejidatarios, they were also subjected to the dictates of government bureaucrats and cooperative administrators who—gradually in the 1940s, and more directly in the 1950s—prioritized profit over these members' interests.

Mexican bureaucrats launched the largest and most productive collectives in the regions of La Laguna (northcentral Mexico), the Yaqui valley (Sonora), the Fuerte valley, and in the states of Yucatán and Michoacán. Despite their idealistic origins, collectives were often run by authoritarian—and often corrupt—administrators who did little to change the unfair structure of local politics or permanently empower their members.[23] By the 1950s this mismanagement, combined with state functionaries' decreasing confidence in collective production, would lead to the SICAE's demise. Yet both the rise of the cooperative as a new, promising power in the Fuerte valley and its fall as an exhausted, corrupt institution came at the expense of Mayo farmers disproportionately.[24]

The Birth and Growth of the SICAE

The SICAE did not start out with the explicit goal of splintering more than a half dozen Mayo villages through manipulating access to irrigation and pressuring collectivists to annex individualists' lands. Yet as a product of the Cárdenas era, the government designed it—like other cooperatives of the 1930s—to support, organize, and control some ejidatarios while excluding others. The SICAE emerged in 1938 from the confiscation and redistribution of thousands of hectares of the United Sugar Companies' (USCOS) land—along with several other large landowners' holdings—that Cárdenas redistributed to newly formed ejidos. Most ejidatarios were subsistence farmers who only produced cash crops irregularly, but members of collectives were the exception. Under Cárdenas's plan, some members of these new ejidos were to become employees of the SICAE and produce sugarcane full time. The government empowered the cooperative with the responsibility of overseeing the clearing, planting, and irrigation of huge tracts of former USCOS land and additional sugarcane property. Its architects intended it to be a benevolent organization that would minimize the volatility of sugarcane prices and make life easier for the crop's growers.

Like many other postrevolutionary state-aligned agencies, the SICAE started off with the goal of empowering campesinos. Yet with minimal presidential oversight after Cárdenas left office in 1940, individual government agencies began to concentrate more on their institutional empowerment and profit at the expense of the citizens they were supposed to protect. As early as the first years of the 1940s, the cooperative had become increasingly exclusionary and tyrannical as the Mexican state slowly diverged from Cárdenas's Indigenous and campesino mobilization efforts and moved toward capitalist development that opened the door to the proliferation of dishonest practices.[25] The SICAE's descent into ejidatario repression in these years reflects this shift, as it increasingly focused on controlling campesinos and their water sources in order to boost the production and sale of a profitable crop on the world market. When the state began emphasizing industrialization and corporatism in the 1940s, cooperatives like the SICAE did not have to drastically change in order to take a more authoritarian approach to local governance. The SICAE's most profound change was shifting its concern from rural producers to urban consumers.[26] These cooperatives were flawed from their inception and the SICAE's land annexation strategies from the 1940s to 1950s were particularly exploitative, but these developments, at least partially, reflected an increasingly corrupt Mexican state.

Why then, when it is clear the SICAE had lost its way in encouraging the empowerment and improvement of small ejidatario farmers, do historians like Lorena Schobert celebrate the cooperative, arguing that its pace of labor and administrative tactics in the Fuerte valley were unprecedented and created a sense of solidarity rarely seen in Mexico?[27] Two factors might explain this. First, this idealized view is true if one privileges the viewpoint of the cooperative. The individualist Mayo ejidatarios victimized by the SICAE had a dramatically different perspective on land and irrigation rights under the cooperative. Second, historians compare the SICAE to what came before it. Two factors defined life for Mayo people in the Fuerte valley in the decades before the creation of the SICAE in the late 1930s: sugarcane and USCOS's domination over the harvest. The sugar conglomerate cultivated nearly one hundred thousand hectares of some of the best land in the valley and had a virtual monopoly on access to the Fuerte River. But while land and control over irrigation figured prominently in USCOS's power in the region, it was its domination over workers that truly rankled people living in the valley. According to Mexican scholar María Eugenia Romero-Ibarra, the USCOS workers "lived in caves like wild beasts, exposed to malaria and other diseases."[28] As the largest employer, the conglomerate had a near monopsony and consequently paid meager wages and mistreated employees.[29]

Thousands of Fuerte valley sugarcane laborers responded to this repression by unionizing, joining the Confederación Regional Obrera Mexicana (Regional Confederation of Mexican Workers, CROM) in the 1920s and 1930s. In turn, USCOS hired thugs known as "white guards," who, in coordination with state police forces, assaulted and terrorized unionists. Lacking allies at the local level, desperate labor leaders reached out to President Cárdenas for help and met with him in 1936. They informed the president of the violence USCOS had ordered, the mistreatment of workers, the illegal attempts to take land from small-scale farmers, and how, in exchange for bribes and favors, the governor of Sinaloa, Manuel Páez (1933–37), planned to cede additional territory to USCOS.[30]

As a result of his discussions with labor leaders, Cárdenas eventually facilitated the creation of the SICAE in December 1938 by assigning a dotación to thirty-five newly created Fuerte valley ejidos and a land extension to four existing ones.[31] Some of the grant came from land the Mexican state expropriated from *hacendados* (owners of large estates), but the largest share—over fifty-five thousand hectares—came at the expense of foreign corporations such as USCOS. The newly created ejidos started off as SICAE-affiliated, and received sixty-one thousand hectares of mostly nonirrigated land overgrown with natural vegetation where they were required by law to harvest sugarcane under the direction of the cooperative leaders assigned and directed by the state.[32] Fuerte valley campesinos and unionized sugarcane workers, both Mayo and Yori, joined forces as some members of the thirty-five new ejidos became collectivist sugarcane growers.[33] Cooperative leaders, mostly consisting of former labor organizers such as Carlos Ramon García Ceceña (who immediately became the head of the SICAE), were tasked with seeing Cárdenas's hopes for the organization come to fruition, yet right from the start they would have to confront tensions between the cooperative's idealistic goals and reality.

Cárdenas placed the newly created National Ejidal Credit Bank in control of managing ejido collectives like the SICAE. Officially, the bank was to provide all ejidatarios with credit for agricultural implements, property, and seeds, as well as to lend technical advice, but Cárdenas understood the bank could do much more. Using the influence of credit, Cárdenas empowered bank functionaries to maintain tight control over collective ejidatarios' economic and political activities.[34] The Ejidal Bank's support became vital to successful harvests, and the bank nakedly favored those who supported the regime over those who opposed it. The Ejidal Bank strengthened its control over collectivist ejidatarios by lending the SICAE five and a half million pesos to acquire United Sugar's land, farm implements, livestock, machinery, water pumps, cane field structures, and other tools necessary for production.[35] Repayment, however, fell on the backs of collectivist ejidatarios who would be responsible for paying it back in ten years.

If the political tension channeled through the Ejidal Bank into the Fuerte valley was new, the tension between capital and labor was not. The state did not confiscate the sugar mill itself, and it remained in the hands of United Sugar, creating an ambivalent relationship between the company and its laborers. Cárdenas did not want to antagonize the U.S. government by cutting out one of its companies completely, as he had expropriated the assets of U.S. oil companies in Mexico earlier that year.[36] Also, as much as he wanted to mobilize campesinos, Cárdenas was reluctant to hand over a multimillion-peso sugar mill complex to laborers with no technical experience. The SICAE-affiliated ejidos became the sole producers of sugarcane and the USCOS sugar mill in Los Mochis their only buyer. As anthropologist Sidney Mintz explains, sugar production requires both "brute field labor and skilled artisanal knowledge."[37] Except for a few ejidatarios who operated tractors, weighed sugarcane, or constructed canals, most SICAE-affiliated collectivists acted as brute laborers growing sugarcane, while United Sugar employees handled the "artisanal" work of operating a vast, modern factory. However upset the collectivists may have been that they had been shut out from the opportunity to graduate to skilled laborers in the mill and would carry on being the "brutes" in the field, they had to have been mollified that instead of the paltry one peso a day wages USCOS traditionally paid, the SICAE compensated its employees with roughly six pesos daily.[38]

The greatest source of tension the SICAE brought into the Fuerte valley was, ironically, within ejidos. Sugarcane demands massive amounts of water, and by 1938 the SICAE controlled virtually all of the Fuerte River's irrigation. As essential as credit was, money and capital meant little to the farmers of the Fuerte valley if they had no water for their crops. And indeed, as had been the case since the late nineteenth century when modern, commercial farming began to displace subsistence farming, there was not enough water to satisfy all. Because of this the collective only took on some of the ejidatarios, creating two ejidal factions: the included collectivists and the excluded individualists. In short, the SICAE, which had been intended to mobilize ejidatarios, birthed an animosity in the region that would only grow over the next two decades.

In sugarcane-growing regions of Mexico, Cárdenas's reforms alleviated but did not eliminate exploitation.[39] This was particularly true in the Fuerte valley, where collectivists—who were certainly appreciative of guaranteed wages and access to water—chafed under dictatorial SICAE administrators who mandated that collectivist ejidatarios grow sugarcane exclusively even when a more diverse crop base would have served the farmers better. With so much power and so little oversight from Mexico City, the SICAE developed a reputation for corruption, and bribes and favors became a common cost of doing business with it. For individualist ejidatarios, there was no alleviation of exploitation. Even if they wanted to grow lucrative sugarcane, they could not because of SICAE water restrictions, the high cost of such operations, and the Ejidal Bank's preference for collectivists. As a result, they had no choice but to cultivate subsistence crops and find ways to stave off poverty.[40]

The SICAE's control over irrigation essentially ensured that collectivist sugarcane crops flourished while individualist farmers struggled to maintain subsistence crop yields, but a qualification is needed in order to understand the extent of this privilege. While the SICAE members enjoyed several advantages, a dearth of collectivist voices in archival records makes it difficult to know how many remained in favor of membership through the 1940s and 1950s.[41] It is also impossible to ascertain if collectivists initially understood that their affiliation with the cooperative meant they would eventually be required to cut off individualists' access to the river. The lack of documentation regarding SICAE members implies a top-down power structure, and collectivists simply either had to follow their supervisors' orders—like it or not—or be cut out themselves.

Individualists not only suffered due to their exclusion from the SICAE in terms of planting but the massive number of petitions they submitted suggests that they also resented the cooperative's maneuvers into local ejido politics. Normatively, executive ejidal committees had the final say in the distribution of ejidal lots and important resources such as water. Although this system had always been hierarchical and imperfect, the SICAE exacerbated this tendency and began pushing its members to vote only for collectivists as committee officers in some ejidos. In this way the SICAE could deliver a block of votes in every affiliated ejido that gave it political domination to match its economic and cultural power. Every ejido's procedures differed slightly, but generally speaking each consisted of a three-person ejidal committee (president, secretary, and treasurer) who made decisions on land and water distribution.

When occasional disputes within an ejido arose, typically all ejidal members would convene and vote on the issue. But that practice changed under the influence of the SICAE. The exact methods are not fully articulated in archival evidence, but it appears that the SICAE began encouraging ejidal leaders to convene select commissions—run, of course, by SICAE members—to bypass ejido-wide voting (which, because collectivists had a majority, would not have changed matters) and weigh in on land annexations and plans to dispossess individualists. It appears that in many cases these commissions, acting under the authority of the entire ejido, proactively granted individualist lands to favored collectivists. Like a small-scale spoils system, the collectivists who enthusiastically supported these commissions—and, by extension, the SICAE—could benefit the most. Those who did not received less, and those who questioned the commissions risked being shut out altogether. Those left out of the SICAE began to openly question village leadership and the structure of the ejido system in general, further fracturing the community.

Mayo collectivists had little choice but to follow the SICAE's orders, even if this meant cutting off their Indigenous, individualist brethren's access to the Fuerte River. As the minority in the Fuerte valley—15,000 of the total population of 130,000—the Mayo people were also demographically overwhelmed by Yoris in both the collectivist and individualist groups.[42] Therefore, while some collectivists were Mayo, most were Yoris, and the local SICAE leadership consisted mostly of former sugarcane-growing Yori foremen who had become members of non-Mayo ejidos. Because of this, in order to enjoy the benefits of belonging to the SICAE, Mayo collectivists had to embrace an allegiance to these leaders and their fellow Yori collectivists that came at the expense of their bond with individualist Mayo ejidatarios. When Yori leaders pushed to marginalize individualist ejidatarios, they paid no attention to whether those ejidatarios were Yori or Mayo and expected the Mayo collectivists to do the same.

Who got to join the SICAE was contentious and reflected life in the Fuerte valley. Yoris typically enjoyed membership in mixed Yori-Yoreme ejidos, but within all-Mayo ejidos affiliated with the

SICAE, such as El Teroque and Los Goros, membership was based on prior sugarcane-growing experience as well as particular leadership and kinship dynamics. According to local SICAE expert Bernabé López, "Because of the guaranteed salary and benefits, ejidatarios wanted to be cooperative members. Those who were already sugarcane laborers, as well as ejido leaders and their families, became collectivists."[43] Logically, the SICAE preferred ejidatarios whose previous occupation qualified them to continue growing sugarcane. But who were the ejidal leaders who ostensibly became cooperative members? The best evidence is that the SICAE also welcomed ejidatarios who had influence within ejidos, knowing that they would need those who could command respect, support, and, most importantly, votes in order to ensure its dominance.[44] The collective may also have known that it would need influential ejidatarios if it was to marginalize large swaths of an ejido.[45] Sugarcane workers became collectivists, but beyond this, membership within the SICAE depended largely on personal relationships and those who could convince their ejidal councils that it was to their benefit to allow them to join the cooperative.[46]

The SICAE's Seasonal Water Monopoly

While ejidatarios took control over former USCOS and other large landowners' plots, the SICAE received something even more valuable: administration over the sugar company's former irrigation infrastructure.[47] This asset was so extensive that it made cooperative leaders the de facto regulators of the Fuerte River beginning in 1938.[48] Ostensibly, ultimate hydraulic authority of the Fuerte valley rested in the hands of the Secretaría de Agricultura y Fomento (Ministry of Agriculture and Development, SAYF), but in practice this was not the case. The cooperative's enormous allocation of irrigation water from the Fuerte River allowed the SICAE administrators to decide the location of new hydraulic infrastructure, how it was constructed, and who would draw water from it.

As if that were not enough, in 1943 the Mexican state encouraged the cooperative's grip over the area by awarding it a four-month monopoly—during the dry months from March to late June—of the irrigation water from the Fuerte River. The decree, signed by Cárdenas's successor, Manuel Ávila Camacho (1940–46), stated that in order to reach the goal of supplying the USCOS sugar mill with at least five hundred thousand tons of sugarcane annually, sugarcane-producing communities would receive all of the water from the Fuerte River for irrigation purposes during those four months.[49] Since communities harvesting sugarcane all belonged to the cooperative, the SICAE was left in charge of administering irrigation water from the river for at least one-third of the year. The monopoly solidified the resentment of Fuerte valley farmers who were not members of the SICAE both to the collective as an institution and their collectivist neighbors who enjoyed unfettered access.

This seasonal monopoly on water solidified the federal government's commitment to the SICAE, to the sugarcane industry in general, and also to the Allies' war effort. The Allied powers relied on Mexico to help increase sugarcane production, not only to provide sustenance to its soldiers but also to compete against Germany's beet sugar production in the world economy.[50] Salomón Eckstein points out that Mexico's declaration of war on the Axis powers in October 1942 resulted in an "urgent need to increase agricultural production due to the demand created by World War II, making imperative the use of all means of production."[51] Mexican politicians recognized their country's role of producing sugarcane as vital, especially during wartime.[52]

Ávila Camacho's goals and priorities initially resulted in his ambivalent support of the SICAE as an institution, yet he soon found a willing partner in the collective to help fulfill his agenda. The president slowed the pace of ejidal land distribution and instead focused on reforming areas such as communications, irrigation, mechanization, and education. He hadn't completely turned his back on the Cárdenas legacy, for in the beginning of his presidency he worked to prevent land transfers—which he feared might destabilize the economy—by solidifying the land rights of small property owners and ejidatarios.[53] Yet he was at cross purposes with his own efforts, for the water monopoly he granted the SICAE to ensure the sugarcane harvest threatened the stability of most of the ejidatarios and small property owners he wanted to protect.

Even after the war, the seasonal water monopoly remained. In large part this is because Ávila Camacho began to support profitable, large-scale production of sugarcane in the Fuerte valley via the SICAE and similar operations in other regions of Mexico over the course of his presidency. A wartime measure, one that marginalized small-scale agriculture and ejidal production, became a fact of life along the Fuerte River. With it came the first glimpse that the state would begin favoring massive economies of scale over less profitable operations in the Fuerte valley.[54] His successor Miguel Alemán (1946–52), in line with his industrial and pro-agribusiness policies, then kept the monopoly in place by signing it into law in 1949. Alemán supported industrialization and attempted to make Mexico's economy more productive and efficient while also establishing monopolies and turning them over to his political allies.

The SICAE's ability to establish a seasonal water monopoly and maintain power in the Fuerte valley underscored its close collaboration with both the Mexican state and its collectivist members. Influential large landowners attempted to repeal the cooperative's water agreement, but the SICAE enjoyed the favor of Mexico's presidents, who ignored the landowners and kept the monopoly in place. The SICAE's power derived from the support of state agencies who gave the organization the freedom to dominate land and water resources while also responding favorably to their petitions and requests. The cooperative also grew powerful thanks to the fact that their affiliated ejidatarios supported all of their efforts and did their bidding by annexing their individualist neighbors' ejidal properties. Collectivist ejidatario backing gave the SICAE the power to impose its will on all nonaffiliated farmers, awakening the political fervor of a diverse array of powerful groups who felt slighted by the water monopoly.[55]

Opposition to the monopoly created strange bedfellows in the Fuerte valley, as disparate entities with opposing political interests formed unlikely coalitions to repeal it.[56] In April 1943 the League of Users of the Fuerte River, the Regional Agrarian Committee

Number Five, fifty-two ejidos, and the Farmers of the Colonized Lands of Los Mochis—groups that had historically feuded with each other over land and water rights—collaborated on creating a leaflet addressed to President Ávila Camacho. The publication, which the groups apparently circulated widely throughout the Fuerte valley, summarized the rights of water users prior to the decree and the harm the monopoly brought to the agricultural sector of the Fuerte valley.[57] For as much as they disliked each other, their displeasure with the SICAE dominating life in the Fuerte valley was even greater.

The next year, others would join the cause against the monopoly. In February 1944 the Ejidal Land Defense Committee—which purportedly consisted of thirty-two ejidos as well as large landowners—sent a letter to President Ávila Camacho asking him to dissolve the water monopoly because it would ruin ejidal lands.[58] Similar to the leaflet from the previous year, this missive did not identify which of the thirty-two ejidos were actual members of this group.[59] By the 1940s Fuerte valley ejidatarios routinely signed their names on petitions they drew up to seek governmental redress, which makes the absence of their names in this letter suspicious. It is not outside the realm of possibility that powerful property owners leading this group wrongfully claimed they had the backing of dozens of ejidos or at least overexaggerated the number.

In October 1943 the leaders of thirteen ejidos, including Los Goros, did in fact collectively write and sign their names on a petition to the SAYF complaining about the misdistribution of water in the Fuerte valley. The ejidal leaders, some of whose ejidatarios were members of the SICAE, complained that the current regulation of water and its distribution would harm the economy of their ejidos and that it prevented them from making their own decisions.[60] This petition was different from the others—which were drafted by private property owners and allegedly included the support of ejidatarios—in that it did not directly call for the repeal of the SICAE water monopoly. Instead, this ejidatario petition more modestly only requested autonomy in choosing irrigation options. The evidence points to this group consisting of

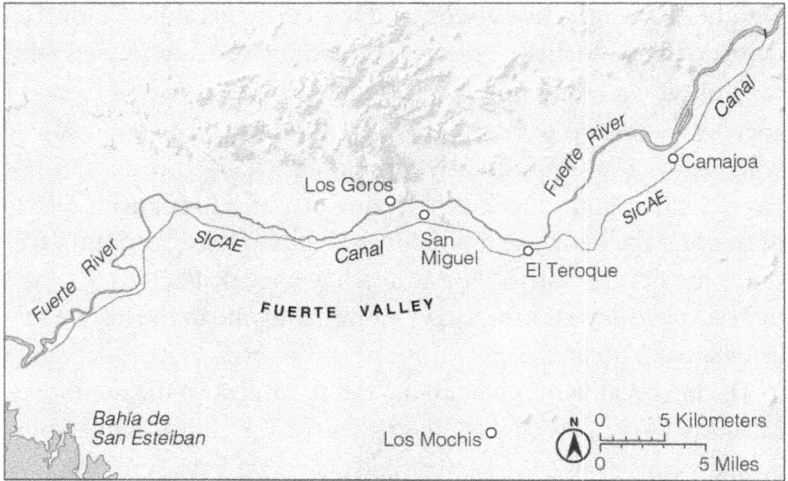

3. Los Goros, El Teroque, and Camajoa on the Fuerte River with the SICAE Canal running parallel. Mapped by Pease Press Cartography.

individualist and independent (members of ejidos in which no one was affiliated with the SICAE) ejidatarios, especially since the SICAE satisfied the irrigation needs of collectivists. In submitting this petition, these ejidatarios responded to both their inability to legally access sufficient irrigation water at all times of the year as well as the fact that the SICAE and private property owners possessed most water concessions.

This petition was an indictment of not just the SICAE river monopoly but the system of water distribution that left individualist ejidatarios out of the equation.[61] Wealthy landowners had the privilege of fighting over how many months of the year they could use their existing irrigation rights in order to increase their wealth, but individualist ejidatarios fought for any trickle that could grow enough crops to feed their families. The SICAE's enforcement of the river monopoly and unrelenting thirst to acquire more land and irrigation concessions therefore had much larger consequences for individualist or independent ejidatarios than collectivists or landowners.[62] This was particularly important for Mayo communities, whose members were usually individualist or independent

ejidatarios. For the individualist ejidatarios of Los Goros, El Teroque, and Camajoa (ejidos depicted here in figure 3) the SICAE's
river monopoly severely impacted their internal village relations.

Indigeneity and the Power of Water in Los Goros

By 1944, and likely sooner, the ejidatarios of Los Goros viewed
themselves as members of either the collectivist or individualist
factions within the ejido and had begun to elect their own executive ejidal committees to administer their respective affairs. They
had become, in de facto terms, two unequal communities. With
support from the SICAE, the collectivists began to pressure their
individualist neighbors into relinquishing their irrigated lots. With
limited access to irrigation water and confronting possible SICAE
land annexation, members of the individualist executive ejidal
committee began to see the fight as a war of attrition. The key bat-
tlegrounds were irrigated lots, and the SICAE's land annexations
in the Fuerte valley convinced individualists that they needed to
consolidate these properties lest the collectivists draw them away
one by one. It is a testament to the SICAE's power that individualist leaders had to take action that harmed the interests of the very
people who elected them in order to stave off a worse outcome.

Situated along the Fuerte River, fifteen kilometers north of the
city of Los Mochis, the Los Goros ejido sits in the heart of the
sugarcane-producing region. Like the proverbial canary in the coal
mine, Los Goros was at the forefront of battles in the 1940s as it
had been in the 1930s. In this case the fight was over the SICAE's
water monopoly and its policies within Mayo communities. Here,
beginning in the 1940s, the SICAE's policies divided the community.
The affiliated and nonaffiliated ejidatarios shared no clear physical demarcation; there was no fence or canal that separated sides
in this fight, as their plots of land were jumbled together. Instead,
water was the great divide, as those ejidatarios with a membership in the cooperative had it and those not members did not. In
response, collectivist and individualist factions formed their own
executive ejidal committees to defend their respective interests.

By the mid-1940s Los Goros, a community that had been so

united in its efforts a decade before, was on the verge of a formal division, but separation would not be easy. First, the leaders had to demarcate the geographic boundaries separating the ejido's collectivists and individualists, as these unclear borders had become an increasingly contentious issue. After a few years of initial discussions, heads of both groups met with the SICAE, the National Bank of Ejidal Credit, and the Agrarian Department to settle the territorial division on March 16, 1945. The two sides agreed on virtually nothing, and only the influence of government officials wrung out the tepid concession that the collectivists would control enough land to produce the sugarcane they were legally required to grow. Yet, even here, there was no agreement as to how many hectares that would require or which plots they would receive.[63]

For those outside the SICAE, the ambiguity of the division spoke volumes. What if cooperative members wanted an inordinate number of hectares? Would they grab the best, most productive land? A fear arose among individualists that with no agreement in place, the SICAE and collectivists would attempt to claim as many hectares as possible, arguing that they needed more property to meet their sugarcane quota.[64] With no clear division of the lands established and with the backing and resources of the SICAE—and thus the endorsement of the federal government—collectivists could practically treat ejidal lands as a blank slate, leaving individualist plots vulnerable.

Left with few alternatives, individualist leaders began infringing on the rights of some of their members in order to protect the rights of the majority. Take, for example, the plight of Ynocente Montiel, an individualist Mayo farmer in Los Goros who reached out to the federal government to defend his land and water rights. On November 18, 1944, he wrote to President Manuel Ávila Camacho on behalf of himself and other ejidatario family members to complain of the actions of the individualist executive ejidal committee. According to the letter, five years before, after striking a deal with General Roberto Cruz to receive irrigation water from his pumping plant, the Montiel family had cleared their land, built irrigation canals, and harvested crops.[65] But the family's victory was short-lived. In July 1944, during a meeting of the individualist group, its leadership announced plans to restructure the entire faction's ejidal land holdings.[66] What that meant in the case of the Montiel family was that they would have to exchange their cultivated, irrigated plots for unirrigated ones. Individualist leaders wanted, as Montiel explained, to "re-fraction" their lands, or, to put it plainly, confiscate the Montiel irrigated lands.[67] The Montiels' struggles within the ejido felt like a war with two fronts: they had to worry about the machinations of the SICAE-affiliated collectivists as well as those of their own individualist leaders.

Supporting documents do not divulge what the individualist executive ejidal committee planned to do with the Montiels' irrigated plots, yet their land was instrumental in the local political power struggles. In January 1945 the committee wrote to the Agrarian Department, informing it that the Montiels' intransigence with the planned restructuring of the ejido was "an anomaly among their peers who all agreed with the 1944 reparceling plan, and the entire ejido [individualist faction] signed the minutes of the meeting where the plan was proposed."[68] Confronting the collectivists' annexation strategies, the individualist ejidal committee expected its ejidatarios to act in the best interests of the entire faction.

But what were these plans, and what motivated the individualist ejidal committee's attempt to confiscate the Montiel properties? The committee could have intended to keep the valuable lots for itself, as the land possessed canals and access to pumps that allowed farmers to produce maize, sugarcane, or other crops year-round. It might seem ironic that in order to stop the collectivist seizure of individualists' land, the individualist ejidal committee should target and seize the Montiel's plots, but there existed good reasons for it. First, transferring the Montiels' irrigated property into the hands of the more politically connected ejidal committee would dissuade collectivists from annexing the land. It was one thing to go after a single family but quite another to take on a group of politically connected leaders. Second, the plot was valuable and could be used as a bargaining chip to entice the collectivists to agree to the formal separation of the ejido. Most likely, the individualists intended to keep the plot and use the Montiels' irrigation infrastructure to distribute water to the rest of the individualist ejidatarios. Whatever their reason, during a 1944 meeting of the individualist faction the ejidal committee convinced the individualists of Los Goros to vote for the confiscation of the Montiel properties.[69]

Though the individualist committee mimicked the collectivists in this case, the semblance between the two is only superficial, for the individualist leaders' motives were defensive in nature. Like a controlled burn intentionally set to prevent a far-worse wildfire in the future, individualist leaders were willing to seize land from members of their own faction to get access to their all-important water rights—rights that could be used to irrigate other individualists' farms and make them more productive. If the land remained fallow—that is, if there was not a well-watered bumper crop grown—collectivists could more easily justify the annexation of these lands and argue that they would have no problem growing ample sugarcane.[70] While the Montiel family lamented their leaders' actions, the individualist executive committee faced a difficult ethical dilemma: Was it fair to impinge on the rights of the few for the benefit of the many? In Los Goros's case, the individualists, after listening to their leaders' arguments, answered yes.[71]

The SICAE-sponsored land seizures influenced every action taken by Los Goros's individualist leaders, testing their faction's faith in them, and even the good news of more land and water did not alleviate their problems. On November 7, 1945, the Mexican state granted the individualists a small six-and-a-half hectare *ampliación* (ejidal land extension) that included irrigation from electric pumps.[72] Mayo elder Alejandro Inzunza of Los Goros recalls how, in 1946,

> the [individualist] ejidal committee let twelve Yoreme families clear out three of the seven hectares and awarded us this land for planting. Clearing the fields of large mesquite trees with machetes and axes was hard work. We planted cotton while clearing the fields

and, with help from irrigation, received a good harvest that first year. Then they told us that we would receive the four hectares of non-cleared land, and not the three hectares as agreed on. We had put all of our resources into clearing and planting the original three hectares, and could not do the same with this new land. We had to abandon it. Our ejidal officers took the three hectares we had cleared, and continued to plant cotton. They should have helped us clear the remaining four hectares. The municipal president could not assist us because we never received land grant paperwork to verify our claims.[73]

In the few short years between 1944 and 1946, the individualist committee transformed from undertaking unpleasant—and unfair—actions on behalf of all individualists to exploiting ejidatarios from its faction. Not officially transferring ownership to the laborers provided the committee with a fig leaf of legality, but the ejidal committee telegraphed its intentions clearly enough: it had used Inzunza and the other families to clear land that it intended to keep for itself.

While the actions of the individualists could be as undeniably ruthless as those of the collectivists, their motivations deserve further elaboration. The pressure the collectivists could summon—through water access, preferred credit terms, and even political sway—meant that individualists and especially their leaders could envision a day in the near future when all ejidatarios would be only SICAE-aligned and all individualists forced out. It led some to seeing the problem as a zero-sum game in which only large-scale, profit-making individualists stood any chance of stopping the collectivists. Whether they deserve censure or not, individualist leaders only took the actions they did because of collectivists' actions.

This situation was not unique to Los Goros. All along the Fuerte River, powerful individualist ejidal leaders employed questionable tactics. Mayo individualist ejidatarios ended up unintentionally providing unpaid labor because their leaders promised them property in return for clearing it. Though they might bemoan the tactics of their leadership, many individualists had no other recourse but to fall in line. The SICAE was too powerful to fight with half measures. By 1946 individualists saw themselves in an all-out war. Though the strategy of fighting a battle of attrition was not uniformly popular, the majority of individualists understood it was inevitable.[74]

Yet, in spite of the divisions and the recriminations thrown around, there is no record of the ejidatarios of Los Goros—individualists or collectivists—questioning their shared, Mayo identity. Individualists in the ejido still acknowledged collectivists as part of the ethnic community, engaged with them in most of their traditional religious rituals, and conversed with them in their Indigenous dialect. Mayo elder Carlos Moroyoqui of Los Goros Uno recalls the troubles haunting the ejido at the time but maintains that "the collectivists were also Yoremes. They stopped performing some rituals with us, but they continued to attend the major ceremonies in San Miguel."[75] Although the struggle over irrigation resources caused Los Goros to eventually split into two ejidos in 1962—individualists became Los Goros Uno and collectivists formed Los Goros Dos—both sides continued to respect one another enough to identify their counterparts as Yoremes and continue to do so today.

El Teroque: Where Mayo Invaded Mayo Lands

The kind of tension erupting in Los Goros occurred wherever the SICAE flexed its muscle, and its aggressive targeting of irrigated land continued into the 1950s. Despite all the tensions crackling through ejidos like Los Goros in the 1940s, a shared mutual recognition of Mayo identity mitigated the harshest feelings and violence was rare. Unlike in Los Goros, the individualists of El Teroque unified in the face of repression by aligning with advocacy groups and collectively petitioning state agencies to defend their land and water rights. Here, there were no individualists turning on individualists. Rather, individualists nurtured solidarity, responded collectively, and worked with local campesino groups as the Confederación Nacional Campesina (National Campesino Confederation, CNC). Leveraging this unity allowed individualists to capture some influence over local hydraulic development decisions.

El Teroque's troubles began in the late 1940s when the sugarcane cooperative's leaders supervised some of their members in the construction of a canal—immodestly named the SICAE Canal—that would expand the ejido's irrigated lands from 190 hectares to 1,328 hectares. Of this land, 506 hectares were already planted with sugarcane, either from new harvests started by the collectivists or leftover fields confiscated from large international companies during the 1938 dotación.[76] However, the canal was a boon for only some in the community. Complaints the individualists filed seven years later claimed their faction never controlled a single acre of that massive chunk of irrigated land.[77] By 1955 individualists were not only minority stakeholders in terms of acreage but they were denied irrigation for what little land they had. Parched, they could only farm with rainfall while they watched their neighbors consume from the Fuerte River's bounty; over the course of the late 1940s to mid-1950s, individualists' frustrations would switch from complaints into action.

Armed insurrection, however, was not their first strategy. Like many Mexicans since the revolution, the individualists of El Teroque appealed to the state, directly reaching out to the general secretary of the Comisión Agrícola (Agricultural Commission) in November 1954. Convinced by their argument, the general secretary then wrote a letter on behalf of the individualists to the Agrarian Department, expressing concern that they did not have access to credits for agricultural inputs or water for harvests. "Individualists," the general secretary wrote, "seek the power to elect their own executive ejidal committee and the separation of their ejido. In affiliated ejidos, the SICAE administration appoints the ejidal committee for the entire ejido, and these leaders only represent the interests of the collectivists."[78] The fact that nothing came from this petition highlights the SICAE's power in the Fuerte valley. Then, as now, farming was a business run on credit, so it is not surprising to read that the individualists needed and wanted more. What is striking is their complaint about irrigation. Farmers the world over complain of lack of access to water, but fewer do so when their farms abut a large river.[79] This agonizing anomaly in El Teroque can only be explained by the SICAE and its appointed officials turning off the individualists' water supply.

The SICAE could do this because of its official backing from the Mexican state and—most troubling—the grip it had on the ejido's executive committee. Those outside the collective faced an uphill battle for water, and, like other ejidatarios in the region facing the same fight, individualists in El Teroque proposed to formally divide their ejido so they could elect their own ejidal commission and make decisions independent from the SICAE. They began in August 1955 by petitioning the Organización Agraria Ejidal (Ejidal Agrarian Organization) for rights to formally divide the El Teroque ejido into two and hold elections for their own ejidal committee. "We cannot," individualist leaders claimed, "obtain credit privately or officially because no institution or company will enter into an agreement under these conditions. . . . With the completed Miguel Hidalgo Dam, we have undertaken an agreement to receive water from the Fuerte River Commission, but who has the power to endorse these contracts? The ejidal leadership will not do so."[80] Water, free of the SICAE's influence, was tantalizingly close, yet individualists lacked the official power to make group decisions in order to secure it. That power rested in an ejidal leadership that refused to take steps that might improve the fortune of individualists.

In September 1955 the Comisión del Río Fuerte (Fuerte River Commission, CRF) supplanted the Secretaría de Recursos Hidráulicos (Ministry of Water Resources) as official regulator of all Fuerte valley irrigation systems. Created in 1951, the Mexican state charged the CRF with developing the Fuerte River's hydraulic technology with an eye toward boosting local agricultural output.[81] State officials, concerned over petitions from individualists and landowners and frustrated with the SICAE's refusal to address them, demanded that authority over the Fuerte River's flow be taken out of the collectivists' hands.[82] While the CRF enacted some changes—notably granting private property owners new irrigation concessions and demanding fees be paid in advance—one thing remained the same: small, individualist farmers still could not secure irrigation, and in El Teroque, time was running out for them to escape their second-class citizenship. Ostensibly, these individualists also had the opportunity to purchase irrigation rights from the CRF and had even reached a preliminary agreement with the CRF before the agency was officially placed in charge of irrigation distribution, but the collectivist-led ejidal committee would not approve the credit individualists needed to buy the water in advance.[83] Once again, the ejidal administration controlled by collectivists thwarted the individualists' hydraulic social mobilization efforts.

Despite their experience, as late as the mid-1950s, El Teroque individualists still employed the petition process to help them gain access to irrigation water. In October 1955 they wrote to President Adolfo Ruiz Cortines regarding their conflict with the collectivists. As their missive explained, "In order to conduct our work we request irrigation for our fields and construction of hydraulic distribution."[84] The demand for hydraulic infrastructure such as pumps, canals, and dams showed that these Mayo individualists had embraced its use in their practices. They needed water, wherever it came from, to grow the crops that earned them a livelihood and kept their fields cultivated and their properties safe—all of which secured them a place within the Mayo homeland along the Fuerte River. Most importantly, despite all that had happened, at this point hydraulic social mobilization in El Teroque still fell safely within legal boundaries.

Matters were tense in El Teroque, but they were no less tense in Los Goros, Camajoa, or any number of ejidos that sought to separate into collectivist and individualist groups. So why was it the only ejido to boil over into violence? One reason may be a change in perspective on the part of individualists. Felipe Buimena, a Mayo elder from El Teroque, recalls that his parents "did not want anyone telling them what they could grow. They also believed the river was for everyone and that nobody had the right to possess it completely."[85] A sense of autonomy and commitment to the good of all were, for these individualist farmers, what made them Mayo. The SICAE's legal control over the river, their abuse of that control to alienate individualist Mayo farmers from their sacred river, and the collective's efforts to dictate what was grown and who grew it were the antithesis of what it meant to be Mayo.[86]

By 1956 El Teroque had split into a collectivist community and an individualist one, but unlike in the ejidos that settled into an uneasy truce, the fight continued on cultural fronts. By the mid-1950s the SICAE was, for individualists in the ejido, the embodiment of all things antithetical to Mayo identity, and this sense of opposition extended to those who benefited from its domination and embraced its dictates. In a letter to the Agrarian Department, the executive individualist ejidal committee of El Teroque used language never before found in the Fuerte valley. In a discussion of unresolved tensions with the collectivist faction, the committee wrote, "There are also antagonistic tendencies on the grounds that the first group [collectivists] are white farmers or 'Yoris,' and the second group [individualists] are purely Indigenous 'Mayo' and speak our dialect."[87] The phrasing was peculiar because both the collectivist and individualist ejidos were, anthropologically speaking, Mayo. But by being such close allies and carrying out the dictates of the SICAE so enthusiastically, the collectivists, in the eyes of their individualist brethren, had made themselves "white." It was not intended as a compliment but instead a label that closed the collectivists off to the goodwill and shared identity that—though having been strained over the previous years—kept the two communities bonded.[88] When this bond broke, so too did the peace between the two sides.

By the end of 1955 the dispute over irrigated land in El Teroque had come close to boiling over. In August individualists demanded the return of a portion of valuable irrigated land that the collectivists had seized from them and planted with sugarcane. On August 31, 1955, their leaders wrote to the National Bank of Ejidal Credit claiming that they were entitled to this irrigated property and that they were willing to devote the land to sugarcane cultivation if the bank provided credit—but only if there were no ties to the SICAE. They explained, "Under the direction of this agency, all affiliated ejidos, except for rare exceptions, have been a resounding economic failure. We ask to stay unconnected to it, or otherwise devote ourselves to other crops."[89] The individualists were confident that, with credit from the National Bank of Ejidal Credit, they could make the land bountiful. The reason for their optimism? If awarded this land, individualists would have had a source of water independent from the cooperative's authority. From the individualists' perspective, if the pernicious influence of the SICAE could just be removed from their lands, their lives and livelihoods would improve.

From the individualists' point of view, the best way to convince the Ejidal Bank to help them recover this land was to prove they had the ability to keep the land profitable, but as poor farmers with limited resources, they needed credit to maintain sugarcane production.[90] By 1955 the Mexican government had no interest in supporting subsistence farming and the individualists knew it. The government and the National Bank of Ejidal Credit would only make loans for sugarcane—a crop that could be exported abroad. If that is what they had to grow in order to make the land bountiful, the individualists would adjust, in part because it allowed them to operate without the heavy, hated hand of the SICAE hovering above them. In another example of the SICAE's still existent power (as well as, in all likelihood, the Ejidal Bank's lack of confidence in the individualists' project), the individualists' request was denied.

Amid rampant inequality, uneven access to land and water rights, and the failure of other tactics, the individualists of El Teroque turned to an ally that had recent success in advocating for campesino communities in the Fuerte valley, the National Campesino Confederation (CNC). Although the CNC was an institution charged with representing all campesinos, in reality not all farmers aligned with it, for those collectivists under the protective arm of the SICAE already had a powerful group that could capture the government's ear.[91] Consequently, by 1955 the CNC found itself championing the individualists.[92] The fact that Mayo individualists aligned with the CNC—an organization run primarily by non-

Mayos—both cautions against exaggerating Yoreme-Yori tensions and shows that, though Yoreme-Yori tensions were real, the Mayo farmers of El Teroque were in such desperate circumstances that they would take their allies wherever they could find them.

In September 1955 the CNC wrote a letter on behalf of individualists to the Agrarian Department to point out the disparity in their land tenure and irrigation access compared to collectivists and to complain about their lack of political representation. The letter argued that collectivists had, over the course of a decade, amassed an additional 1,000 hectares of sugarcane land to add to their holdings, which now totaled over 2,300 hectares. By invading their plots and planting the cash crop, the 120 collectivists left the 104 individualist ejidatarios—just under half the 224 ejidatarios in El Torque—to scrape by with a mere 200 hectares. In terms of acreage, the collectivists had a dozen-to-one advantage, but this paled in comparison to their advantage in irrigation access. Individualists simply had none and therefore lived under the constant threat that their holdings, as slim as they were, could be taken away.[93] And while individualists managed to hold onto their meager 200 hectares of dry land, even the CNC's petition could not contend with the SICAE's political sway, and thus it fell by the wayside.

Individualists contended that they and the collectivists of El Teroque had met and reached agreements for property reinstatement in the months leading up to the individualists' 1956 invasion but that collectivists broke their promise by withholding anticipated land transfers.[94] Accounts do not specify what they armed themselves with, but in early 1956 individualist El Teroque farmers took control of the collectivists' pump and canals and occupied some of their plots planted with sugarcane. Using threats of violence, they prevented the collectivist farmers from tending to the land. The individualists were not after the sugarcane crop but rather the system of pumps and canals that fed the crops.[95] Indeed, their original intent was to destroy the sugarcane plants and replace them with *milpa* crops. Only the arrival of a commissioned engineer from the Agrarian Department and a promise that his agency would arbitrate an agreement between the two groups convinced the individualists to hold off on obliterating the sugarcane.[96]

While the seizure of land had obvious significance as a gesture of political protest, the individualists targeted this particular property for the simple reason that it enjoyed irrigation. They had tried through official channels to mobilize and lobby for access to water, but with the SICAE impeding their efforts they had no choice but this extreme form of hydraulic social mobilization. Individualists informed state functionaries from the Ejidal Bank, Agrarian Department, and even the president on several occasions leading up to the invasion that—though the collectivists' encroachments rankled them—their most pressing need was irrigation. The SICAE obstructed any deals they might have made with government functionaries for irrigation water.[97] Keeping with what they and their advocates had announced to the government for the past decade, access to irrigation water from the Fuerte River, more than access to land, catalyzed their desperate action.

The importance Mayo individualists attributed to irrigation infrastructure raises questions about the sociocultural impacts of development. For Mayo ejidatarios who found themselves lumped into the individualist camp, life had changed along the Fuerte River. As late as the mid-1920s Indigenous farmers in the Fuerte valley did not have access to irrigation infrastructure. But by the mid-1950s—one generation later—irrigation had become so essential to earning a livelihood that some were willing to risk their lives and freedom to gain control of it. Farmers had previously been able to raise subsistence crops and leave portions fallow as necessity dictated, but by the 1950s leaving land unexploited allowed collectivists to claim it. It was a vicious cycle created not by nature but by Mexican law, technology, and regional demographic/economic growth. And like in Los Goros, the resource war within El Teroque eventually led to a formal, legal separation. In 1963, seven years after their first petition for separation was denied, the individualists of El Teroque formed an ejido named El Teroque Viejo and the collectivists created a separate ejido named Cinco de Mayo.

In the end, the Agrarian Department did not punish those who led or participated in the occupation, and the agency awarded the individualists 607 of the more than 1,300 hectares of irrigated land in El Teroque—roughly proportional to their numbers in the ejido. Notably, this included the section of the ejido they had invaded.[98] Yet the individualists of El Teroque were an exception in being granted so much irrigated land compared to other non-affiliated ejidatarios of the Fuerte valley. Individualists in other ejidos employed hydraulic social mobilization tactics to recover annexed properties—such as petitioning state functionaries—but none were as successful as El Teroque individualists' risky strategy of invading their adversaries' lands. The agreement to end the standoff had not only awarded the individualists land and water access but also the right to decide how water was distributed, what crops received it, and whether new hydraulic infrastructure was necessary.

The action in El Teroque was more than a lost battle for the SICAE, it was the end of the war. After the Agrarian Department worked out a solution in the community, the government no longer turned the other way as the SICAE coached collectivists into annexing individualist properties. Instead, it withdrew its support for the collective and began to give hydraulic priority to private landowners engaging in large-scale commercial agricultural operations. The historical record reveals that the El Teroque individualists' achievement in 1956 eliminated any chances the SICAE had of reviving its political power. A year later the government dismantled the agency permanently.

Camajoa: A Divided Ejido Stays United amid Inequitable Access to Water

The ejido of Camajoa was unique in the Fuerte valley in that all the ejidatarios had been members of the SICAE since its inception in 1938. As stipulated in its 1938 dotacion, the sixty-one Mayo ejidatarios would be required to grow sugarcane collectively.[99] As explained earlier, the limited amount of water from the Fuerte River allowed the SICAE to harvest a finite amount of sugarcane, and thus only some of the local ejidatarios could join the collective. Most likely due to the small number of ejidatarios in Camajoa and the fact that most had experience in harvesting sugarcane, every ejidatario was allowed to become collectivists. Early ejidal unity, along with the value Camajoa's leaders placed on irrigation infrastructure helps explain why it did not split into two ejidos like Los Goros and El Teroque.

Of the 950 hectares Camajoa received, only 84 were mechanically irrigated.[100] This low number should have resulted, as it did elsewhere, in only some of Camajoa's ejidatarios becoming collectivists. But the community was committed from the beginning to sharing what little they had—with the plan to use the SICAE's influence to gain more. Their commitment paid off a decade later when the SICAE Canal opened and allowed all ejidatarios to harvest an additional 160 irrigated hectares in 1948.[101] While the additional irrigated acreage was welcome in Camajoa, it was also a bit of a disappointment. A year prior, engineer Adolfo Orive Alba, the former head of the National Irrigation Commission (CNI) and now director of the Ministry of Water Resources, boasted that the SICAE Canal would irrigate 40,000 additional hectares after it was completed, enough to satisfy the irrigation needs of 50 percent of ejidatarios affiliated with the SICAE.[102] When they heard these numbers, the ejidatarios of Camajoa experienced visions of immense expansion, but instead they received only a modest enlargement.

Camajoa's slight expansion in sugarcane production was not reflected in regional production. Indeed, something quite strange occurred after the completion of the SICAE Canal. While several ejidos now had the capacity to grow more sugarcane, there was actually a massive decline in the amount collectivists harvested, from 10,316 hectares in 1947 to 6,800 in 1957.[103] The drop in production had many causes, including the rise of political infighting, labor disputes between the SICAE and United Sugar, the growing informal market for sugar, and clashes between individualists and collectivists. Yet the most important reason from the perspective of collectivists in Camajoa was that SICAE officials never intended—despite official pronouncements—for the water in the canal to be exclusively for collectivist ejidatarios, as they planned to sell off a large share to large landowners. The SICAE was not supposed to sell off collectivist irrigation but water was too precious and the contracts too lucrative to turn down.[104]

The fact that Camajoa actually received enough water to irrigate an additional 160 hectares suggested that the SICAE valued the ejido and their loyalty more than the profit it could earn from selling the water. Keeping the ejido happy kept an essential ally in their camp. Camajoa now had 244 hectares of irrigated land where they continued to harvest sugarcane. By 1948, the number of ejidatarios grew by twenty, meaning that eighty-one ejidatarios held ejidal rights, and the fact that they continued to grow sugarcane collectively suggests that the entire ejido remained affiliated with the SICAE.[105] Disappointed though they may have been that the canal failed to live up to its promise, the SICAE had done enough to keep Camajoa's ejidatarios content. It may not have been as dramatic as the hydraulic social mobilization undertaken in El Teroque, but leveraging their unity and working with the SICAE was an effective strategy for Camajoa.

Camajoa's contentment with the SICAE through the late 1940s changed by the mid-1950s as mistreatment at the hand of the cooperative led to disillusionment. Regionally, the SICAE spent 150,000 pesos on medical services and 100,000 pesos to construct school buildings, in addition to erecting 285 houses for employees, but it did not distribute these resources to members equally.[106] Going beyond aggregate figures, Mayo elder Daniel Galaviz of Camajoa recalled that although workers received credit from company stores and had access to hospitals, there was always a ceiling on how far the collective wanted to improve the lives or uplift the standing of some members. "The schools," he recalls, "were only primary and secondary, and although some Yoremes learned arithmetic and became leaders of their ejido, education was limited. The SICAE only wanted our labor, it deceived Yoremes and paid us less in wages than other members."[107] Archival documents point to other Mayo collectivists similarly complaining to state functionaries about the SICAE disenfranchising them.[108] As some of Camajoa's ejidatarios lost confidence in the collective, despite all the benefits membership allotted them, they left and became the nucleus of an individualist faction within the community.

By 1955 individualists in Camajoa expressed complaints of land and water right abuses. In June of that year Rufino and Refugio Aqui, both individualists by that time, wrote a letter to the Agrarian Department arguing that many of the ejidatarios of Camajoa had no rights within their ejido and that they had been sanctioned—meaning they were being punished for not supporting the SICAE. They added that nobody was held accountable for the poor administration of the ejido and that their (presumably collectivist) leaders were renting properties to "individuals"—meaning large-scale private farmers—even though the ejido had a limited amount of irrigated land with which to grow crops.[109] If leaders did in fact rent some of Camajoa's ejidal plots to outsiders, then this violated Article 27 of the 1917 Constitution, which stipulated that only ejido members could cultivate these lands. By 1955 the individualists were not simply disappointed in the SICAE but accusing collectivists of knowingly violating the law. It had taken well over a decade and a half, but the toxic influence of the SICAE had finally created the animosity seen in other ejidos in Camajoa.

The disagreements between individualist ejidatarios and the SICAE came to a head in June 1956 when groups of Mayo individualists reclaimed their lands in the ejidos of Camajoa, Charay, and Pochotal. The Culiacán daily newspaper *La Palabra* reported the story of Indians in these three ejidos claiming possession of some of the SICAE sugarcane lands, and although SICAE officials "vigorously contested" the validity of the individualist claims, the Agrarian Department divided the land tracts and turned over the occupied land to the Indians.[110] The paper made it appear that these Mayo farmers were outsiders—or at least not originally members of this ejido—and omitted that the threat of SICAE annexation forced these individualists ejidatarios into asking for individual titles that certified their usufruct rights to particular plots within the ejido.

In August 1956, when individualists requested the Agrarian Department to send an engineer to officially mark off their plots, they took the first step on their path to autonomy.[111] The next step occurred on October 8, 1956, when seven members of the Aqui family wrote a petition on behalf of individualists asking the Agrarian Department for the formal separation of the Camajoa ejido.[112] The family pointed to collectivist demagogues who inflamed social differences between the two groups. Missing in this initial petition but very much a force in the call for separation was the desire for individualists to secure their own water supply and not have to rely on demagogic collectivist leaders for it. To achieve this, individualist leaders began by doing their homework and approached Leon Garduno, an engineer with the Agrarian Department, to inquire about the quality of canals used by the ejido and the volume of water assigned to Camajoa.[113] Garduno, for one, could see immediately what these ejidatarios were after: knowing how much water the ejido received meant that they could calculate how much of a proportion they should request from the Agrarian Department upon separation. This was a calculated and shrewd maneuver that once again relied on establishing relationships with state agencies.

Individualists attempted to leverage their new connection with Agrarian Department officials and knowledge of Camajoa's water concession in order to simultaneously break away from collectivists and secure water rights. With knowledge of Camajoa's water concession, the individualist ejidatarios would not risk upsetting their new connection with Agrarian Department officials—whose favor would be essential to securing a separation—by making an outrageous demand. They felt comfortable enough that by August 1957 they approached José Luis Torres of the Agrarian Department to assist them in defining the necessary steps needed to form their own ejido and separate from the collectivists. Arguing that they could not sufficiently grow their corn and other vegetable crops with the land and water resources they currently held, individualists asked the Agrarian Department to divide the irrigation concessions equally between both factions and then split the ejido into two.[114]

The summer of 1957 would mark both the clearest, most assertive demonstration of individualist identity and political strength in Camajoa and, ironically, its last. In March 1958 Torres concluded that the Fuerte River Commission (CRF) controlled the ejido's irrigation concessions and that the matter was therefore out of his agency's hands.[115] From this information individualists inferred that they would need to petition the CRF if they wanted to secure water rights before breaking ties with collectivists. This gave the individualists reason to pause. It was one thing to seek irrigation concessions from the Agrarian Department, which the individualists had established ties with, but quite another to petition the CRF—an agency that notoriously valued private landholder rights over that of any ejidatarios. Soliciting water rights from the CRF proved to be a tall task that Camajoa's individualists were not ready to undertake, and they never would be.[116] The CRF and the Agrarian Department, while both ostensibly working to boost Mexico's agricultural production, were often at cross purposes, fighting over funds, resources, and political clout. But it would be farmers like the individualists of Camajoa who fought on the front lines of these battles. They would have to use their knowledge and political savviness to navigate these bureaucratic battlefields.

No trace of individualist petitions to the CRF seeking water concessions exists, and the attempt to divide the ejido's water resources soon fell by the wayside. Had the individualists gone through with a separation, they would have had to petition a state agency that would not only have denied them any water concession but might also have reduced the collectivist concession as well. Rather than draw unwanted attention to their ejido's water rights and risk the CRF's intervention and a possible change in their concessions, the individualists chose to table their petition for formal separation and remain connected to collectivists. The differences that had compelled the individualists of Camajoa to divide their ejido remained, but they were not ready to risk the entire ejido losing access to irrigation water. When asked why Camajoa did not split into two in the late 1950s, Daniel Galaviz recalled, "Even though we [the entire ejido] disagreed, we needed water, so the ejido had to stay together."[117] While Galaviz did not provide specifics on the factors that went into these leaders' decisions, his memory points to the major role water played in not pursuing separation. Instead, individualists focused their struggle on winning back positions of power within the ejido so that existing irrigation concessions were distributed more equally. The fact that the SICAE, whose backing had been essential to collectivists' ascension to ejidal positions of power, was defunct by this point would have given individualists more confidence that change from within was indeed possible.

If any ejido had the best chance to survive the infighting and factionalism of the postwar years, it was Camajoa. But even here the SICAE's influence strained the bonds that held the community together. Though the ejido did not separate, the ejidatarios can claim no great distinction in this for they would have done so if circumstances had allowed. Rather, their strategy of hydraulic social mobilization was to swallow their pride, brush away the hurtful rhetoric hurled at them over the last few years, look past the unfair and inequitable treatment large swaths of the community had suffered, and stay together. In the end, water mattered far more than all those other things. Conceding their plan to form their own ejido in favor of maintaining their water rights was not only a sacrifice but also a form of hydraulic social mobilization that fully expressed the value Mayo farmers attributed to water.

Conclusion

Being affiliated with the SICAE was a mixed blessing for some Mayo ejidatarios of the Fuerte valley from the mid-1940s to mid-1950s. The cooperative paid Indigenous collectivists a decent salary; invested in canals, pumps, dams, and aqueducts; and granted its members reliable irrigation access to cultivate sugarcane. But the SICAE's benevolence came at a price. Cooperative members had to prove their loyalty by maneuvering within ejidal laws to annex individualist lands and commandeer whatever access they had to irrigation. These actions created tensions that exploded into division and violence in El Teroque, division in Los Goros, and a near division in Camajoa.

Ostensibly, land was at the heart of the battle between individualist and collectivist ejidatarios, but in the arid Fuerte valley land meant little without water. From the late 1920s to early 1940s Indigenous farmers either paid third parties for irrigation water or applied to the postrevolutionary Mexican state for water concessions, but that changed with the arrival of the SICAE. Its four-month-per-year water monopoly and virtual control of the Fuerte River politically marginalized unaffiliated Mayo farmers and severely restricted the availability of irrigation water by the mid-1940s. While the SICAE ordered the clearing and occupation of properties in the Fuerte valley, the excluded individualist Mayo farmers continued to seek irrigation rights. They had to, for collectivist land annexation pushed them onto less productive lands where, ironically, their only chance of producing crops depended upon deepening and expanding the region's irrigation infrastructure.

The history of water in the Fuerte valley during the 1940s and 1950s demonstrates how Mexican Indigenous people survived cultural and physical challenges through hydraulic social mobilization. Time has tested this survival, for in the half-century since Camajoa's near split the Yori population of the Fuerte valley has exploded to nearly a million people while the Mayo population has remained constant at around fifteen thousand. This transformation is evident in the makeup of the El Teroque, Los Goros, and Camajoa ejidos. At the close of the 1950s all three ejidos were still completely Indigenous, but today only 36 percent of ejidatarios in El Teroque Viejo and only 31 percent in Cinco de Mayo define themselves as Mayo. The ejidos that split from Los Goros appear to have retained their traditions more fully, as 80 percent in Los Goros Uno (Oro Pinto) and 28 percent in Los Goros Dos claim to be Mayo. Interestingly, the only ejido to remain united, Camajoa, also managed to remain largely Indigenous, as 79 percent of its inhabitants self-define as Mayo today.[118] It appears that the acute divisiveness within El Teroque left a legacy of mistrust among Mayo ejidatarios that allowed other commonalities such as class or political leanings to overtake Yoreme identity as the bonds of community. Yet even while other alliances have emerged, the culture of Mayo inhabitants in these particular ejidos has remained strong, becoming a source of local pride.[119]

The postrevolutionary and postwar Mexican state intended to promote water distribution strategies to both mobilize campesinos and generate a thriving agricultural economy. Instead, state-sponsored institutions like the SICAE sugarcane cooperative—founded with relatively idealistic aims—exacerbated irrigation disparities they were designed to fix. While the state's hydraulic distribution plans in the Fuerte valley were flawed from their inception, marginalizing campesinos instead of empowering them, some Indigenous farmers leveraged every aspect of their agency to resist. At the heart of their efforts was the issue of water. With it they stood a chance, but without it they were virtually powerless. The SICAE and the corrupt ejidal leadership it cultivated forced Mayo individualists to mobilize. In so doing, some—such as the individualists of El Teroque—found a voice in local development decisions.

By the early 1950s the SICAE's heavy-handed monopoly over water in the Fuerte valley was crumbling. By 1956 the organization was defunct—but not entirely gone. Officials from the agency pivoted to other powerful government posts and brought with them insights and attitudes born of their experience with the SICAE. The SICAE's irrigation manager Calderón Nieves Caparro, for example, made a seamless shift into a high-ranking functionary of the CRF, where he joined new colleagues eager to marginalize Mayo communities.[120] His experience would prove valuable as the state charged the CRF with the goal of squeezing all ejidos' precious water concessions and directing them to large-scale private agribusiness.

The SICAE deserves credit for doing something no one else in Mexican history—not conquistadors, not missionaries, not waves of Yoris, not even United Sugar—had been able to: fracture Mayo solidarity. In the middle of the twentieth century, hydraulic social mobilization for Mayo ejidatarios often meant turning against other Mayo ejidatarios. The cultural wound the cooperative left was deep but not deadly, and though it healed with time the scar is still felt today. The rifts and divisions Mayo individualists had to navigate and respond to were painful on many levels, but the anxiety they felt about not knowing if their land and water would be taken from them pales in comparison to the struggle independent ejidos—those who had no connection to the SICAE—faced. For them, as the next chapter explains, their trials would be so fierce and their options so few that they would scale back their reliance on political avenues and protest and instead have to rely on otherworldly strategies.

THREE

When the State Fails the Gods Remain

Independent Mayo Water Control Strategies, 1944 to 1957

On a hot summer day in the early 1950s, Indigenous farmer Julián Valenzuela and others from La Misión crossed two trickling rivers en route to the Mayo ceremonial center of Tehueco. There was virtually no water left in the two rivers—the Fuerte and Alamos—because the SICAE and private corporations had drained most of it. In Tehueco they joined a half dozen other Indigenous villages to participate in the Yuco Conti ceremony. Long before the postrevolutionary state granted these villages an ejido, generations of Mayo people had met annually in Tehueco during the dry season to watch dancers mimic animals and the natural cycle of rainfall in an effort to coax rain from their gods. For Valenzuela's generation, however, the Yuco Conti ceremony had taken on an importance that had not been felt in decades. When he crossed the rivers, Valenzuela and his compatriots carried with them a particular, collective sense of desperation, for they had become increasingly reliant upon rainfall to harvest their bean, squash, and corn crops.[1] Their embrace of traditional customs like the Yuco Conti was not simply to reinforce or celebrate community—although that is present in their story—but because of the simple fact that they had nowhere else to turn for water.[2]

Like the two crossings Valenzuela had to make, Mayo farmers of the Fuerte valley confronted a double obstacle from the mid-1940s to mid-1950s. The first challenge was the Mexican state. In

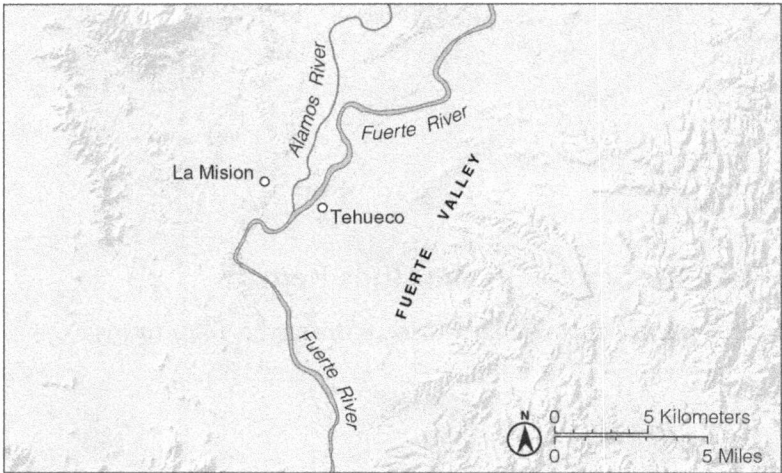

4. Two rivers separate La Misión from Tehueco. Drawn by Pease Press Cartography.

an attempt to transform the Fuerte valley into a breadbasket of Mexico, the state retreated from a combination of ejido-based subsistence farming and cooperative sugarcane harvesting under the SICAE sugarcane cooperative, in favor of clearing land and turning irrigation resources over to large-scale, private agricultural production.

As part of this developmentalist program to "modernize" agriculture in the valley, state agencies such as the Fuerte River Commission (CRF) and Ministry of Water Resources (SRH) began diverting water from canals and pumps away from ejidos like Tehueco and toward private landholders. For La Misión, which never had the right to pump any water to this point, the hope of gaining one completely disappeared. The vast majority of farmers in Mexico at this time depended on rainfall, but the arid conditions of the Fuerte valley had always made this untenable. Historically, Mayo farmers had solved this dilemma by relying on floodplain farming complimented by what little rain fell, but the hydraulic infrastructure of the twentieth century put an end to that. Successful farming now required pumps and canals—and dozens of Mayo villages, like other farmers in the region, had become dependent upon them. But as they lost access to these technologies in the early 1950s, these villages confronted the same difficulties as those who never benefitted from irrigation infrastructure.

Mayo farmers confronted a second, related challenge. As the state appropriated water for private farms, desperate Indigenous farmers became too reliant upon rainfall and came to conclude that large landowners' recent clearing of natural vegetation had reduced local precipitation.[3] As explained below, there may have been reasonable, objective reasons for Mayo farmers to think that less rain fell in the region in the middle of the twentieth century, but the simplest explanation for why they believed this was that they had concluded that Yoris were at the root of all their problems. For Mayo farmers, the same force that left them with too little rainfall to support their crops had also shoved them away from the river and syphoned its precious water elsewhere. If true, their only leverage was to appeal to the gods for more rain. Squeezed on two fronts, Mayo farmers had to look, paradoxically, beyond modern technology and back into their past to solve their current problems.

Apparently, the ceremony in Tehueco that Valenzuela attended did not bring sufficient rainfall, because two weeks later, for the first time ever, the leaders of La Misión hired the same dancers and musicians to reenact the Yuco Conti ritual in their village.[4] The performance of this ceremony in La Misión represented one— but not the only—mobilization strategy farmers used in order to control water. While not as dramatic as seizing irrigated lands (as in chapter 2), bringing the Yuco Conti to La Misión was certainly an act of hydraulic social mobilization.[5] The fact that La Misión, a community just getting by, spent scarce funds to reenact the ceremony exemplifies just how desperate it had become. After all, those living there had come to believe that petitioning their gods for water was as effective as petitioning the Mexican government.

By the 1940s Mayo farmers constituted three categories in the Fuerte valley. As described in chapter 2, ejidos affiliated with the SICAE split into two groups: collectivists who received a decent wage for harvesting sugarcane versus individualists who were

poorer, lacked the political connections of the collectivist ejidatarios, and were consequently pressured out of their lands. Yet
there were also members of ejidos not affiliated with the SICAE
at all who comprised a third category: independent ejidatarios.[6]
This chapter tells the story of how Valenzuela and other "independent" Mayo farmers adapted to massive changes in the political
and physical environment in the Fuerte valley during the crucial
years of the mid-1940s to mid-1950s.

Independent Mayo farmers found no prosperity outside of the
SICAE. Rather, they became collateral damage as the sugarcane
cooperative battled back against the state's preference for and investments in private farmers. Water was the weapon of choice in this
fight, and neither the SICAE nor large, private estates cared how
little the independent ejidos received. Some independent ejidos, in
a fashion that appears to have been systematic, compounded their
problems by cultivating divisions among themselves. For example, in Jahuara, an ejido discussed below, all the ejidatarios were
independent—they had no formal affiliation with the SICAE—
yet the ejido had its own small forest cooperative of which only
some were affiliated while others, who were generally less elite and
politically connected, were not. Understanding how independent
Mayo farmers used different water gathering strategies than sugarcane collectivists and individualists attests to the heterogeneity
of Indigenous practices of the Fuerte valley in the 1940s and 1950s
and exemplifies how, of the three groups, their goals and concerns
were least important to the Mexican state.

No one came away unscarred in this battle for authority in the
Fuerte valley, including the SICAE. Even though it still retained a
four-month monopoly on water from the Fuerte River, the state's
developmentalist polices from the mid-1940s to mid-1950s began
undermining the cooperative's authority. This wrestling for power
altered the political, physical, and social landscape of the Fuerte
valley in ways that independent farmers never predicted. While
the postrevolutionary state (1927–42) encouraged independent
Mayo political mobilization and organizations like the SICAE that
were supposed to help other small farmers advance economically,

postwar-era developmentalist hydraulic projects actively ignored small farmers and undermined institutions intended to strengthen them. The forces at play in this chapter appeared, rather, to expect their submission.[7]

Despite these obstacles, independent Mayo farmers refused to be mere spectators to the fight. Rather, they employed their knowledge of the political and natural landscape to navigate the new irrigation laws that the state created with an eye toward stripping them of their control over water. Because of the distinctive personalities within each community and the diverse challenges they faced, independent Mayo villages responded differently to these changes. Yet their reliance upon the ancient and the new was a common denominator that speaks to Mayo people's ability to embrace change by reaching into the past—a trait not uncommon among other Indigenous people of the Americas.

Jahuara: What Is Old Becomes New

By the early 1940s the Mayo farmers of Jahuara, like all the independent ejidatarios in the Fuerte valley, faced limited options to access water. They also had a unique problem: the ejido had a pump but the group controlling it was unwilling to share it with the rest of the ejido. A portion of the 4,606-hectare dotación Jahuara received in 1938 included 160 hectares of land irrigated from a pump owned by a Yori farmer named Cecilio Román.[8] For the first few years of the ejido's existence there appears to have been no significant problem in distributing water from the pump, but that changed in the early 1940s when several dozen ejidatarios of Jahuara created the Sociedad Cooperativa Forestal Ejidal (Ejidal Forestry Cooperative, SCFE). The SCFE aimed to supplement members' incomes from farming with selling wood harvested from their pastureland and forests.

Like a smaller version of the SICAE, Jahuara's most powerful ejidatarios comprised the cooperative, and, like the SICAE collectivists, SCFE cooperative members (referred to as loggers from this point forward) leveraged their relative power and backing from state agencies like the Banco Ejidal (Ejidal Bank) to claim the best farmland, pushed nonmembers (non-loggers from here on out) out of irrigation rights, and prevented others from joining.[9] This pattern appears to have prevailed elsewhere in postrevolutionary and postwar Mexico, for as environmental historian Christopher Boyer argues in the cases of Chihuahua and Michoacán, "Cooperatives established a means for communicating the ideals of scientific forestry to the 'people' and, if necessary, for sanctioning illegal behavior."[10] Like other cooperatives across the nation, Jahuara's loggers straddled the lines of legality, often victimizing non-loggers who refused to accept their marginalization.

Loggers had a powerful ally in the Ejidal Bank, which in addition to offering advice and preferential credit, also provided them with irrigation water from the pump it controlled.[11] Since the entire ejido had access to the pump in the late 1930s, it appears the loggers had gained control of the device and then ceded it to the bank as collateral for credit to fund their forest cooperative. In a blatant act of favoritism, only loggers affiliated with the bank received irrigation water from the pump. In turn, they leveraged this influence to gain power within the ejido, acting as the decision makers for the entire ejido.[12] The Ejidal Bank provided the loggers every advantage possible to ensure that they could pay back their debts.

The Ejidal Bank did not have formal permission from the Secretaría de Agricultura y Fomento (Ministry of Agriculture and Development, SAYF) to operate this pump, yet Jahuara's loggers continued to draw water from it until 1948.[13] The leeway the SAYF granted to the Ejidal Bank showed the immense power the state apparatus awarded certain institutions in its attempts at redesigning the Mexican countryside to maximize economic efficiency. There was, of course, also an ethnic component to the way it wielded power. Like other state-backed institutions such as the SICAE, the Ejidal Bank's administrators were primarily Yoris, whose policies did not express concern for Mayo rights or identity. As the 1940s wore on, these high-placed Yori administrators saw Indigenous farmers as a barrier to improving Mexico's agricultural production. While they might occasionally favor particular groups like the Indigenous loggers, Yori-dominated agencies excluded individualist farmers from decisions regarding hydraulic development projects as a rule. Simply put, Yori administrators, even those in institutions that were supposed to help all ejidatarios, had little concern for Indigenous farmers who did not directly serve their interests.

With the loggers of Jahuara receiving all of the water from the pump, non-loggers became compelled to find imaginative ways to get water. In September 1944 non-loggers proposed to SAYF officials a plan to use a canal to drain water from a lagoon that flooded with the rains and divert it to one hundred hectares of garbanzos. Once they had drained off the flooded portion, they planned to grow corn and beans in the damp earth.[14] Their petition took care to point out that their ambitions would not interfere with any other powerful player in the region, explaining, "We will discharge flood waters from rain into the river and build a drainage canal over the SICAE's irrigation canal, where it intersects. . . . After cooperative leaders [loggers] left Ejidal Bank offices they delayed our project, even burying a portion of the drainage canal to stop our progress."[15] On the one hand, the petition was a straightforward solution to a water shortage problem, but it also shows the non-loggers' bureaucratic savvy. They took great care to point out that they would in no way affect the SICAE's existing hydraulic structure. As the petition states, they already had the Ejidal Bank for an enemy, and the last thing they could afford was to incur the wrath of the powerful sugarcane cooperative as well.

The use of lagoon land to grow crops was an adaptation of the traditional Mayo floodplain cultivation. While the technique had not been in use for over a generation, the knowledge had not been lost. However, in contrast to their ancestors who relied on the annual flooding and receding of the Fuerte River to water land for planting, the non-loggers of Jahuara intended to use modern technology to drain flooded sections of the ejido and plant crops there. Thus there is a strange, almost poetic, irony to the petition. In the previous few decades, canals and pumps along the Fuerte River had diverted water and reduced the river's flow, preventing it from annually overflowing its banks and essentially ending Mayo floodplain agriculture. Now the same canal and pump technology that had eliminated traditional Mayo irrigation would help resurrect its practice, even if only on a smaller scale.[16] The plan, which drew from historical Mayo farming techniques, showcased how these Indigenous farmers moved between traditional and modern worlds and the growing hybridity of Mayo practices.

Likewise, other time-honored practices, such as identifying the enemies of one's enemies and leveraging alliances from that knowledge, had never left the Mayo people. Several Mayo groups, such as Jahuara's non-loggers, became quite adept, particularly during the SICAE's ascendancy, at exploiting existing divisions between the Ejidal Bank and the SAYF. Like many state agencies of the 1940s, the two vied for federal resources and the power to distribute them, and it was no coincidence that the non-loggers, who had been marginalized by the Ejidal Bank, sent their petition to the SAYF. The September petition warned the SAYF to remain cautious of unnecessary delays in moving forward with the project as it gave the loggers time to create obstacles and bring in the influence of the Ejidal Bank to stop it all together.[17] Standing up on their own to the influence of the bank was never a realistic option for the non-loggers, but they could with the support of the SAYF. Their relative vulnerability did not deny them viable strategies.

This infighting among state-backed organizations characterized the struggle during the mid-1940s for limited federal funds. Mayo farmers seemed to have grasped what Timothy Mitchell contends in *Rule of Experts*: that modern states take on the appearance of uniform entities when, in fact, they are a collection of multiple, sometimes conflicting logics.[18] For example, it was SICAE officials who reported to the Secretaría de Recursos Hidráulicos (Ministry of Water Resources) in 1948 that the Ejidal Bank did not have official permission to use the pump in Jahuara.[19] Elsewhere the Ejidal Bank and the SICAE had collaborated, flexing their political muscle to empower affiliated sugarcane collectivists, but as there were no SICAE collectivists in Jahuara, the SICAE had no investment in protecting members of Jahuara's forest cooperative. Rather—in an almost paranoid effort to control as much of the Fuerte River as possible—the SICAE viewed Jahuara's irrigation concession as detrimental to its irrigation monopoly.[20]

The ejidatarios were not the only ones who could employ divide and conquer strategies—state agencies could just as easily. While Jahuara's non-loggers turned state agencies against each other, the Ejidal Bank took a cue from the SICAE and provided loggers with the tools necessary to hoard natural resources and force non-loggers to fend for themselves. Ironically, the SICAE and the Ejidal Bank, both designed to provide opportunities for ejidatarios, created the conditions that caused conflict and contention between ejidal factions.

The 1944 lagoon-canal proposal showed that, despite their growing marginalization within the federal bureaucracy, leaders of the non-loggers in Jahuara believed they could align with state agencies to get water—but not all Mayo farmers were as optimistic. As water concessions became more difficult to obtain and hopes dimmed, dozens of Indigenous farmers elsewhere began to embrace other less-than-legal strategies. For instance, Indigenous elder Gustavo Aguilar of Los Goros describes how some individualist (relative to the SICAE) Mayo farmers from his ejido constructed unsanctioned small canals that drew water from larger canals or directly from the river. Similarly, Francisco Jacinto recalls how non-loggers in Jahuara illegally opened canal floodgates so that the irrigation water ran onto their fields and then held makeshift partitions to keep the water in place long enough to seep into the ground.[21] In a sense, these farmers put into action a hydraulic social mobilization practice similar to the 1944 petition only without state sanction. But what was that to them when state functionaries were clearly losing interest in their rights and well-being?

Fortunately for the non-loggers in Jahuara, the SICAE took no position on their petition to drain the lagoon—their opposition would have all but assured the project's termination—but in January 1945, four months after the non-loggers submitted their petition, matters worsened. That month the Ejidal Bank sent a letter to the SAYF in an attempt to strengthen the loggers' ejidal water monopoly. The letter voiced the bank's opposition to the proposed construction, with the implicit message that it threatened the power the loggers' water monopoly gave them over the ejido.[22] The Ejidal Bank claimed to represent the best interests of the ejido, yet by formally opposing the petition, the bank gave credence to the non-loggers' claims that loggers' efforts to stall construction came at the behest of the bank.

The SAYF dismissed the claims of the Ejidal Bank and, heeding the non-loggers' accusation that the bank and its loggers sought to sabotage the project, monitored the undertaking closely. Sensing that it was on shaky ground, the Ejidal Bank withdrew its explicit opposition to the non-loggers' plan. In March 1945 Raymundo Enríquez Cruz, an engineer with the SAYF, informed his superiors that the work was "moving ahead without incident and benefits the entire village of Jahuara. Opponents of the project have agreed to give consent."[23] Sensing the project was gaining momentum, the Ejidal Bank appears to have pivoted from overt condemnation of the endeavor to more subtle tactics. Still, from the bank's perspective, power in the ejido was a zero-sum game; whatever benefited the non-loggers came at the expense of the loggers it supported.

The last hurdle for the non-loggers of Jahuara was to secure the formal support of the SAYF, for with that they could rest assured that no one could steal away their hard work. In August 1945 the Departamento Agrario (Agrarian Department) helped the non-loggers on their way by writing a letter to the SAYF that precisely outlined the non-loggers' construction plans, explaining, "The 32 individualists [non-loggers] plan to divert water from the Jahuara lagoon to irrigate 100 hectares of garbanzos. They are installing a gate and spillway and have built 1,430 meters of the drainage canal, and 1,845 meters of the irrigation canal."[24] Much of what was in the letter would have been known by the SAYF's own observers, but there was a new element to this letter: at no point did the Departamento Agrario mention the drainage canal crossing the SICAE Canal. It appears that non-loggers found a way to avoid threatening any of the sugarcane cooperative's infrastructure. With the Ejidal Bank and the SICAE indifferently on the sidelines, the non-loggers made it easy for the SAYF to formally agree.

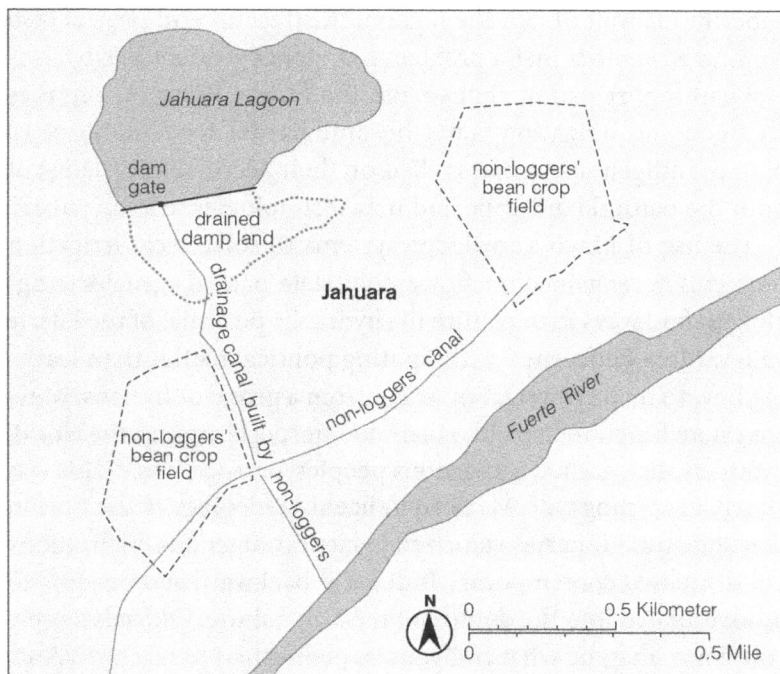

5. Non-loggers' irrigation project in Jahuara, 1945. Originally drawn by Engineer Benjamin Castro Tinoc, June 1945, AHA, Aguas Nacionales, Caja 1313, Expediente 17668. Redrawn by Pease Press Cartography.

The addition of an irrigation canal allowed the non-loggers to grow corn and beans on the recently drained, moist land, and use the diverted water to irrigate one hundred additional hectares of garbanzos. The blueprint represented in figure 5, included in the non-loggers' proposal to the SAYF, shows the construction completed by June 1945. Non-loggers set aside the southern "L" shaped tip of the lagoon, in the upper left corner of the blueprint, to harvest corn and bean crops in the damp earth, separating this section with a gate to prevent water from seeping back in after they drained it. These independent Mayo farmers also intended to use the irrigation canal below the lagoon, running parallel to the Fuerte River to divert water and irrigate garbanzo bean crops in the areas marked "non-loggers' bean crop field."[25] By using the superfluous water from the lagoon, this resourceful project also eliminated another major problem facing independent Mayo farmers: gaining irrigation rights from the Fuerte River. As regimes changed and irrigation water became harder for ejidatarios to obtain, Indigenous farmers relied on their accrued knowledge of both the natural landscape and new technologies to keep pace.[26]

The use of Mayo knowledge systems to solve local irrigation problems never gained traction among state-backed agencies struggling to find ways to maximize the hydraulic potential of the Fuerte valley. More concerned with fighting political battles than learning how to manage irrigation water from a group of Indians, Mexican state functionaries, like their counterparts around the world, routinely disregarded Indigenous peoples' perspectives.[27] This was largely in keeping with Mexican indigenista ideology of the time in that state functionaries valorized ancient Indigenous civilizations but dismissed contemporary Indians as backward and needing to be assimilated into the dominant mestizo culture. Officials simply could not imagine what Indigenous people had to teach.[28] While such disdain for local irrigation practices undermined the very democratic principles most modern states claimed to uphold, it also limited technocrats' development options. In the Fuerte valley, state-mandated use of Indigenous hydraulic innovation would have provided campesinos more water and could have led to a more egalitarian system of irrigation distribution. Yet by shunning native hydraulic knowledge, the state followed a preconceived path to modernity because it allowed for more political, social, and environmental control.[29]

Whatever confidence the non-logger ejidatarios had accumulated at the beginning of 1945 had largely dissipated by the end of the year. Despite the earlier report of SAYF engineer Raymundo Enríquez Cruz, in which he claimed all parties approved of the project, it appears that the Ejidal Bank did not actually support the non-loggers' water rights but had adopted a judicious silence, waiting for the right opportunity to turn the non-loggers' efforts into an advantage for the loggers. In October bank officials asked the SAYF to suspend construction so that they could conduct a census in Jahuara to determine who had rights to the proposed irrigation water.[30] This was more than just a mere stalling tactic, for there never was a question as to who the bank would find had the requisite rights. The maneuver was a blatant effort to marginalize farmers by finding ways to give most, if not all, of their loggers access to the water and denying non-loggers' water rights. If the non-loggers had an autonomous source of irrigation, they could be equal partners in ejido decisions and potentially push back against the privileges the loggers had secured for themselves.

The bank had already made sure that loggers of Jahuara were the sole beneficiaries of water from the ejido's pumps, and now the bank wanted these cooperative members to profit from the irrigation infrastructure that the non-loggers had constructed with their own labor and funds. One explanation for the bank's intrigue is that Mexico's emerging developmentalist plans had adversely affected it, too. Like many state institutions at this time, the Ejidal Bank was under enormous pressure to get its numbers in the black, so it did all it could to ensure that its debtors had every resource necessary to pay back their debts.[31] Yet by doing so, the bank eliminated opportunities available to other Mayo groups— like non-loggers—and eroded the ejidatarios' faith in state agencies generally.

Corresponding documents do not reveal if Jahuara's non-loggers ever completed their project, but oral sources suggest that the state never granted them the opportunity to utilize water from the lagoon. As Mayo elder Flor Escalante of Jahuara remembers, "Some ejidatarios had irrigation in the 1940s, and the Yoris kept the rest from getting it. By the 1950s, none of us had irrigation."[32] Historical evidence corroborates Escalante's claims. It was not until 1948 that, at the behest of the SICAE, the state shut down the Ejidal Bank's pump. If, as Escalante asserts, no ejidatarios had irrigation water by the 1950s, then the lagoon drainage plan never came to completion. The lack of project documentation after 1945 appears to substantiate this claim.

Besides providing evidence as to the fate of the petition, Escalante's recollection also reveals the distrust that Jahuara's independent Mayo farmers had for state agencies by the late 1940s. It is significant that Escalante remembered the "Yoris" as responsible for keeping Mayo farmers from accessing irrigation water.[33] The fact that Yoris managed the Ejidal Bank and that the agency consistently refused to promote projects that benefitted all Indigenous people led independent Mayo farmers to equate such state institutions with Yoris. In a sense the judgment was fair, as these agencies had caused the immediate suffering of the independent Mayo in Jahuara. First, the Ejidal Bank, looking to ensure that its affiliated ejidatarios had all the resources they needed, targeted non-loggers and denied them irrigation. Next, the SICAE, looking to protect its power vis-à-vis other government agencies, targeted the entire ejido by having the pump shut down. However, it was ultimately a losing battle for both agencies, as faith in the two declined in rough correlation to their waning influence.

Changes in state hydraulic bureaucracy and new irrigation projects of the mid to late 1940s enabled the private sector to cut into the authority and power of both the SICAE and the Ejidal Bank. The key to this shift lay in President Miguel Alemán Valdés dismantling the SAYF and creating in its place the Secretaría de Recursos Hidráulicos (Ministry of Water Resources, SRH) in 1946. Driven by the goal of promoting economic development, Alemán tasked the SRH with finding ways to distribute water resources, especially to regions with untapped economic potential. Alemán's administration saw the Fuerte valley as one of these regions, and soon the SRH adopted policies which facilitated land grabs—and the water resources that came with them—by large commercial agricultural operations. For instance, Filiberto Quintero, a large estate owner in the region and consistent critic of the SICAE's water monopoly, began to buy properties in the Fuerte valley with the SRH's encouragement beginning in the late 1940s. With these lands, he also secured water rights and effectively broke the monopoly which had dominated economic life in the valley for the previous decade. Quintero's gains went only to himself; no ejidatarios—not even collectivists—benefited from the change in water rights.[34]

The SRH's actions reflected a trend of state-backed private invest-

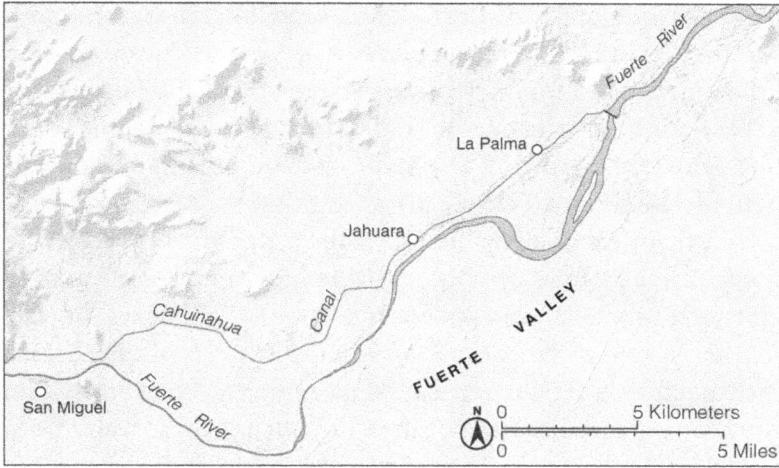

6. Jahuara and La Palma are located on the banks of the Fuerte River, with the Cahuinahua Canal running through them. Drawn by Pease Press Cartography.

ment that gave Yori landowners rights to irrigation infrastructure in hopes that their large-scale agricultural ventures would be more efficient than the ejidos. The SICAE's seasonal water monopoly was still in place, but internal strife, corruption, grassroots opposition, and the increasing power of private landowners and corporations challenged the cooperative's dominance. When the state and large landowners began collaborating on the construction of canals and dams in the late 1940s, it signaled the beginning of the end for the SICAE.[35] It also created new hydraulic obstacles for independent Mayo farmers in such unaffiliated ejidos as Jahuara's neighbor La Palma, where a new, celebrated canal brought water in an unwelcome way.

Flooded by Indifference in La Palma

The proliferation of canals and dams fulfilled the Mexican state's developmentalist agenda in the late 1940s, but they did not bring much benefit for independent Mayo ejidatarios. Despite their proximity the irrigation canals never poured a drop out onto independent Mayo farms but instead rushed by on their way to large, private estates. In the case of La Palma, the problem was not merely the state's indifference to its irrigation needs but the fact that projects the state did endorse and underwrite wreaked havoc on what little water the community came in contact with. The ejidatarios of La Palma confronted either a shortage of dependable water throughout the growing season or else too much all at once—both of which ruined crops.

Like many ejidos along the Fuerte River, La Palma's history with water and the state is complicated. The state granted La Palma its first water permit in 1942, but due to the SICAE's influence the state refused to renew the concession when it expired in 1944.[36] Like their neighbors in Jahuara, La Palma exploited divisions within government agencies and began to illegally purchase water from the Ejidal Bank in 1944. In 1948, when the SICAE discovered the purchases, they forced the bank to end the agreement.[37] As was the case in Jahuara, the SICAE looked to tighten their grip on water, and this meant there was no reliable irrigation water available for independent or individualist ejidatarios. In La Palma's case, however, the situation grew worse, for in that same year, state and private investors collaborated to construct the Cahuinahua Canal running parallel to the Fuerte River just south of La Palma.

A cornerstone of the state's plan to modernize the Fuerte valley, government engineers intended the canal to supply only private landowners with irrigation water in the expectation that they would not only feed the local population but also produce a surplus for export.[38] The daily local newspaper *El Debate de Los Mochis* explained that the Secretaría de Agricultura (Ministry of Agriculture) paid for the canal's construction through a four million peso loan from the Banco de Crédito Agrícola (Agricultural Credit Bank) and, ironically, the Ejidal Bank.[39] The article explained to its readers that the engineers designed the structure to irrigate an additional thirty thousand hectares of land for local farmers, but also added, tellingly, "It will benefit farmers who will ultimately pay for this [hydraulic] work, because the money that banks contributed will only be a loan."[40] State agencies therefore put up the capital to construct the canal, but rights to its use would be determined by the amount farmers contributed. Poorer subsistence ejidos would not have the funds to so much as dip into the new canal.

The construction of the Cahuinahua Canal marked a turning point in the Fuerte valley. From that moment on, the Mexican state curtailed its support of the SICAE's irrigation projects and instead began funding the erection of hydraulic infrastructure that would serve massive agribusinesses and occasionally smallholder farmers. Water availability equaled dominion. By flexing their financial resources and collaborating with the state, Yori landowners found another way to further consolidate their power in the region and begin to push aside the sugarcane cooperative. Even a weakened SICAE could have still been a valuable ally for La Palma, but as independent ejidatarios, they were on their own. They had to witness the brutal sight of the canal literally passing by their ejido, carrying valuable water to those with more clout. Painful as this sight was, the ejidatarios of La Palma had another, more pressing problem: when heavy, seasonal rains came, water pooled up and overflowed or broke through the sandy banks of the canal, drowning their crops.

In an attempt to seek assistance and prevent disaster, the head of the executive ejidal committee of La Palma sent a petition via telegram to President Miguel Alemán and the Federal Treasury in July 1948. Their petition asked the president and treasury to remove the canal, arguing, "The placing of the Cahuinahua Canal near our ejido is irresponsible, and, since it is poorly constructed and made of sand, it causes unpredictable floods in our village that have ruined our crops."[41] The committee still held onto the hope that they could, despite limited success in the recent past, appeal to the Mexican state to be a fair arbiter of the situation.

Like their Mayo neighbors in Jahuara, ejidatarios in La Palma knew that flooding could be a viable source of irrigation, but the poor construction of the canal caused capricious inundations that diverged from the expected annual Fuerte River flooding that Mayo farmers had depended upon for centuries. Before canals began diverting river water in the early twentieth century, Mayo farmers had calculated the coming and receding of the flood waters

7. This photo of the unfinished Cahuinahua Canal, kilometer 8, taken on May 1, 1951, displays its porous sandy banks, which caused ruptures in the sides and made surrounding areas susceptible to floods. CONAGUA-AHA, Fondo Consultivo Técnico, Caja 739, Expediente 7110, Legajo 1, Foja 11.

within days and stood ready to plant seeds in the wet soil as soon as the water receded. They knew when to expect deluges, ensuring that they harvested their bean, squash, and corn crops before the next one struck. With the canal both causing inundation in some places and blocking receding water in others, there was no clear pattern to planting and harvesting; some areas could be bone dry while others sat under deep pools of water.

What La Palma's leaders expected from their petition is unclear. The federal banks, Ministry of Agriculture, and even President Alemán had already showed enthusiasm for the canal by helping to create it, so they were unlikely to side with an Indigenous community looking to remove it. At the least, the submission testifies to the limited options at the disposal of independent Indigenous ejidatarios during the late 1940s. They likely understood where the interests of each of these state institutions lay, but without wealth or influence of their own or a powerful ally like the SICAE or the Ejidal Bank, they had little other choice than to try. The petition's authors knew they faced long odds and were likely unsurprised when their petition met with silence.

La Palma's ejidatarios experienced a particularly difficult year in 1948. Within the course of just two months, the SICAE's complaint resulted in the termination of their water concession and the newly built Cahuinahua Canal caused an excess of floodwaters. Maintaining productive lands without the use of canals and pumps was challenging but having to produce crops during times of unpredictable flooding was a nearly insurmountable obstacle. It put the community into a political and economic vice. If these farmers did not plant because of the risk of flooding, a lack of crops meant that there would not be food to put on the table. Worse yet, the land left fallow would become vulnerable to seizure. However, to risk planting only to see the plants drown could also spell economic ruin. La Palma's leaders had tried petitions but met only with indifference from state functionaries. As a result, ejidatarios embraced escalating protests over the next few weeks.

By the late 1940s, as common as Mayo petitions for the redress of injustices were in the Fuerte valley, so too were protests and political actions outside the legal norms. However, as in the case of La Palma, these actions must be understood as a last resort that independent ejidatarios embraced only after failed attempts to work within the system.[42] They still saw themselves as valid partners and valuable assets to Mexican agriculture, but state functionaries viewed Indigenous groups like the Mayo as unfortunate remnants of an earlier political regime and obstacles to improvement.

The tension between the views of the state versus those of La Palma's ejidatarios became increasingly unavoidable. In the same busy month of July 1948, the official director of construction for the canal wrote a letter to the SRH about the potential threat of unrest in La Palma. "This situation," he warned, "has been caused by the bad faith of some individuals who have incited the Indigenous people of La Palma, for purely political purposes."[43] The letter and corresponding archival documents do not reveal what these protests entailed or the identity of the alleged outsiders who incited the Mayo ejidatarios of La Palma, but the government had been put on notice.[44]

Oral sources paint a different picture, refuting the director's claim that outsiders incited the Indigenous ejidatarios of La Palma. As Librado Cuadros, an Indigenous elder from La Palma explains, "We were behind the protests. We did not need anyone else to tell us the problem. We could see the destruction was coming from the canal they put in our village."[45] It is possible that Cuadros remembered these events retrospectively and assigned ejido members more agency by claiming that they initiated the protests without being incited. However, Mayo elders of the Fuerte valley proudly boast about their political savviness and the alliances they forged to this day; they did not require outsiders to egg them on.

Local officials wanted to quell any political unrest because it made them appear incompetent and could jeopardize the canal. After all, the state's efforts to modernize the Mexican economy were extensive in most cases. But in La Palma, at that point, modernization consisted of just a few inches of packed sand and dirt—the sunk costs were low enough that the state could have walked away from the project. Perhaps this helps to explain why federal officials and especially local Yori elites pushed the narrative of outside agitators: they did not want another Mayo revolutionary like Felipe Bachomo—as discussed in chapter 1—to emerge and rally Indigenous farmers against modernization efforts. The 1948 La Palma protests were one of the few documented examples of Indigenous people in the Fuerte valley opposing the construction of hydraulic infrastructure.[46] Through most of the twentieth century Mayo villagers commonly supported canal construction with the hope that they would be able to use them. The protest in La Palma was a measure of dimming hope as the community came to the realization that, in addition to the floods it caused, the Cahuinahua Canal would never benefit them. Only three years separated Jahuara's 1945 petition from La Palma's, but it might as well have been different eras. Whereas non-loggers in Jahuara had been able to at least get a hearing regarding construction of new irrigation infrastructure and pit state agencies against one another, the Mexican government simply dismissed La Palma's petition.

One reason state functionaries could afford to ignore La Palma's petitions was that not all farmers in the region agreed with the ejido's perspective. Other ejidatarios and small property owners sent letters to President Alemán expressing their support for the canal. For instance, in April 1948 a Yori farmer named Antonio Caballero wrote a letter to Alemán on behalf of local small property owners, thanking him for the Cahuinahua Canal. According to the letter, the canal brought great agricultural opportunities to smallholders who all agreed on their approval for the structure.[47] Not only did private property holders sing the canal's praises but even other ejidatarios supported the canal's construction. In March 1949 a Yori ejidal farmer named Lorenzo Robles also wrote to President Alemán and urged him to continue the construction of the canal on behalf of the ejidatarios of the municipality of Ahome.[48]

Both letters ostensibly expressed support for the canal, yet there is a small—but telling—difference between them. In the case of Robles's letter on behalf of ejidatarios, it further asks the president for help with procuring pumps to divert water from the canal to their fields.[49] Simply put, there was a large discrepancy between private landholders and ejidatarios in their ability to use the canal. Landowners often had the means to use this canal immediately, but financial constraints forced ejidatarios to depend on the state to help them gain access to pumps. To make matters worse, ejidatarios generally did not help fund the construction of the canal, so—pumps or no pumps—they would not have legal rights to the structure's irrigation water.

It would take time before other ejidatarios came to understand the reality that the farmers of La Palma already grasped. Until then, enthusiasm for the canal and hope for what it could provide was the norm in the Fuerte valley. In this respect, the region's farmers held attitudes toward irrigation projects much like other agriculturalists throughout the world. Mark Fiege explains in his book *Irrigated Eden* that farmers and technocrats in Idaho marveled at their ability to control nature and the flow of water and believed it would improve the lives of all. Yet, as in the Fuerte valley, Fiege reveals that attempts to manipulate Idaho's natural landscape did not always go according to plan. The inability to regulate water and local ecosystems to meet irrigation expectations in Idaho forced proponents there to tone down their rhetoric and refer to their relationship with nature less as "control" and more as "housekeeping."[50] The Cahuinahua Canal demonstrated that a similar rhetorical dampening was due in the Fuerte valley. Though they never used the language of the people Fiege quoted, the Mayo leaders of La Palma believed that since the Mexican state was liable for the mess that the construction of the canal created and because it was unable to control the flow of water through the natural landscape, it should spearhead "housekeeping" operations.[51]

The timing of the La Palma leaders' 1948 petitions and another letter the following year suggest that the unexpected flood waters coming from the Cahuinahua Canal ruined both the summer crop of 1948 and winter harvest of 1949. As they were in uncharted territory, the community took unusual steps. On March 22, 1949, La Palma's ejidatarios formally asked the government for monetary compensation for ruined land and fruit crops.[52] The request indicated that, though the canal had been in existence for just under a year, the floods had grown worse and more erratic and left the ejidatarios of La Palma in a precarious position. They were reluctant to plant anything for fear that unpredictable flood waters would destroy crops.

This context makes it easy to see why the protests in La Palma could escalate so easily. Up until the late 1940s the ejidatarios of La Palma had never requested monetary compensation from the state and only minimally protested against the construction of canals. Rather, with the government's encouragement, the ejido had adapted to changes in the physical and political landscape in the postrevolutionary era by using canals and pumps to draw water, extending their connection to the Fuerte River. When the state responded to their petitions and approved land grant and irrigation concessions in the mid-1930s to early 1940s, the state brought La Palma's ejidatarios into the social, political, and economic system of the Fuerte valley, but this encouragement lasted just over a decade.[53]

By the beginning of 1949 it was clear, at least to the ejidatarios of La Palma, that Mexican policies favored corporate development over subsistence farming and that the flooding caused by implementing this agenda was the responsibility of the state. La Palma's hydraulic social mobilization strategy had evolved from seeking the right to access irrigation and becoming a partner in local development, to pleading to the state for help in adapting to an agenda that excluded and endangered them, to finally demanding compensation and protesting. By midcentury La Palma's situation was becoming dire, but it was not alone. Many other Mayo villages were also being squeezed by state developmentalist agendas and La Palma was unfortunately notable only in that it was at the forefront of these changes.

Their experience with the Cahuinahua Canal did not, however, turn the Mayo farmers of La Palma into Luddites. The documents and oral interviews analyzed here reveal that even into the 1950s independent Mayo farmers embraced irrigation infrastructure that they believed could advance their village's interests. For example, in 1951, after fighting against the installation of the Cahuinahua Canal for years (apparently the state finally fixed the problem by lining the canal with concrete), the ejidal leaders of La Palma requested permission to install a pump along the north bank of the Fuerte River.[54] Despite the Cahuinahua Canal ruining ejidal land, independent ejidatarios of La Palma were able to draw a distinction between beneficial and detrimental hydraulic infrastructure.

While their belief in the usefulness of technology persisted, the ejidatarios of La Palma's faith in the Mexican government had been shaken by the time they requested to install a pump. There is an element of desperation in their request for pumping rights, as though they might leverage their unconventional demand for compensation with a more conventional request for an irrigation concession. Unsurprisingly, it did not work, and the Mexican government turned down La Palma's petition.[55] Water was a valuable resource and state functionaries wanted it to go to the large, private farms they believed were more efficient. This last petition reflected the close of an era in La Palma and in the Fuerte valley more broadly. No longer would independent Mayo farmers look to the government as a disinterested arbiter in the region—let alone a potential ally—they would leverage other systems of knowledge to secure their water, land, and lives.

The Perception of Decreased Rainfall in Mayo Ejidos

"Because we could not get irrigation water, this [rainfall] became the life of most Yoremes [Mayo] by the 1950s. When it rained we took advantage of the water; working our parcels, we planted beans, squash, and corn."[56] Mayo elder Sabás Ynustrosa of La Mojonera recalls the fate of independent, Indigenous ejidatarios as the state stopped approving their irrigation concession requests and instead helped large landowners build hydraulic infrastructure to be used exclusively for large-scale agricultural ventures: they relied increasingly—exclusively in some cases—on rainfall, the only equitably distributed source of water in the Fuerte valley. As their reliance on it increased, Mayo attitudes and perceptions of rain changed. For roughly two decades, beginning in the late 1920s, hundreds of independent Mayo farmers in villages like La Palma had used pumps and canals to draw water from the Fuerte River, virtually ending their reliance on rain-fed agriculture—at least temporarily. But now, as the state denied them the right to use canals and pumps to irrigate and as that same hydraulic infrastructure prevented the possibility of floodplain irrigation, this generation of Mayo farmers rediscovered the importance of Mayo rain traditions and ceremonies like no generation before.

Even their best efforts to call upon and harvest the rainfall, however, could never compete with modern hydraulic infrastructure. SICAE-affiliated ejidos, or at least the collectivists in them, could rely upon the power of the cooperative to acquire water and ensure their lands never became fallow, but the independent ejidos had no such assurance. As the state took their water and gave it to large estates, the size of their fields diminished while private

landholdings expanded. For instance, in the early 1950s Sara Herrán Viuda de la Vega, the owner of a vast, private farm, was able
to recover some of the lands the state had originally confiscated
from her deceased husband in order to form part of the La Palma
ejido.[57] In fact, private holdings in the Fuerte valley—such as Viuda
de la Vega's in La Palma—increased so much that, in addition to
encroaching on ejidal lands, large landowners also began clearing
thousands of hectares of natural vegetation. From the Mayo perspective, this outsider encroachment stung. First, annexed "fallow"
ejido lands were likely never going to return to the community.
Second, and equally insidious, the clearing of trees and other vegetation seemed to have an impact on the only remaining source
of water for the independent farmers: rain.

Independent Indigenous ejidatarios noticed decreases in
annual crop yields beginning in the late 1940s, and most came to
believe that the cause was reduced rainfall. As Mayo elder Roberto
Escalante of La Palma contends, "There was more rain before the
1950s, but we did not rely on it, because we had access to a pump.
But after, there was less rain and we did not have enough water.
It often stopped raining before the crop was ready, and the corn
was dried, or beans, squash, or watermelon crops were ruined."[58]
Escalante's claims of a dual curse—elimination of irrigation rights
and decreased rainfall—are echoed by others who lived through
the period. But were these Mayo farmers doubly burdened? And,
more pointedly, were the two curses somehow connected?

Independent Mayo ejidatarios blamed the decrease in precipitation levels on Mexico's developmentalist agenda, particularly its
ravenous appetite for acreage. As Mayo elder Juan Valenzuela of
Camajoa, recalling the period from the late 1940s to the early 1950s,
asserts, "There was more vegetation before Yoris, in the name of
progress, cleared trees and shrubs to make way for farmland and
animal pastures, resulting in less rain here. But it was dangerous for
those of us who needed rain to grow the crops we relied on to survive."[59] The growth of the economy in the Fuerte valley meant the
expansion of cultivated land and the reduction of forested land, all
of which, in the minds of the Mayo people, adversely reduced rain-

fall. It was not only the large private estates that were to blame. As wealthy landowners expanded their large-scale agricultural operations and cleared land in the late 1940s, they began to encroach on ejidal lots, and as their farmlands diminished annually due to this encroachment, independent Mayo ejidatarios had to carve cultivatable plots out of land that had been forested with natural vegetation.[60] Irrespective of Mayo claims that it led to less rain, it is undeniable that during these years thousands of acres of natural flora fell in the Fuerte valley in a race for farms and pastures.

Mayo elders such as Juan Valenzuela never specified where they derived the notion that deforestation resulted in decreased precipitation. Mayo cosmogony dictates that nature—animals, plants, weather, and water—is made up of several intertwining parts and the elimination of one puts the others in jeopardy, but anthropological studies, folktales, and oral histories do not fully explain how Mayo villagers came to believe in desiccation theory, or that the removal of vegetation leads to a decrease in rain. Since Mayo cosmogony does not address this topic, all indications suggest that this notion came from both contemporary observations and sources outside the Fuerte valley.

In the late 1940s, when the idea began to circulate in the Fuerte valley, a scientific connection between deforestation and rainfall was only in its speculative infancy, but the notion has remained a provocative area of research and time has given it some credence. In "How Forests Attract Rain," Douglas Sheil and his collaborators address the link in more scientific terms by suggesting that forest cover can influence rainfall amounts and that forested regions generate large-scale flows in atmospheric water vapor.[61] Scientists have trended toward accepting the link between deforestation and a decrease in precipitation levels for decades, yet such connections are still inconclusive. Some Mayo elders believe that the prevalence of such outside theories encouraged other elders to believe that the clearing of Fuerte valley vegetation, including forests, resulted in less rainfall.[62]

There are documented cases of Indigenous people of Mexico establishing a link between deforestation and precipitation decline.

Anthropologist Andrew Matthews has found such a connection, arguing that the Serrano Indigenous people of the Sierra Juárez mountains of Oaxaca have appropriated desiccation theory and other environmental theories more broadly.[63] Mayo people, like Serrano communities, likely observed these changes themselves while incorporating information from outsiders, adding it to a body of knowledge that helped them understand new developments. In both cases, Indigenous communities had been cut off from sustainable and historical sources of water and forced to rely on sources that provided too little for even subsistence agriculture. It is no wonder that the cry went up that there was too little rainfall, for rain had never in the history of the Mayo people been asked to do so much for them. Rather than see that the limited amount of rain was being stretched over acreage it could never be expected to sustain, Mayo farmers, like other Indigenous people, instead implemented both exogenous theories and endogenous observations to argue that the acreage was not the issue—it could not be, for they had to feed themselves. Their problem was the limited amount of rain.

Yet nature had not turned its back on the Mayo people, the Mexican state had. Rainfall measurements prove it was the sociopolitical situation Yoreme farmers were in—that is, the state's decision to not grant enough irrigation for even subsistence farming—and not changes to rainfall that made matters so dire. Official statistics provided by the Fuerte River Commission show that the El Fuerte precipitation station recorded an annual accumulation of 445 millimeters in 1945, followed by a gradual increase to 775 millimeters in 1949, and then a gradual decrease to 493 millimeters in 1952.[64] In fact, there is no major discrepancy in the amount of precipitation in the Fuerte valley from 1930 to 1952 as compared to 2000 to 2021.[65] Despite the claims of dozens of Mayo elders, there is little evidence that the clouds bypassed the Fuerte valley in the latter half of the 1940s.

We should not critique Mayo farmers too harshly for their claims that there was less rain. While memory can be imperfect and independent Mayo farmers struggling through the mid-1940s to mid-

1950s may have well remembered (and continue to remember) the 1930s and early 1940s as bountiful, there were valid reasons for the impression that they received less rain.[66] First, in the early 1950s drainage projects drastically decreased the amount of water that pooled above ground for long periods after a rain storm. Whereas people could visually gauge the amount of rain in large, standing puddles and swollen lagoons before these projects, after them, even though the rains had not significantly changed, it may have looked as if there was less rain falling on the ground. Second, the Fuerte River itself had changed. The proliferation of canals and dams reduced the river's flow, eliminated streams and creeks, and lowered the number of floods during the rainy season. Finally, northern Mexico suffered a severe drought from 1945 to 1953, and although it did not hit the Fuerte valley particularly hard, it may have limited the amount of water that accumulated in the Fuerte River above northern Sinaloa, reducing its flow.[67] Even if it had no impact upon the Fuerte, the drought dominated the nation's press and—more importantly for predominately illiterate Indigenous communities—word of mouth, and was on everyone's mind in this still overwhelmingly agricultural nation.

Dismissing the Mayo people's claims as a mere misperception of less rain in the absence of fact misses an important point. Measuring the millimeters of rainfall each year would never illuminate the Mayo perspective, for they were not looking at the problem from the vantage point of a modern hydrologist. Geographer Randy Peppler proposes that traditional knowledge systems "emanate from different orientations to and historical paths through the world, possibly causing the knowledge used in such comparisons to be inadvertently decontextualized or deemed lacking."[68] Mayo people could not separate out and treat individually the interconnected elements of rainfall, river levels, crop yields, and, ultimately, community vitality. A shock to one element rippled out and had an impact on all.

During the late 1940s, as the state began actively revoking irrigation concessions to ejidatarios and denying their new requests, Mayo villagers might have even woven the political strength of the community into that fabric of essential natural elements. Appreciating this holistic perspective helps to explain their allegations of diminishing rainfall. River levels, field sizes, and crop yields were all, to various degrees, in the hands of the Mexican state, but not rainfall. The latter, therefore, became the one element essential for community vitality that was not stacked against them. Through all the challenges of the late 1940s and early 1950s they remained proud Mayo people, but in their complaints of less rainfall one can hear their equal concerns for their community. This concern helps to explain why traditions and religious ceremonies centering on rainfall underwent a renaissance in the late 1940s to mid-1950s.

A Mayo Cultural Renaissance: Rain Predictors

As Mayo farmers turned, by default, to rainfall and worried over its quantity in the late 1940s, they naturally renewed their interest in their culture's ancient knowledge systems of rainfall prediction, for what little rain had fallen could not afford to be wasted. Indigenous elder Mauricio Mejías of Huepaco explains, "They [Mayo farmers] channeled our ancient ways of reading nature, predicting good or bad seasons for planting. During good seasons they prepared the earth in May, awaiting the June rain. All Yoremes, being one with nature, had this knowledge. It was the only advantage we had with land."[69] Predicting rainfall was no mere curiosity. Ejidatarios invested heavy labor in the hottest months based on the predictions of their elders. For Mayo farmers, these predictions were as factual as a daily weather report might be for a Yori. Even today, Mayo respondents such as Mejías still celebrate their weather predictions as proof of their balanced, reciprocal, and better relationship to nature compared to Yoris. For them, these traditions are more than a performance; they are proof of a strong connection and a demonstration of their "natural" rights to water in the Fuerte valley.

More impressively, ejidatarios remember the predictions of their elders getting better and more accurate. Mayo elder Jorge Robles of San Miguel recollects that by the mid-twentieth century, Yoremes based their seasonal planting cycles on the moon: "They could tell when it was going to rain, and how much, based on the color of the moon's portholes. When the portholes of the moon are very orange, this signifies the coming of the cold. The next shade of orange signifies that there will be a lot of rain."[70] Mejías's testimony explicitly, and Robles's implicitly, boast that the independent Mayo farmers had an advantage that Yoris were not aware of. Despite the power and wealth that allowed Yori farmers to monopolize irrigation water and cultivable lands, these Yoremes had an understanding of nature that, if it did not completely compensate for their irrigation losses, at least mitigated the worst effects. For independent Mayo farmers, the fact that Yori landowners were ignorant of this knowledge was an advantage; the Yoris may have expected Indigenous communities to flounder and fold, but they would hold on.[71]

Independent Mayo farmers were not alone in relying upon traditional techniques to overcome problems caused by government policy. In the early 1950s, at the same time that the Mayo people of the Fuerte valley were rediscovering rain prediction, some Native Americans in the United States were also deeply engaged with predicting weather patterns based on their observances of the natural landscape such as cloud color and animal and plant behaviors.[72] It is impossible today to gauge the efficacy of these methods or to tell how much of an advantage they gave independent Indigenous farmers in the late 1940s and 1950s, but that is largely beside the point.[73] More importantly, the revitalization of such practices shows that Mayo farmers, much like native people elsewhere, were willing not only to channel ancient knowledge systems in times of crisis but also believed their relationship to the natural landscape helped them cope with a changing political and economic environment. The ultimate test of these methods would be if they helped Mayo farmers remain on their lands.

Oral accounts tell us that some independent Mayo farmers believed their relationship to the natural landscape helped them cope with a changing political and economic environment when their hydraulic opportunities began to decrease in the late 1940s. The growing relevance of this rain predicting strategy is another example that explains the immediate effects of independent Mayo farmers losing irrigation rights and therefore their connection with the Fuerte River. The result was a reconfiguration of their relationship with rain that relied on their cumulative Indigenous knowledge of the local ecosystem. Mayo farmers continually displayed a propensity for using hydraulic knowledge to move between ancient and modern worlds. Rain prediction acted as a vital component of Mayo hydraulic social mobilization, showing how these Indigenous farmers created the best possible outcome with the limited resources available to them.

From Petitions to Prediction to Prayers: The Yuco Conti Ceremony

In this time of crisis, independent Mayo ejidatarios could not afford to merely tap into passive forms of ancient knowledge but had to dig deeper into active forms. What, after all, were these desperate farmers to do when the predictions were poor? Fortunately, for centuries Mayo villagers had practiced a rain-requesting ritual known as the Yuco Conti that had diminished in importance for most of the twentieth century but never entirely disappeared.[74] Beginning in the late 1940s that trend changed and the ceremony underwent a dramatic renaissance, taking on new significance as not just an expression of cultural heritage and unity but a viable strategy of hydraulic social mobilization.

The ceremony, like much of Mayo culture, is a fascinating hybrid of ancient Mayo beliefs mixed with more recent historical influences. Despite a multitude of intrusions, Mayo people maintain an Indigenous cosmogony that, while containing significant elements of Catholic practices, relies very little on church officials.[75] Mayo Catholicism has evolved over hundreds of years and differs greatly from the formal religion Jesuits introduced in the sixteenth century. Cultural autonomy is a hallmark of Mayo life, and their religion is no different. Anthropologist Charles Erasmus points out that the Yoremes of Sinaloa and Sonora "maintain a religion which is almost independent of the official Roman Catholic Church, except for baptism and marriage, which are performed by an ordained priest."[76] The Yuco Conti lays beyond the authority of a priest and instead, like most religious ceremonies, is led by an Indigenous *tenachi* (prayer teacher). A tenachi is a holy man who remains at the center of Mayo religious life by conducting Indigenous religious rituals in ceremonial centers, essentially replacing a Catholic priest.[77] The religious rituals that the tenachi conducts ensure the survival of Mayo identity—including their relationship to water and the natural landscape in general. Even while the meaning and importance of Mayo river ceremonies changed over the centuries, the tenachi's essential functions have not.[78]

Before the late 1940s Mayo villages honored the Yuco Conti ceremony as crucial to their cultural heritage but not crucial to their economic well-being. As the state denied farmers irrigation water in the mid-twentieth century, however, the rain-requesting ritual became more frequent and well attended. Even today, Mayo people still gather at a few central locations in northern Sinaloa just before the rainy season, and although the number of Mayo attendees is not as high as in the early 1950s, the crucial elements of the ritual remain.[79] Mayo elder Horacio Pitahaya of Boca de Arroyo explains, "We invoke [the saint] San Isidro Labrador who derives from the [Mayo] river God Bawahamjuna. Before we only enacted Yuco Conti in ceremonial centers, such as Tehueco or San Miguel. But the lack of rain compelled some ejidos to pay ritual performers to conduct the ceremony in their villages."[80] Like most of Mayo culture, the ceremony reflects the mixture of influences that form their fundamental Indigenous identity.

The growing prevalence of hiring performers to conduct the Yuco Conti ceremony in unaffiliated Indigenous villages shows just how crucial rainfall had become in the life of independent Mayo farmers by the late 1940s to mid-1950s.[81] Poor farmers spending their limited funds on ceremonies to bring rainfall is a great measure of what they thought to be the most crucial at this time—especially since they had never had to sacrifice their scarce resources on this ritual before. While the reemergence of the Yuco Conti helped to reproduce Mayo identity, the fact that impoverished independent farmers started to pay for individual ceremonies in their ejidos suggests not just the need to normalize a cultural practice in a period of large-scale change but a recognition that they were desperate and could no longer depend on alliances with the state to provide resources.

Then as now, dancers participating in the ritual take on the characteristics of animals through their movements. Mayo elders Narciso Bachomo and Carlos Salcedo of Camajoa explain that in this ceremony, "Musicians play music alongside traditional dances, *matachines, pascolas, venados*. Musicians hit drums to signify thunder, and on every drum beat, dancers stick their tongues out to imitate a lizard, they also splash water up and around, representing rainwater hitting the ground."[82] Even today, Mayo elders claim that a rain shower soon follows the performance of this ceremony.

By all accounts, Mayo villagers danced with sincere engagement in the Yuco Conti and saw themselves as vital participants in a natural cycle of life in which rain played a crucial role. As anthropologist Gabriel Uriarte describes, the world of Mayo dance "breaks with our dimension to enter the magical, making tangible the old cosmogony. The human is an animal and vice versa. Plants, water, sun, earth, appear on stage, contextualized by various transformations of dancers who represent everything belonging to Juyya Annia [nature]."[83] During the Yuco Conti ceremony and other rituals that involved dancing, the performers' movements mimicked and represented animals, thus transporting the dancer into the realm of the animal and, at the same time, manifesting the spirit and power of the animal to the human realm where it can be beseeched and called upon. Then as now, Mayo people took pride in their symbiotic relationship with local ecosystems and invoked all of the elements of the natural environment into the Yuco Conti ceremony despite the vast changes to the physical landscape taking shape. By the midpoint of the twentieth century this cultural pride was as important to Mayo villagers as the assurance that the rains would come—for they depended upon both.

The need for rain was so great by the 1950s that Mayo villagers began to adjust the ceremony so that the Juyya Annia would be certain to understand their plea. For example, the representation of toads, which had not been a central feature within the ceremony before, became prevalent during the crisis of the 1950s. Toads, as Elder Laura Apodaca of La Misión points out, "came to find a place within these ceremonies because they symbolize the coming of rain. Some Yoremes also think it will bring rain if you kill a toad and hang it."[84] Mayo people always revered toads—as they did most animals—but because they observed these animals coming out into the open when rain showers started, they thought it judicious to include them explicitly and even privilege them in the ceremony. Whether the inclusion of toads made the ritual more efficacious is far less important than the fact that independent Mayo were willing to tweak and even experiment with different versions by the 1950s. Indeed, it is one measure of their desperation for water.

It was never the government's intention, but denying Mayo farmers' use of hydraulic infrastructure helped spur a renaissance in Mayo traditional practices. While today some elders lament that Mayo culture is disappearing due to a lost relationship with nature, the increased use of the Yuco Conti ceremony in the 1940s and 1950s underscored two fundamental points. First, Mayo villagers had become reliant upon rainfall for their crops, despite available technological advances. Second, traditions could, under the right circumstances, return and occupy a meaningful place in Mayo life. There are no accurate means of measuring the efficacy of the Yuco Conti—and the Mexican government left them with little choice but to embrace it—yet Mayo people believed sincerely in its usefulness. It reminded them of the continued, vital role they played in their ecosystem and reflected their universal cosmogony of cause and effect.

Conclusion

After inheriting a legacy of colonialism, independent Mayo farmers in the mid-1940s faced a particularly challenging set of circumstances as the state initiated plans to transform the Fuerte valley into one of the most productive agricultural regions of Mexico. Already, the SICAE controlled irrigation from the Fuerte River and had used that power to muscle out independent and individualist ejidatarios, but when the state began backing private hydraulic infrastructure development designed to bypass all ejidos, independent Mayo farmers faced not only political but economic disaster. From their perspective, the pumps and canals that had been available from the mid-1920s through early 1940s metaphorically disappeared by the mid-1940s. Physically, however, they remained in plain view, often running close to independent Mayo villages. As their number multiplied, they became a painful reminder to the independent Mayo of their second-class citizenship and that their hydraulic social mobilization strategies were becoming less effective. Their responses had a rough evolutionary arc: They began with petitions, some of which stressed their legal rights and others of which simultaneously embraced both contemporary and ancient technology. They then moved to protest. When the state ignored them, independent Mayo fell back upon their connection to ancestral traditions. First, they tried to predict rain but when they came to believe that there was less precipitation, they requested it in ceremonies.

The two independent ejidos under review in this chapter, Jahuara and La Palma, never found mobilization strategies as effective as the individualists in El Teroque. There, ejidatarios voiced their needs and concerns within local development decisions.[85] By contrast, government agencies never took the demands of the independent ejidos of Jahuara and La Palma seriously—the details of La Palma's protest failed to even enter the historical record. One lesson to take from this is that it may help to have influential enemies. The individualists of El Teroque had the SICAE as their adversary and consequently had the cooperative's political opponents as allies. Ironically, without the benefit of a nemesis like the SICAE, ejidos like Jahuara and La Palma could not reach out to or cultivate the support of the cooperative's rivals. Literally on their own, independent Mayo villages were marginalized even more than individualist ejidatarios, and their hydraulic social mobilization strategies reflected their tenuous predicament.

Beginning in the mid-1940s and continuing well into the 1960s, the Mexican state put far more thought and effort into the planning and funding of irrigation projects than into how those projects would impact independent Indigenous communities or their historic ties to the Fuerte River and the landscape of the valley. Certainly, state officials had to have known that once they decided that these expanded projects would syphon most of the available water off to private, corporate farms, Indigenous ejidatarios would be in an untenable situation. But this was, after all, their goal, for if small farmers only had rainwater to cultivate crops, they then would be forced to keep smaller and smaller plots, leaving the remainder fallow and available to be handed over to larger and, so these officials believed, more productive entities. Yet Mayo farmers like Julián Valenzuela and other independent ejidatarios from La Misión would not succumb easily and pushed back in ways that not even the state could have expected. From the outside it may have appeared these independent farmers only had tradition to fall back upon, but for them it was a real source of power that might even save them. Whether it could was an open question.

The next chapter will look into how Mayo farmers reacted to the state pushing its developmentalist policies. Much like this chapter, it explores how Mayo villages maintained and adapted religious ceremonies as a tactic of hydraulic social mobilization. It also delves into diverging hydraulic social mobilization strategies through the lens of a religious revival movement in Indigenous communities in the Fuerte valley and its neighboring Mayo valley. And finally, it also asks the difficult question: Why, when they were facing land loss and political and cultural marginalization on a scale that had not been seen for fifty years, did Mayo laborers continue to construct irrigation infrastructure for private entities?

FOUR

The Inward Turn

Mayo Hydraulic Labor, Millenarian Movements,
and Changing Rituals, 1947 to 1963

At some point in the early 1950s, independent Mayo farmer Mauricio Mejias surveyed his ejidal lot and realized that he could no longer feed his family merely by growing corn, beans, and squash. His problem was not that his lot was too small or his family too large; his problem was a lack of water. As Mejias and other Indigenous farmers of the Huepaco ejido lost access to the canal that had irrigated their lands from the 1930s to the mid-1940s, they were compelled to rely on rainwater—which could come in deluges or trickles but rarely with the sufficient consistency to guarantee a good harvest. Huepaco was not an outlier, for most independent Mayo ejidatarios of the Fuerte valley beginning in the 1950s abandoned cultivating their ejidal lots full time in order to search out supplementary work. They found few promising choices. The two most common options for augmenting their income were constructing canals for large landowners or renting out their lands to Yori farmers. While both offered more frustrations than funds, choosing to build irrigation infrastructure compounded the difficult situation farmers found themselves in.[1] The very hydraulic structures they constructed, the ones that could have brought Indigenous ejidatarios the water they needed to grow crops on the land the postrevolutionary state granted them, were closed off. Instead, they built canals and had to watch as the water rushing through them brought wealth to large, private farms. Even decades later, Indigenous elders such as Mejias unsurprisingly regard this moment in the mid-twentieth century as a turning point in their history: the period in which Yori outsiders used their control of irrigation to encroach on independent Mayo farmers' autonomy and way of life.[2]

While chapter 2 outlined the hydraulic struggles between individualists and collectivists in response to the SICAE's power and chapter 3 examined the state's anointment of large, Yori landowners as sole beneficiaries of Fuerte River water, this chapter addresses a particularly vicious cycle that emerged from these shifting water rights. The state's encouragement of large landowners to close the spigot on Indigenous farmers forced independent Mayo farmers like Mauricio Mejias to sell their labor, but only rich, Yori landowners were hiring. As Mayo farmers had less time and resources to work their ejido plots, wealthy, private farmers would then point out to state officials that large portions of ejidal lands were fallow and therefore legally available for annexation. And who would annex these plots? Landowning Yori farmers who had the irrigation and capital to make "fallow" lands bountiful.[3] As Mayo farmers carefully balanced the wages they might earn against the land that they risked becoming fallow, they gravitated into more dramatic responses that included altering their riverine religious rituals and even participating in a millenarian movement. Trapped between desiccated fields and opportunistic neighbors, Mayo farmers found solace in adapting religious rituals.

Then as now, however, Mayo identity was not monolithic. Though both Mayo people of the Fuerte valley and their northern brethren of the Mayo valley in Sonora faced a process of state-sponsored marginalization that scholars have called "enclavement," the two communities responded to the crisis in different ways. Manuel L. Carlos argues that enclavement in the Fuerte valley, beginning in the 1940s, was a process through which the dominant society—in this case, mestizo farmers—conspired with the state to "encapsulate, marginalize, and subordinate ethnic groups," most notably,

Mayo farmers. But far from folding in the face of this pressure, Carlos contends, "Groups like the Mayo in turn develop[ed] parallel rituals and belief systems . . . to intensify their cultural and ethnic identities and thus guarantee themselves some degree of cultural integrity and continuity."[4] Carlos's analysis is a welcome challenge to previous histories that overlooked Mayo responses, but it still does not go far enough, for the Mayo people of the Fuerte valley and those of the Mayo valley had different ideas of what "integrity and continuity" looked like.

By the 1950s and 1960s both Sinaloan and Sonoran Mayo communities realized that the state was not sympathetic to their legal complaints. So, in a fascinating mix of mystical Catholic and native beliefs that constituted religious syncretism, they reached out to other sources of authority. Unfortunately, in this battle between scarce resources and calls to cultural and spiritual assistance, earthly powers had the upper hand. Both communities gravitated toward increasingly supernatural solutions as their legal and economic options diminished, but the degree and shape of that supernatural turn reflected their unique experiences and understanding of the recent past. In the Mayo valley a famous millenarian movement erupted that promised God's direct intervention in the water crisis, but the experience in the Fuerte valley Mayo community was not comparable. There, villages adapted and tinkered with existing rituals to cope with the political and environmental changes that had unfolded over the previous twenty years. The simple explanation for this divergence is that each community had a different historical experience with irrigation infrastructure, the state, and, consequently, hydraulic social mobilization. Despite their best and varied efforts, Fuerte valley Mayo farmers continued to experience ejidal land loss and, as a result, increasing numbers entered the ranks of wage laborers. As other—generally private and Yori—farmers argued that they should take over ejidal land, claiming they could boost agricultural production, Mayo farmers coped as best they could but had to prioritize what was most important to them. In the end they chose autonomy, ethnic affiliation, and cultural connection.

Irrigation Access, Vulnerability, and Land Dispossession

In 1951 the Mexican state tasked the newly created Fuerte River Commission (CRF) to maximize the region's economic potential. In turn, the commission privileged commercial farming. As large, private farms grew in the late 1940s through 1960s, the CRF not only ignored the Mayo ejidos of the Fuerte valley but actively negated most of the advancements ejidatarios had made during the postrevolutionary era. The commission expanded on the encroachment of ejidatario hydraulic rights begun in the mid-1940s and embraced outright favoritism of large landowners' irrigation projects. Independent Mayo ejidatarios were unprepared when private, corporate agriculture arrived, exacerbating endemic hydraulic inequalities.

In fact, inequity in hydraulic resources was not just a problem in the Fuerte valley but a regional and even national one. Ejidatario loss of land and water rights was essentially national policy beginning in the 1940s. Steven Sanderson argues that during the counter-reform years of 1940 to 1970 the federal government was "dedicated to the eradication of the minifundio [small farm], regional isolation of the ejido, and cost-benefit criteria within the land-reform bureaucracy that effectively negated the promise of 'social obligation' to the countryside under the Revolution."[5] At that time the hydraulic power and consequent political influence of the SICAE mitigated the policy's impact on ejidatarios in general and delayed the counter-reform in the Fuerte valley. But it did so only temporarily—and it might not have been much of a blessing.[6] As shown in chapter 3, by the late 1940s the SICAE had lost much of its political clout and could no longer protect its members, who then became some of the least prepared to deal with the jarring transition to commercial agriculture. In the years after the 1950s, all ejidatarios faced land dispossession, but for former SICAE farmers the transition came with such force that they were nearly powerless in its face.

The Mexican state was not a monolithic entity that collectively conspired to dispossess Mayo ejidatarios. While each state agency responsible for the economic development and physical transformation of the Fuerte valley in the mid-twentieth century pursued their own, differing agendas, however, the diversity of their efforts led to a common outcome: the marginalizing of local Indigenous inhabitants. By the 1950s even Yoreme ejidatarios who had been affiliated with the SICAE had felt the sting of mistreatment and turned against the collective. The Instituto Nacional Indigenista (National Indigenous Institute, INI), a government agency charged with advocating on behalf of native communities, generally eschewed intervention in the Fuerte valley in the mid-twentieth century. Even in other regions where it was active, it often prioritized economic development over genuine Indigenous community advocacy. The Ministry of Water Resources (SRH) supported the hydraulic efforts of large landowners, rejected both Yori and Mayo ejidatario irrigation petitions from the mid-1940s to mid-1950s, and, after that point, referred petitions to the CRF, where they were routinely rejected. Beginning in the 1950s the CRF, undoubtedly the worst perpetrator of Mayo ejidatario oppression, supervised the construction of irrigation infrastructure that they denied to Indigenous farmers, while also siding with large landowners in land and irrigation disputes and turning a blind eye to Mayo land dispossession.[7] So even while the goals of different agencies changed and their fortunes waxed and waned, the one thing they appear to have agreed upon by the early 1950s was that small farmers— and particularly small, Indigenous farmers—slowed the nation's march to prosperity.

During this transition to commercial agriculture, when Indigenous ejidal lands of the Fuerte valley became susceptible to annexation, Mayo farmers were, in a word, vulnerable. Scholars have spent a great deal of time analyzing the concept of vulnerability. Like Indigenous identity, vulnerability is not static and changes over time, so much so that Bruno Messerli and his coauthors assert that there is "a trajectory of vulnerability through which all societies pass as they develop economically, technologically, and socially, that influence their relative vulnerability."[8] Therefore, it is possible to trace varying degrees of vulnerability both within populations at any given moment and throughout their history.

In the Masserli model there are different levels of vulnerability to change with which, historically, every society contends. For example, a nature-dominated society (such as the Cáhitas that Spaniards encountered in northern Sinaloa during first contact) was particularly vulnerable to change, but in the Fuerte valley the gradual technological development during the colonial era allowed local Indigenous groups necessary time to adapt.[9] Like an inoculation, successive generations of Mayo farmers adopted outside practices into their traditions a little at a time, becoming less vulnerable with every iteration. By the early twentieth century Mayo farmers not only embraced change but proactively transformed their local ecosystems radically by clearing land for planting. Hundreds of Indigenous farmers from the Fuerte valley then secured these changes in the postrevolutionary era by constructing dams, canals, and aqueducts to bring their cleared land under cultivation. This ability to exploit the Mexican state's momentary receptiveness to ejidatario needs demonstrates a perfect example of Mayo adaptability, or, in the parlance of the Masserli model, their relative invulnerability.

Looks, however, can be deceiving. Even changes that appear radical can in fact be deeply conservative, for some societies throughout history have modified natural landscapes and accepted outside technology into their practices and traditions only to create a "buffer" that protected what they most treasured.[10] In the case of the Mayo people of Sinaloa, they embraced dams, pumps, and canals, but not as a fingerhold from which they could ascend to modernity. Rather, they used them as a buffer to protect a host of cultural practices and their traditional group identity. This identity was rooted in both the land of the Fuerte valley and the equally important river. Mayo farmers expanded their fields and changed their cultivation methods but only in order to secure their right to stay in their ancestral lands and keep their cultural practices involving the river alive.

Yet there was a paradox to the Mayo people's successes after the Mexican Revolution, for while the use of irrigation infrastructure increased agricultural productivity and allowed Indigenous farmers to defend ejidal territories from annexation, it left them dependent and vulnerable. The Masserli study discusses how the adaptations and adjustments some societies make over time leave them more vulnerable in the long run.[11] This was the case in the Fuerte valley, where hydraulic technology helped some Mayo farmers during the postrevolutionary era adapt to their changing surroundings in the short term but left them exposed in the long term, especially in the postwar period.

Simply put, hundreds of Mayo farmers embraced hydraulic technology in order to stay on their ancestral lands, but once they became dependent upon dams and canals for irrigation, they found themselves critically vulnerable to the state shutting off access to water. When irrigation trickled to a stop, independent Mayo farmers found it difficult to keep ejidal lands productive and avoid outside encroachment. The buffer that was supposed to make them safer became the vehicle of their own oppression. For an independent Mayo village like La Palma—which had enjoyed access to canals—this transition was debilitating. For other Fuerte valley villages, such as El Añil, which had never used canals and pumps, the shift to residing in a commercial agricultural zone in the 1950s was not as drastic. Either way, independent Indigenous ejidatarios with previous access and those without it both found themselves facing outsider encroachment and no buffer system to protect them.

Recall from chapter 3 the floods that the Cahuinahua Canal caused in the La Palma ejido, leaving it in economic ruin; this was just the start of their troubles. After the floodwaters subsided, in came a new, equally unwelcome inundation: wealthy, politically powerful Yori neighbors who eyed Mayo land enviously. The construction of the Cahuinahua Canal and other privately funded irrigation infrastructure for sole use by large commercial farmers in the late 1940s marked a turning point in the social, political, and physical landscape of the Fuerte valley. Elder Roberto Escalante of La Palma recollects that before the canal came, they used a pump for irrigation and had fertile land for planting, but then, "Yoris cut off our access to the pump and brought in the

Cahuinahua Canal, it flooded our land, ruining houses and crops. Yoris then moved in, monopolized all water from the canal, and planted crops. Some Yoris even became members of our ejido."[12] For La Palma, the arrival of the Cahuinahua Canal signaled the beginning of an era that put Mayo ejidatarios on the defensive against outsider incursion.

The historical link between commercial agriculture, the growth of private irrigation construction, and Indigenous land dispossession is well established in other Mayo communities as well. Indigenous elder Mateo Quintero of Tehueco explains that "the new irrigation modules modified all land because the federal government supported canalization for private development, giving rich landowners all the property that they needed. The beneficiaries bought and stole lands from Yoremes."[13] Quintero does not clarify the process by which outsiders stole Mayo lands, but his words suggest that everyone understood that the state's encouragement for commercial farmers to develop the countryside gave them implicit permission to dispossess Mayo ejidatarios. A parched plot of land was not worth much on its own, but a farmer privileged with hydraulic access could develop its full potential.

The state understood the economic potential of this region and provided large landowners of the Fuerte valley with the tools necessary to commence commercial agriculture: loans, equipment, research, and, most importantly, hydraulic infrastructure. Mexican scholar Alejandro Figueroa argues that during the mid-twentieth century the Mexican state aimed to boost the production of large agricultural owners in the Fuerte, Mayo, and Yaqui valleys. "They," Figueroa claims, "received most official credit at very low interest rates, enjoyed the contributions of technological and genetic research aimed at increasing productivity, and were the main beneficiaries of infrastructure works such as the construction of roads, dams, and irrigation canals."[14] Northwestern Mexico thus became a showcase of the nation's agricultural development, a model of increased productivity that the state used to justify similar development initiatives in the rest of the country.[15] From the perspective of Presidents Adolfo Ruiz Cortines (1946–52) and Adolfo López

Mateos (1952–58), if they could break the influence of ejidal organizations and empower large agricultural owners in this region, they could do it anywhere.

By 1960 the changes were obvious. Large properties dominated the landscape of the Northwest, and states like Sinaloa had a larger degree of commercial agriculture than most areas of Mexico. In fact, nationwide, of the nearly 1.4 million Mexican properties in 1960, only 32 percent were larger than five hectares, whereas 66 percent were smaller than five hectares (ejidos made up the remaining 2 percent). This was almost the exact opposite in Sinaloa, where, out of 13,387 properties, 73 percent were larger than and 23 percent were smaller than five hectares (here, ejidos made up the remaining 4 percent). Ejidos were their own category at the time because—though ejidos were massive collectively—hundreds of individual ejidatarios controlled small plots, usually averaging under five hectares. In the agricultural sector, ejidos were still, even as late as 1960, large actors, constituting 26 percent of all Mexican properties and 35 percent of those in Sinaloa. This large percentage of ejidal property in Sinaloa can be explained by the fact that its ejidos possessed immense acreage, as 366 ejidos or 67 percent of them were in the one-thousand-to-five-thousand-hectare range.[16]

Because water was as important as land—if not more immediately important—it is unsurprising that the disparity between ejidos and large private properties were just as striking in regard to irrigation as landholdings. Keeping with general landholding patterns, of the 183,392 irrigated lands in Mexico, only 34 percent were larger than 5 hectares while 63 percent were smaller. However, of the 3,170 irrigated properties in Sinaloa, 79 percent were larger than 5 hectares whereas only 21 percent were smaller. There was a diversity in the size of irrigated lands in Sinaloa, but properties in the 50-to-100-hectare category constituted 21 percent of all farms, making them both the largest group in Sinaloa, a state characterized by large, irrigated farms. By contrast, of the more than 1.4 million hectares of ejidal land in Sinaloa, only 110,000 hectares, or less than 8 percent, were irrigated. This number may seem small at first glance, but it far exceeded the national figure of only 0.8 percent of ejidal lands enjoying irrigation. Only 11 ejidos in Sinaloa had less than 50 hectares irrigated, and 202 ejidos had more than 100 hectares irrigated, of which only 74 ejidos had more than 400 hectares irrigated.[17]

From a national perspective, ejidos in Sinaloa were in an enviable situation in terms of irrigation, but even that did not help stem the tide of change. While Sinaloan ejidatarios had far better access to water than those in the rest of Mexico (8 percent versus 0.8 percent), this statistic hides much. By 1960 a number of ejidatarios had, out of necessity, begun to rent their lands to outsiders. Most renters were large, neighboring commercial farmers, who were much more successful at retaining irrigation rights than the ejidos.

A number of conclusions can be gleaned from these raw statistics. The first is that, by 1960, in Sinaloa and northwest Mexico generally, large private properties prevailed over small properties and ejidos as compared to the rest of Mexico. The majority of these large lands in northwest Mexico, many in the fifty-to-one-hundred-hectare range, enjoyed access to irrigation. Second, this transformation of landholding patterns happened quickly once the state embraced developmentalist policies after 1951. Third, the ejidos of Sinaloa were not outright forgotten, just neglected. Like ejidos throughout the nation, they received some irrigation but not enough. The majority of Sinaloan ejidos controlled between one thousand to five thousand hectares, but only 25 percent of irrigated ejidos had more than four hundred hectares irrigated—proof that control over water was perhaps a better gauge of political power than mere acreage. Plus, not every hectare of land in the Fuerte valley was (or is) equal. Private farmers not only received most of the water, they also typically held more and better land.

Again, the example of La Palma ejido is instructive. The La Palma *ejido* consisted exclusively of Mayo ejidatarios in the 1950s, but the *town* of La Palma did not. There, the population was both ejidatario and non-ejidatario small property owners or renters who were both Mayo and Yori. Under the new rules promoted first by the Ministry of Agriculture and Development (SAYF) and then the CRF, the non-Mayo residents of the town of La Palma were showered with favoritism. Other Mexicans recognized that fact and moved to the town to take advantage of it. These new Yori residents had the state's blessing to acquire irrigation rights, especially since functionaries in the SAYF and CRF believed their agricultural activities were more efficient than Mayo ejidatarios engaged in subsistence farming. In the early 1950s outsiders poured in to capitalize on the new hydraulic opportunities offered by the CRF. It did not take them long to realize they could go further and encroach upon and eventually exploit Indigenous ejidal lands.

Oral sources indicate that this influx of outsiders was directly related to opportunities that arose from the destruction of ejidatario lands in La Palma. According to Mayo ejidatario Roberto Escalante of La Palma, after first flooding and then the elimination of their irrigation rights made lands unproductive in the late 1940s, "Yoris moved in, planted crops on our property and stole it from us. Some Yoremes could not grow crops without irrigation water, so they rented out ejidal lands to Yoris, who became ejidatarios, making most of the decisions within our ejido."[18] Escalante could have been referring at least partially to communal ejidal lands, which all ejidos received. Whether these plots were held communally or individually, Escalante's account suggests that outsiders took advantage of declining productivity to acquire La Palma's ejidal lands.

Since Yori outsiders had access to pumps and canals, they had a better chance of attaining productive harvests. They also had, through state and private avenues, privileged access to credit to make payments on land. La Palma ejidatarios were desperate for money after the flood—ruined lots were expensive to bring back into cultivation—and Yoris made tempting offers to rent sections of ejidal lots as well as communal pasture lands. These dynamics allowed people like Maria del Rosario del Ahumada and Jesús Soto to encroach closer to ejidal lands. In June 1952 del Rosario rented six hectares of riverbank land in the town of La Palma at ten pesos per hectare.[19] In March of the same year Soto rented land on the banks of the Fuerte River in La Palma that was bordered by the properties of Anselmo Soto to the north, Pablo Soto to the south, and the Fuerte River directly to the west.[20] While renting ejidal lands was illegal and thus not recorded in the official record, these examples show how outsiders moved increasingly closer to Mayo lands, increasing the possibility of both renting and annexing ejidal lots.[21]

Indigenous ejidatarios' had few options. Not only were outsiders arriving to take advantage of government policies and exploit ejidatarios' situation, but they also faced longstanding local threats. Hacendados who clung to the remnants of their former empires in hopes they could restore them still existed in places like La Palma. In the early 1950s a Yori named Sara Herran Viuda de la Vega—as mentioned in chapter 3—reclaimed a portion of the 2,032 hectares of hacienda property that the SAYF had confiscated in 1937 to create the bulk of the La Palma ejido.[22] In 1932 Viuda de la Vega inherited the property from her husband Eduardo, who had purchased several thousand hectares in 1915—during the height of the revolution—to create the Buerocahui (or Parnaso) hacienda.[23] As late as the 1940s the widow's numerous legal maneuvers to regain her properties fell on unsympathetic ears, but by 1950 the government began to listen.[24] Viuda de la Vega's allegations that ejidatarios rented out their plots and did not personally cultivate it convinced the CRF to return some of her land and relocate twenty-seven ejidatarios in 1951.

The return of a fraction of Viuda de la Vega's land after more than a decade of petitions demonstrates the state's shifting political loyalties in the 1950s. Engineer Heriberto Valdez Romero of the CRF, who was in charge of this reassignment, rationalized his decision by stating that ejidatarios had been unsuccessful in cultivating this (newly assigned) portion of land despite what he claimed were "numerous steps taken with this motive."[25] It was no accident that forty of the one hundred hectares were of valuable land along the river, reflecting the state's commitment that large landowners have whatever resources they required for success. Removing and reassigning twenty-seven ejidatarios to new, less desirable lots sent a clear message that the CRF viewed campesino subsistence farming as inefficient; they would tolerate it only so long as it did not literally get in the way of "modern" agriculture. In contrast to the enthusiasm shown to larger landowners, the CRF and the state more generally could offer ejidos like La Palma little more than an indifferent shrug. They did not necessarily go out of their way to shut them down in most cases, but they did nothing to ensure their success.

Outsiders commonly alleged that the ejidal land they desired was "fallow" or "damaged," such as lands ruined by floods. They were so successful that by the mid-twentieth century ejido demographics had changed. Indigenous communities nearest the river usually saw the largest changes. Both Roberto Escalante and Librado Cuadros contend that outsider encroachment in La Palma slowly transformed it from entirely Mayo to a mixed membership ejido.[26] State records support this claim. Engineers charged with determining La Palma's ejidal boundary lines in the mid-1930s reported that the overwhelming majority of inhabitants were of Mayo descent.[27] Today, while some sources claim that half of La Palma's eight hundred inhabitants are Indigenous, local experts and residents view Mayo people as the minority population.[28]

Geographic location and adjacency to the Fuerte River were prime factors in determining the types of tactics Yoris employed to dispossess ejidatarios. State bureaucrats perpetually invoked Article 27 of the 1917 Constitution when rejecting ejidatario petitions for concessions to riverbank land, as they were technically not supposed to assign such plots to ejidos.[29] Yet some Mayo ejidos such as Pochotal and El Teroque inexplicably received dotaciónes that abutted the Fuerte River. Elsewhere, ejidal properties were not always contiguous, and even though the majority of an ejido did not border a river, some smaller, separate plots might. This was the case in La Palma (see figure 8) where scattered ejidal lands sat next to non-ejidal properties. Here, non-ejido neighbors coveted these smaller ejidal holdings—especially as they were bathed in river water for part of the year.

As river shore property became increasingly valuable, outsiders used their advantage as landowners to leverage out Mayo eji-

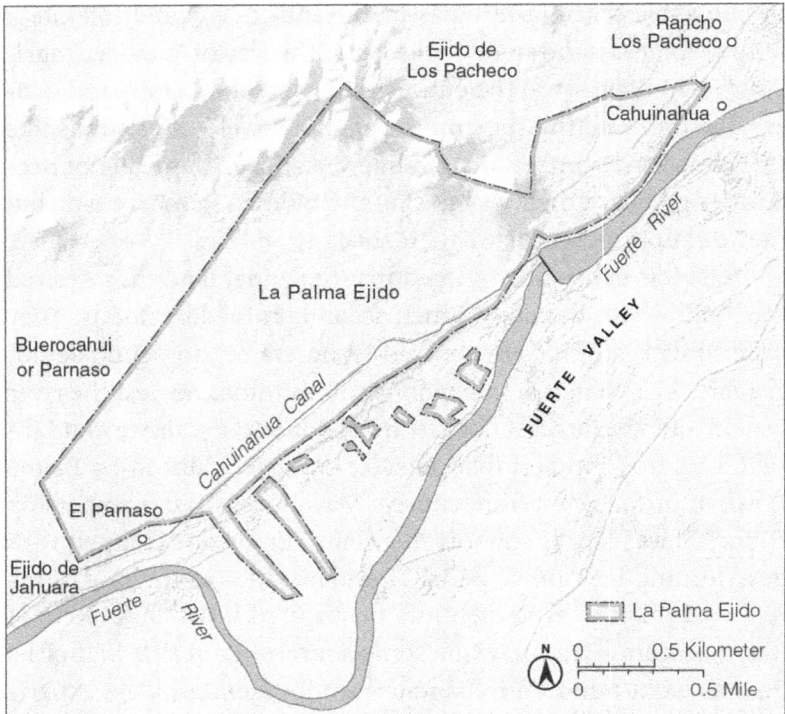

8. La Palma ejido is surrounded by small private properties and Hacienda Buerocahui or Parnaso. Drawn by Pease Press Cartography.

datarios. Indigenous elder Jorge Robles of San Miguel remembers some Yoremes like his parents owning valuable ejidal lands on the river shore in the 1940s. Yoris also, according to Robles, "bought river shore land and set up canals directly from the river. My parents struggled producing crops because they no longer had access to irrigation water from the river, so they started selling pieces of their ejidal land to outsiders, until it was all gone."[30] Without the legal power to draw water from the river and the financial resources to build their own canals or pay water providers, Mayo ejidatarios with riverbank access soon found it difficult to hold onto their plots. Yori landowners slowly acquired most of this river shore property, used their capital to set up pumps and canals on the river, and further exacerbated inequities in the Fuerte valley. Keeping with the developmentalist policies of the times, they increasingly had the direct assistance of the state. Beginning in the 1940s bureaucrats from the SAYF and its successors, the Ministry of Hydraulic Resources (SRH) and CRF, not only denied ejidatario requests for riverbank concessions but hunted for earlier, erroneous allotments of riverbank land. Federal officials enthusiastically began renting these properties to outsiders around the same time and did so increasingly in the 1950s.[31]

These new Yori arrivals not only abutted against and rented lands from ejidos, they also physically moved into Indigenous communities in the mid-twentieth century. By the early 1950s the town of La Palma alone had become home to dozens of relocated Yoris, many of whom looked to become ejidatarios. Legally, ejidal communities could expand membership, but doing so could cause problems and division, especially if ejidatarios were not unanimous in voting for an outsider's inclusion. However, an informal avenue existed for Yoris seeking entrance to a Yoreme ejido: simply by remaining they became de facto ejidatarios. This was not supposed to be the case. Article 27 of the 1917 Constitution states that only members of an ejido receiving a dotación could harvest and benefit from these land grants, but the law was frequently ignored.[32] Archival documents do not explain how a Yori could become a de facto ejidatario in a Mayo ejido, but from oral sources it appears that over time someone renting the land became simply associated with it and practically earned full ejidal membership. In La Palma this happened enough that Yoris came to govern the ejido.

Not all Yoris were so patient or earned a place in ejido society so benignly; some took advantage of Mayo farmers' desperate situations and then forced themselves upon ejido governance once recognized as the de facto holder of a plot. As was the case throughout the Fuerte valley, water provided excellent leverage. Indigenous elder Laura Apodaca of La Misión recalls childhood memories of her family's experience with thirsty plants, poverty, and Yoris who looked to take advantage of the community's plight:

With few options, we built roads and irrigation structures for Yoris in the 1940s and 1950s. We fended off Yori influence for years, knowing how they destroyed our culture and Indigenous values, but soon they got involved in our community. Crops did not grow, so like other poor and struggling Yoremes, my dad sold some ejidal land for 80 pesos a hectare. We also could not afford to fight legally against other Yoris stealing our lots, we did not have money or enough weapons to defend ourselves. After we lost those lands Yoris were always here putting their noses into ejido meetings, trying to divide us.[33]

Unscrupulous Yoris, like the ones who plagued Apodaca's family could reliably apply pressure with threats and promises of irrigation to sow division within the ejido. It was a subtle but consistent stress in Mayo people's lives.

Numerous oral testimonies like Apodaca's detail how ubiquitous stealing ejidal land was in the 1950s, yet court cases addressing such crimes in the Fuerte valley do not exist. The fact that an immense number of Mayo elders recall land theft in the mid-twentieth century without it appearing in the official record reveals the disadvantages that the independent ejidatarios of the Fuerte valley encountered. At the same time, archives abound in documented cases of outsiders legally gobbling up huge portions of territory, usually while simultaneously accessing newly available canals and pumps. Rather than evidence that land theft did not happen, the lacuna in the court records reflects three simple facts. First, most Mayo ejidatarios were illiterate in the 1950s and several did not even speak Spanish. Second, most independent Mayo ejidatarios did not have the resources to fight against land dispossession and, in any case, did not perceive the judicial system as a welcoming ally. Finally, unlike some individualist Indigenous communities like El Teroque that aligned with campesino advocate organizations such as the CNC, most independent ejidos, including La Misión, did not trust Yori-led associations to help defend their rights and interests. It is impossible to specify how many acres Yori farmers illegally confiscated from Mayo ejidatarios, but even if the number of legally taken acres was the same as those illegally taken, it all felt wrong to Indigenous farmers.

Complicity also helps explain the absence of Indigenous ejidatario complaints against land theft in the official record. With no access to pumps or canals, Mayo farmers often had a difficult time eking out a living by relying on rainwater alone, and some ejidatarios, such as Apodaca's father, had no other choice but to illegally sell or rent their ejidal lands to outsiders. Having entered, at the very least, the legally murky—if not outright illegal—area of renting lands to outsiders, ejidatarios like the Apodacas had little recourse once the Yori newcomers began to break the rules themselves. What could possibly be gained by drawing the attention of an increasingly hostile state to a dubious situation?

Unfortunately for these independent Mayo farmers, there were few opportunities to tell their stories of land theft before these oral interviews six decades later, but their voices still help complete a picture of mid-twentieth century Fuerte valley social history. After modest gains in the postrevolutionary period that included securing ejidos and sometimes water rights, independent Mayo farmers experienced diminishing state support in the postwar era. Without water rights, credit for seeds, rifles to keep interlopers off their property, money for lawyers, or political capital to gain support from state functionaries, independent Indigenous ejidatarios watched in despair as powerful Yori outsiders occupied chunks of their ejidal properties. Often their best defense was to retreat back into the core of their ejidal lots and focus their meager resources on making what land they had left productive. With theft in some cases all but inevitable, independent Mayo ejidatarios sometimes made the best of a bad situation by selling or renting land to colonizing Yoris.

These Yori arrivals not only had no compunction about what they did, they celebrated it. N. Ross Crumrine describes how the mestizo population who swept in during the wave of commercial agriculture of the 1950s saw themselves as noble frontier people bringing into production land that they claimed had gone to "waste." To do so, they found it necessary to dominate not only the land but especially the native populations that had allegedly left it so unfruitful. This mentality and their subsequent actions forced Indigenous ejidatarios to engage in a "deal" with Yori money lenders that made Mayo farmers peons on their own land.[34] This mestizo frontier mentality emerged everywhere in northwest Mexico during this period, but in the Fuerte valley, with its substantial population of marginalized Mayo ejidatarios, the exploitation was particularly pronounced.

Because selling or renting ejidal land was illegal, transactions between Yori and Yoreme farmers rarely entered into the official record. This absence makes it impossible to gauge just how complicit Mayo farmers were in ceding their lots to outsiders. But it would be short-sighted to blame Mayo ejidatarios for taking advantage of their best short-term opportunity to alleviate their woes given how meager their options were. It would be equally wrong to blame the region's expanded hydraulic infrastructure. The expansion of irrigation did not in and of itself have to be an economic and social disaster for Mayo farmers. Rather, it was Mexico's developmentalist agenda and the state's commitment to "modernizing" the nation's agriculture that proved ruinous.

Ejidos may well have continued being viable agricultural units for Mexico's farmers in the mid-twentieth century, but the opportunity for them to compete and demonstrate their potential never got a fair chance from a government who gave every opportunity instead to private landholders. Irrigation became an effective cudgel to beat down small-scale, Indigenous farmers. Even allowing the ejidos to have some regular, reliable irrigation water might have been enough for them to prove their worth, but developmentalist thinking in government circles had no place for these quasi-public, quasi-private hybrids. For Mexican officials in agencies such as the CRF and SRH, mid-twentieth century modernity gave no place to Indigenous culture or institutions.

Mayo Laborers: A Hydraulic Army?

If the Mexican government envisioned any place for small farmers like independent Mayo ejidatarios by the mid-twentieth century, it was solely as laborers. Firmly committed to introducing large-scale hydraulic infrastructure to even the most remote regions of the nation, government agencies such as the SAYF, SRH, and CRF needed the manpower to build them. In much of northwestern Mexico, it would be independent Mayo farmers who dug the canals and aqueducts, piled the earth, and poured concrete to build the dams. With diminishing options for their farms, Mayo farmers took on this work even though it became quickly clear that the infrastructure they built would serve large landowning Yori farmers at their expense. Yet a wage of any sort was better than losing one's land, and Mayo laborers roamed the Fuerte valley and other parts of northwest Mexico, erecting structures that ultimately would send vital water to competing farms.

Several Mayo elders recollect traversing the Fuerte valley to help build dams and canals. Some elders such as Librado Cuadros of La Palma recall the construction devices they used, how this technology improved over time, and how hard the work was:

> When I was only sixteen, in 1948, I built canals all over this valley. At first, we opened the earth with just axes and eventually used an old, jalopy-like tractor with small tires, that whistled like a calf. After clearing the land, we built six-meter-high walls of the canal, using huge rocks and filling them in with concrete, then Yori owners installed pumps to drain water for irrigation. I also helped to construct the bridge near Charay. I tried every job because it was hard to survive by just farming. I got great work experience building these structures.[35]

Mayo hydraulic workers benefitted from new development projects insofar as it gave them valuable experience with modern construction equipment that they might use in other future employment, but new restrictions on pumps and canals in the late 1940s made their primary employment—milpa agriculture—more challenging. It is not a coincidence that a young Cuadros sought employment in the same year that his family's ejido both lost access to a water pump and flooding from the Cahuinahua Canal ruined La Palma's crops. Cuadros was not alone. The deteriorating prospect of subsistence or small-scale agriculture became so acute that the number of wage earners in northwest Mexico grew to nearly 50 percent of the region's labor force by the mid-1960s, nearly double the amount nationally.[36]

The growing supply of laborers pushed down wages and allowed for frequent mistreatment. In response, some Mayo ejidatarios left northern Sinaloa altogether and went to neighboring Sonora looking for work. In a limited respect these migrations into the Yaqui and Mayo valleys of Sonora were not necessarily new. As early as the 1930s a trickle of Sinaloan Mayo laborers had gone north to take advantage of the higher minimum wage in the region, but the scale of the migration in the late 1940s was larger, as were the consequences of the work.[37] Once there, Mayo laborers from the Fuerte valley often encountered other Indigenous laborers trapped in the same dynamic, and despite their shared economic circumstances and Yoreme identity, they had to navigate subtle differences that made being far from home difficult. Roberto Escalante of La Palma recounts the cultural diplomacy that accompanied the migration: "We traveled north of Obregón to work on a big dam in the late 1940s, because unlike here, they guaranteed wages. Other Yoremes working there treated us like family, because we shared a language and customs. Their food was too sweet, but they were our brothers, so we said we liked it."[38] The cordial cultural exchange between Mayo laborers from Sinaloa and Sonoran Yaqui was common in twentieth century northwest Mexico. Despite some minor differences, Yaqui and Mayo people recognized each other as Yoremes with not only a nearly identical language and culture but as people facing the same legal and economic trials. In much the same way that Mayo laborers did not want to have to leave the Fuerte valley, Yaqui people would have preferred if they were not there as competitors. Yet that friction never overwhelmed their shared identity, one that, Escalante points out, the migrant Mayo laborers were eager to encourage.

Escalante obliquely mentions one of the primary forces driving Fuerte valley laborers north and far from home: Yoris underpaying or even refusing to pay for services rendered. Rumors of particular Yori employers not paying workers circulated constantly in the Fuerte valley, and though independent ejidatarios obviously avoided an employer known to renege on his obligations, the limited employment opportunities in the Fuerte valley meant that ejidatarios often had few choices but to offer labor where they could and hope for compensation. Because state officials never welcomed or looked too deeply into ejidatarios' complaints of nonpayment, this vicious tactic frequently left economically stressed and emotionally demoralized Mayo laborers to seek employment outside the Fuerte valley. Leaving home was, quite literally, the last thing they wanted to do.

As desperate as these actions were, some Mayo villages took even more extreme measures. Unable to gain official irrigation rights or strike deals with third-party users as they had in the postrevolutionary era, some communities looked to the emergence of hydraulic technology near their ejidos in the postwar period with hopeful eyes, eager that they might secure water concessions. Yori newcomers recognized both the ejidatarios' desperate situation and their hope in new irrigation infrastructure and took advantage of both, convincing independent Mayo ejidatarios to construct canals for free in exchange for vague promises of irrigation once the canals were completed. Indigenous elder Sabás Ynustrosa of La Mojonera recollects how these deals uniformly turned out badly for the ejidatarios, "My friends, family, and other Yoremes constructed the canals in the early 1950s after property owners promised them free irrigation access upon completion. Then they broke their promises, did not pay them, and refused to make deals for irrigation water. This kind of lying was typical of Yoris."[39] Ynustrosa's family members and friends were not simple, bucolic farmers; they understood the value of hydraulic infrastructure and wanted it in their community. Desperate times indeed called for desperate measures, and these Mayo farmers gambled that if they constructed the structures for free, Yoris would follow through on their promises. It was a gamble they had no choice but to take, but it did not pay off.

Such deceit was part of a strategy among canal and pump owners to cut off water to ejidos. Before large-scale canal construction in the 1950s, pump owners and irrigation permit holders had frequently worked out arrangements with Mayo villages, often exchanging water for a percentage of the ejido's harvest. However, by the 1950s canal owners adamantly refused to negotiate deals with Mayo ejidatarios for access to water. Irrigation had become too valuable to exchange for a percentage of rapidly diminishing ejidatario crops, and more importantly, the owners had targeted Mayo farmers as a source of cheap labor. The simplest way to establish a pool of workers was to eliminate irrigation, make it more difficult for Indigenous farmers to cultivate crops, force them to illegally sell or rent their ejidal lands, and finally, to become laborers. Little archival evidence exists that definitively proves Yori landowners conspired to make ejidal lands less productive in order to then annex or rent these properties and turn Mayo farmers into full time laborers, yet even if they were not all conspiring en masse, the state had given them, individually, the tools and motivation to create a rural proletariat. This, combined with the Yori farmers' view of themselves as rugged pioneers that set out to make "wasted" lands bountiful and to be an example to the "indolent" Indigenous population, was more than enough motivation to push Yori farmers to ruthless ends.

It did not have to be this way. In the postwar years, however, the Mexican developmentalist agenda operated on the assumption that for Yori landowners to prosper, Mayo ejidatarios must fail. Though given many opportunities, no state agency after 1950 ever took initiative to defend the relatively meager rights of Mayo ejidos. And as mentioned earlier, state agencies did not act monolithically. Rather, they took different approaches to heaping further advantages upon private Yori farmers. The CRF was busy directing the Fuerte's waters to large commercial farms. The Ejidal Bank—while still distributing limited loans to some ejidos—was also funneling credit into already well-capitalized farms. The INI officials rarely entered the Fuerte valley and generally relied on their own ideas on how to assist Indigenous communities rather than listen to community leaders. No agency had either the time or incentive to worry about displaced ejidatarios, and these Mayo farmers knew it. The back-breaking labor that the ejidatarios of La Mojonera undertook, for example, to build a canal—with only a faint promise of water as repayment—testifies louder than any document how effectively marginalized independent Mayo ejidatarios had become.

In fact, the Indigenous laborers who constructed dams and canals in the Fuerte valley resembled what historian Karl Wittfogel has described as a hydraulic army. Ancient empires across the world drafted or conscripted a *corvée*, or hydraulic army, of unpaid peasants assigned to communal work teams. These groups constructed large irrigation structures as a form of taxation imposed in the name of the common good to further enrich the state.[40] While Wittfogel's classic definition of corvées does not perfectly describe Sinaloan Indigenous laborers of the mid-twentieth century, in the six decades since his work first appeared scholars have redefined and applied his ideas in ways that more accurately resemble the pressures facing the Mayo hydraulic labor market.[41] In particular, Donald Worster builds on Wittfogel's hydraulic army thesis by showing how, in the western United States, the federal government empowered some farmers and subjugated others via massive water projects. Worster's discussion of crony capitalism, in which state functionaries disenfranchised vulnerable constituencies ceding irrigation rights to powerful landowners, fits the circumstances of the Fuerte valley well.[42] Whether ancient Chinese despots, the U.S. Army Corps of Engineers, or the Fuerte River Commission, when representatives of the state anoint a winner— someone who will benefit from centralized water policies—they often also, implicitly, pick a loser. That fact is made doubly painful when, as in the case of independent Mayo farmers, the losers are made to carry out (however indirectly) the hydraulic policies that will harm them.

The ability of Yoris to convince large numbers of Mayo campesinos to construct canals and dams for cheap—and, in shockingly frequent cases, even for free—fostered the economic growth of the Fuerte valley. Indigenous elder Mateo Quintero of Tehueco explains how projects presented to Yoremes were deceitful and hidden under lies and broken promises: "Yoris did not keep promises that Yoremes could use canals after constructing them, and often did not pay Indigenous laborers. They promised a lot, but throughout our history Yoremes could not predict just how far Yoris would go in taking what they pleased. This valley was built on those lies."[43] Quintero identified his account as part of "our history," a phrase he uses to distinguish Mayo people's memories of this period from Yori accounts. But Yoris were so favored by the state and became so influential that he might as well have used the phrase to signify the difference between Mayo history and official histories.

Scholars such as Mario Gill reflect this difference in published histories. In his seminal work, Gill fails to recognize land dispossession and dishonest labor practices in the mid-twentieth century Fuerte valley. In fact, Gill understates the realities of water distribution in the 1950s so much that, at one point, he contends, "In the valley, class differences are incidental; all are linked to the earth and water; if there is drought all lose; if there is water everyone wins."[44] Every Mayo person who lived through this period knew this was not true. Because large landowners monopolized water sources, Indigenous farmers did not "win" when new irrigation infrastructure arrived. "Class" may have been incidental within the ranks of Yoris, but the cleavage between the Yoris and Yoremes amounted to a class chasm. Simply put, the triumphalist narrative claiming that elites used dams and canals to propel the Fuerte valley into one of the most productive and ostensibly egalitarian agricultural regions of Mexico is inaccurate.

Rather, the truth is that as large landowners gained control of irrigation water in the mid-twentieth century, they used this leverage to marginalize the Mayo farmers who had long been there. The Mexican state either turned a blind eye to or—as a stack of denied petitions grew into an impressive pile—were complicit in the process of Indigenous land dispossession. That Indigenous ejidatarios were frequently complicit in the emergence of shifting land and water rights—either by selling or renting land illegally or by building the hydraulic infrastructure that would serve Yori farmers—occurred only because, in the short term, they had no other choice. During the turbulent decade of the 1950s, Mayo farmers looked for any fingerhold with which to cling to their land. The long-term consequences were tomorrow's problem; they had to make their way through today.

In this story of desperation, there was still a glimmer of hope for some. Numerous Mayo farmers of the Fuerte valley engaged the very system that subjugated them because it also generated aspirations. Jeffrey Banister reasons that "centralized water governance is also a production of hope, or the constitution of a 'hydraulic subject' who identifies with and continues to act on the promise of a better future through federal irrigation programs."[45] Several Mayo farmers of the Fuerte valley had seen canals and pumps boost crop productivity in the mid-1920s to mid-1940s and hoped that the trend would continue. Of course, not all Mayo farmers hoped to be "hydraulic subjects"—as we will soon see, some wished that the region's entire hydraulic infrastructure would be wiped away. Yet there were enough who, despite the political reality that they were not preferred recipients, looked upon the massive projects of the 1950s and calculated that even if they only received a fraction of it all, they would still have enough with which to plant a future.

San Juan Ritual: The Limited Response of the Fuerte Valley

The impetus behind Mexico's developmentalist programs of the mid-twentieth century—which, in the large agricultural sector, centered on the proliferation of irrigation infrastructure—was undoubtedly economic, yet a cultural motivation also drove the state's initiatives. As anthropologist Mary O'Connor argues, "Weber's idea that rationalization of the social structure would bring about a general cultural modernization was the basis for Mexico's economic development programs."[46] Mexican policymakers wanted to do more than steer the inputs of agricultural production to the supposedly "modern" Yori farmers. They also wanted a more mobile, fluid, and flexible rural labor force, one that did not see the land—including rivers—as a spiritual or cultural asset but as physical capital to be bought, sold, and employed in the most profitable pursuits. Mayo villages refused to agree, especially when it came to the Fuerte River.

One dimension in which Mayo villagers manifested their refusal to acquiesce to Yori cultural expectations was in their riverine rituals, which reproduced community by binding participants to each other while paying homage to the Fuerte River as the source of elements essential to life. But this connection came under threat as Yori farmers and the state pushed Mayo ejidos away from the shore. However, similar to how they transformed the Yuco Conti rain-requesting ceremony, independent Mayo also altered riverine rituals in the 1950s and 1960s. As forests fell, irrigation infrastructure and large estates expanded, Yoris stole Indigenous lands, and access to an increasingly polluted Fuerte River grew limited. In order to ensure their cultural survival, independent Mayo villages changed the locations where they performed the San Juan Bautista ritual, another ceremony that linked them to their sacred river.

The San Juan ritual, celebrated on June 24, originated in Europe to commemorate the birth of Saint John the Baptist. The Catholic Church deliberately set its official observance six months prior to Christmas at the summer solstice so that it would coincide with pre-Christian European harvest ceremonies. Anthropologist David Guss proposes that the church's openness to observing the San Juan (or Saint John) festival in late June "resulted in not merely one of the most widely diffused holidays, but also one of the most syncretic."[47] San Juan allowed these newfound Catholics to create ceremonies essential to reinforcing community bonds. After it crossed over the Atlantic to Latin America, the holiday continued to help forge thousands of communities out of Afro-Latinx, Indigenous, and European populations.[48]

Long before Yori colonists renamed the río Zuaque the río Fuerte, its waters had been a meeting place for the Indigenous inhabitants of the Fuerte valley. The change in name did not affect the reciprocal relationship Indigenous people enjoyed with the river: it still provided water for them, their plants, and the animals they hunted and raised. Mayo people believed the waters had the power to heal.

More than that, the river was a sacred oracle that they alone knew how to speak with in order to gather pertinent information about life.[49] In turn, Mayo villagers paid homage to the river through rituals and viewed themselves as its protector. Because of this, Mayo elders only partially attribute the origins of their version of San Juan to Christianity, although most agree with anthropologists that the modern form of the ceremony is syncretic.

If the origins of San Juan in fact predate the Spanish and relate to earlier planting rituals, then this could help illuminate the festival's popularity and resilience throughout the years. As Oralia Flores of Pochotal explains, "San Juan is associated with Saint John baptizing people in the Jordan River. The Yoreme adopted it from Spaniards, modified it, and made it an important tradition of our own."[50] Perhaps because of her deep-rooted Catholicism, Flores notably evades the issue of an Indigenous antecedent to San Juan, but the modifications she refers to has to have come from earlier Mayo practices. Regardless of the ritual's origins, the Mayo version of San Juan mixes elements of Roman Catholicism, such as entering and bathing in the water, and pre-Hispanic Indigenous beliefs such as prayers in the Mayo language and speaking to the river.[51] So while the form is Catholic, the ceremony holds, maintains, and preserves ancient Mayo traditions.

The first recorded description of the San Juan Festival in the Fuerte valley came from anthropologist Ralph Beals in the early 1930s. He described how people arrived at the river about three o'clock in the morning and that "when entering the water, they said 'God has permitted us to arrive at this day.' Then they splashed water at one another, singing three times in one tone, 'San Huanta bapo yewe' (Saint John playing in the water). Then they returned home and prayed."[52] Beals's account captures just one version of the ceremony. Even in the 1930s, each Mayo village and ceremonial center practiced the San Juan ritual with slight variations. These differences still persist today, and although the ceremony has changed slightly, it still binds Mayo people to each other and the Fuerte River.[53]

Beals argues that although the San Juan ritual was Christian, it probably derived from an aboriginal planting or harvest ceremony. This assumption likely stems from his claim that Mayo people viewed San Juan as the "owner of seeds," which fits the timing of the ceremony: the festival of San Juan comes at the end of June, the start of the rainy season.[54] Beals's description does not reveal whether this Indigenous antecedent included bathing in the water and, if so, how the ceremony was intended to boost crop yields. Perhaps the San Juan ceremony's Indigenous antecedent expressed the connection between rainwater, river water, and crops given that generations of Mayo farmers depended on the planned overflow of the river, as well as on rainwater for planting and harvesting beans, corn, and squash.

For centuries, the Mayo people living along the Mayo River in Sonora—in an almost exact way Sinaloan Mayo approached the Fuerte River—shared the belief that river water was sacred, as reflected in the way they renewed their commitment to the river through the San Juan ceremony.[55] Anthropologist N. Ross Crumrine suggests that the Mayo people have long conveyed the notion that water from the Mayo River may become the means of the supernatural castigation of the people. They also have claimed that since the river is very old, it is also the site where all Mayo have been baptized.[56] And while Crumrine does not mention it as one of the reasons why river water was sacred, the very fact that he observed festival participants speaking directly to the Mayo River during the San Juan Ceremony in Sonora implies that they regarded this body of water as a respected, living entity that they could communicate with directly.[57] If alive, a river also could die, and it fell to Mayo people to not just pay it reverence but to protect it. It was an ancient obligation that had become vital to Mayo identity in both Sinaloa and Sonora over generations.

In the Fuerte valley, the San Juan celebration demonstrates how Mayo people protected Indigenous religious beliefs and identity by fusing them with Christian practices. In so doing, pushed this celebration's meaning past its Catholic roots. To this day, participants in northern Sinaloa mark the ceremony by bathing in the Fuerte River to cure ailments and clean and energize the soul.[58] In the centuries after Spanish conquest, the ceremony became central to Mayo life, and oral testimonies suggest that, as late as the mid-twentieth century, nearly all Indigenous people of the Fuerte valley participated in this ritual.[59] But, according to elders, since then enthusiasm has waned and the number of participants declined as river water became contaminated and access limited. Others argue that, while absolute numbers of participants declined in some villages, the constraints independent Mayo faced spurred a cultural and religious revitalization of the San Juan ceremony. There may have been fewer people each year in some locations, but those who attended invested a deeper significance into the ritual and it became a key practice that bound Mayo people together—regardless of faction or ties to the SICAE—during the massive changes to the natural landscape in the 1940s through 1960s.[60]

In response to having less access to river locations in the mid-twentieth century, Mayo villagers began to gather at less than a half dozen Indigenous religious centers in large towns such as Mochicahui and San Miguel to practice San Juan. Mayo participants still converge on these riverbank sites to carry out similar ceremonies that use the banks and water of the Fuerte River. When possible, Mayo villages also conduct their own versions of riverine rituals. For instance, Mayo people of La Florida baptize Fariseo (Pharisee) dancers—participants invoking evil characteristics in the ceremony—on the river shore during Holy Week in mid-April. Carla Bacosegua, an elder from that ejido, describes how Fariseos dress up and reenact the imprisonment and crucifixion of Jesus as well as how "a tenachi creates a circle, lights candles on the riverbank, and fills pots with river water. Fariseos walk on the riverbank sand to accept baptism as Christians. The baptism, the sand, the water, and the location all connect us to the river, and unite us as Yoremes."[61] Whether performed in the waters of the Fuerte River or on the riverbanks, the religious ceremonies still tie Mayo villagers to this body of water and to each other.

Even today, Mayo elders like Laura Apodaca of La Misión believe that on June 24 the water from the river takes spiritual significance. "We call it," Apodaca claims, "the Golden River. We know that the rays of the sun bless the water on June 24, giving it extra curative properties and making it more sacred that day. Yoremes bathe in the river to grow their hair, to cure sores."[62] Unlike Yoris, for Mayo people the gold in the "Golden River" references not wealth but the spiritual power they have recognized for centuries.

Throughout the second half of the twentieth century, the degree of reverence with which Indigenous people of northern Sinaloa treated the Fuerte River, particularly during San Juan, continued despite changes to the natural landscape, decreased access to the river, and, especially beginning in the 1950s, increased pollution. Some Mayo elders such as Felicitas Mejía of Vinaterias assert that "all Yoremes bathed in the river on June 24 to treat their ailments and receive spiritual energy. Some cured others with the waters' magical properties, but healers are now rare, and less go to the river to perform the ritual."[63] Other sources corroborate Mejía's complaint that there are fewer participants in the ceremony. It appears that a paradoxical dynamic developed over the last sixty years in Sinaloa: the importance of the San Juan ritual to Mayo identity appears to have increased for those who arrived at the river on June 24, but the numbers who participated has declined in some villages.

One reason for this apparent decline in many villages is that pesticides and unregulated animal waste seeped into the river, gradually deteriorating its quality until, by the end of the 1950s, few Mayo villagers dared bathe in its waters. Mayo elder Horacio Pitahaya of Boca de Arroyo explains, "Every Yoreme used to bathe in the river during this ritual, but water became contaminated, and we lost faith in its curative properties. We used to be able to drink directly from the river, but many of us stopped bathing in it because we were afraid the poison that began draining into the water would harm us."[64] As they saw swirls of rainbow-colored blooms in the water and watched fish and other animals die, a disturbing number of Mayo people came to doubt the water's healing properties.

Complicating the problem was the fact that while more pesticides and runoff crept in, there was less water volume to dilute what was accumulating. A few decades before, Mayo villagers used canoes to navigate the river for most of the year, but over the years large landowners' canals and pumps drew enough water from the Fuerte River to reduce it to almost a trickle near many Mayo ejidos.[65] Some elders recall the absurdity of attempting to bathe in a dribble of water that hardly resembled a creek, let alone the powerful river they had come to depend on over generations. As large farmers syphoned off ever greater quantities of the river, what they left behind was increasingly toxic. Potential San Juan participants had demonstrably less water—sometime just pools—in which to immerse themselves, and what remained had become noxious and poisonous.

Runoff and lower water levels pushed away some, but there were many who argued for the necessity of ancestral traditions. Their challenge was to find a place that had enough water to bathe in but was not visibly contaminated by animal feces or toxic waste (let alone the hidden dangers of pesticide contamination). Mayo villagers living on the banks of the Fuerte River had a long history of allowing everyone—including other Indigenous groups—access to the river, believing that it belonged to all and provided life, information, inspiration, and energy. They viewed the Fuerte's banks as a "space of effective appropriation of the ecosystem, that is, as spaces used to satisfy community needs and to bring about social and cultural development."[66] But the Yori newcomers to the valley did not share their Mayo neighbors' tradition of access, even if it was merely ceremonial.

San Juan participants were met by landowners who railed that they were violating private property with their ceremonies. Mayo elder Mauricio Mejías of Huepaco reminisces how Yori riverbank landowners disrespected them and "chased off Yoreme ritual participants at gunpoint or hit them with belts, while the government did not protect Indigenous ceremonial centers. Yoremes also lost access to river shores because Yoris profited from extracting construction aggregate materials there, such as sand and gravel."[67] With the government's support, Yori landowners pushed off independent Mayo farmers in the 1940s. They also fenced in valuable lots—including the river banks—and blocked off vast swaths of the river by the 1950s.[68]

As Mayo villagers' identity—which they were adamant in their refusal to forfeit—was largely based on a ceremonial interaction with the Fuerte River, those carrying on the San Juan ritual converged upon the few sites available. This brought an unexpected benefit. As Indigenous elder Ronaldo Baisegua of San Miguel recounts, "Yoremes reduced the number of locations where they performed San Juan, there used to be more places, but we had to stick to sites like San Miguel that were not cut off by the Yoris. Seeing more of us together united us through those hard times."[69] Unlike the Yuco Conti rain ceremony, which evolved from a centralized ceremony to one dispersed across several villages to increase efficacy, San Juan celebrations went from being diffused throughout the Fuerte valley to increasingly concentrated. Participants understood the important role the ceremony played in their community and refused to concede to Yoris this key cultural performance.

The story of the San Juan ritual thus far reads like a defensive bunkering—a last stand of Mayo culture in an increasingly hostile world. While true, this is not the whole story, for (as exemplified by the transformation of the Yuco Conti ceremony) Mayo villages were adept at adapting. As the riverbank became less available and welcoming, hydraulic structures like canals took on new religious and cultural significance. Some independent Mayo farmers extended their connection to the Fuerte River by treating any hydraulic infrastructure that carried its waters as part of the river. According to Mayo elders Narciso Bachomo and Carlos Salcedo of Camajoa, during San Juan in places like Mochicahui in the 1960s, "We started bathing in a canal instead of the river. We were lucky to have a source of water to use for ceremonies and not have to interact with Yoris owning river bank land. They cut off access to our ceremonial centers on the river, limiting our rituals and threatening our identity."[70] Yori farmers used irrigation infrastructure to expand their wealth and relegated Mayo farmers to using such structures to defend their cultural autonomy. While these adaptations may not have been ideal—no Mayo source celebrates this change—they at least allowed Mayo villagers to continue drawing sacred river water that was essential to the survival of such ceremonies central to their identity.

Mayo culture expanded and contracted throughout the twentieth century as they adapted existing traditions to new challenges and brought in new practices, leading to more heterogeneous customs. Today, select Mayo ejidos continue to practice the San Juan ritual—and not just in the ceremonial centers. After the trials of the mid-twentieth century, the San Juan ritual slowly expanded out again and villages renewed their individual celebrations with their own unique flair. These subtle nuances in practices, including San Juan celebrations, have helped villages maintain their own character, and no two villages have the exact same ritual. In La Palma, for example, Mayo elder Librado Cuadros explains that "we bathe in the irrigation intake and cut our hair to symbolize a cleansing. Yoremes from Cahuinahua join us to maintain our ancient rituals by performing Pascola and Matachin dances under a wooden shelter on the river bank."[71] By contrast, in the ejido of Pochotal, the San Juan celebrants would never cut their hair, as they believe the sacred waters of the Fuerte aid in health, including hair growth.[72] Despite its decline in some villages during the crisis of the 1950s and 1960s, San Juan's revitalization and consolidation in ceremonial centers tied villages together and—however tenuously—to the Fuerte River. The ability of independent ejidatarios in La Palma, Cahuinahua, and Mochicahui to use irrigation infrastructure to perform the San Juan ritual exhibits a form of adaptation that defines Mayo identity in the twentieth century.

Independent Mayo villages led the charge in adapting the San Juan ritual largely because they were the most negatively impacted by commercial farming. It is ironic that cultural revitalization started with the group that had the least leverage with the state, as if their hopelessness pushed them first into these necessary responses, and it is no coincidence that all information available regarding adaptations to the San Juan ceremony come from recent interviews with elders who were members of independent Mayo villages in the mid-twentieth century. Such dialogues reveal that independent Mayo farmers responded to their loss of control over irrigation infrastructure and banks of the Fuerte River with something they could control: the manner and location in which to perform their religious ceremonies. As their connection to the modern, commercial world diminished, independent Mayo farmers were the first to fall back on their traditional identity.

By the 1960s it was not just the independent Mayo ejidatarios of the Fuerte valley who converged on the limited ceremonial centers to participate in the San Juan ritual—the majority of Mayo villagers, regardless of their affiliation with the SICAE, attended. Individualist and collectivist Mayo factions had shared a contentious existence within villages controlled by the SICAE, but by bathing together in the San Juan ceremony both sides signaled and reaffirmed their shared Mayo identity. Notably, however, it was independent Mayo farmers from villages not embroiled in squabbles over the SICAE's attempts to dominate the valley who led the efforts to revitalize the San Juan ceremony and determined where it would be held. All of which signals two facts. First, that though there was real acrimony within villages split by the SICAE's heavy-handedness, in the end, despite feelings of betrayal, the bonds of religiosity and culture overcame conflicts of economics and self-interest. Second, as the SICAE threat ended by the mid-1950s, the state's developmentalist policies united Mayo ejidatarios against a universal threat of limited access to the water and banks of the Fuerte River.

Mayo farmers found in their rituals a way of anchoring themselves in a rapidly changing world. Bathing in a canal may seem at first blush to be a far cry from immersion in the river proper, but it allowed Mayo people to continue using sacred river water and carry on what was essential in their symbiotic relationship with the river. By converging on traditional ceremonial centers to conduct San Juan, participants also ensured their spatial connection to the geographic location of the river. The San Juan ceremony was, in the end, what the living participants invested in it. The fact that they had fewer river shore sites to utilize—or had to use hydraulic infrastructure—reflected the legal and physical relationship the state allowed them to keep with the river. Though the state might try, however, it could not puncture the essential ontological bond that Mayo people had forged with the river and, through it, with each other.

Antonio Bacosegua's Vision for the Fuerte and Mayo Valleys

In 1957 God spoke to Antonio Bacosegua, or so he claimed. At first few believed him, but soon people beyond his family heard about his experience and word spread outside his Fuerte valley village of La Florida. By the following year Bacosegua, an independent Mayo farmer, was a phenomenon in the Fuerte valley and had become a lightning rod within the Indigenous villages of northwest Mexico. While Bacosegua prophesied that God would right the wrongs perpetrated upon all Mayo people, not all Yoremes rallied to his vision. In particular, because of differences in their political experiences and histories of hydraulic social mobilization, the Mayo people of the Mayo valley in Sonora embraced Bacosegua's prophecy but those in the Fuerte valley in Sinaloa did not. This split proved that identity, economics, and spirituality intersected in complicated ways in the two valleys and that there was no monolithic response among Mayo villagers to Mexican developmentalist policies.

As this book's introduction explains, God appeared to Antonio Bacosegua in 1957 in the ejido of La Florida, located along the Fuerte River, and commanded him to make more religious *fiestas* in His name, a task Bacosegua and his followers took seriously. Mayo fiestas require prayers, music, and dancing to express the community's dedication to God, and Bacosegua and his followers understood that the consequences of their failure to create these fiestas would result in catastrophic events that could spell the end of mankind. The god they knew was wrathful, notoriously punishing and destroying those who refused his commands. In their cosmogony, Mayo people saw themselves as stewards tasked with maintaining a balance in their natural landscape both because it benefited them and because God's punishment awaited them if they failed.

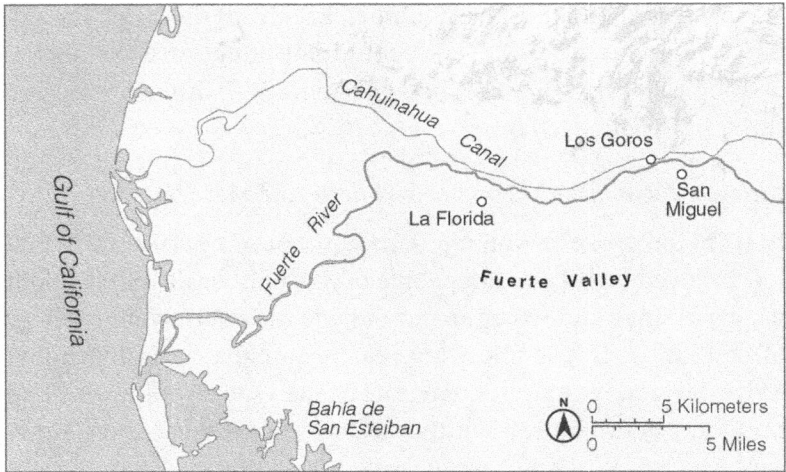

9. La Florida ejido next to the Fuerte River. Drawn by Pease Press Cartography.

The subject of some scholarly studies, Bacosegua's vision and the millenarian movement it spawned are still fondly remembered by Mayo elders today.[73] Antonio's goddaughter Carla Bacosegua, an Indigenous elder from La Florida, recalls her godfather as a man who was both a mystic and someone rooted in the Mayo world. "He was," she recounts, "a healer who organized religious rituals every eight days in May. While followers played the drum, he performed miracles and healed grateful Yoremes. This movement revolved around both religion and preserving Yoreme culture, the two were synonymous."[74] Whether Bacosegua actually cured people is a matter of debate, but he did use his vision and status as a healer to unite Indigenous people during a challenging era.[75]

Restrictions on accessing the Fuerte River led to the emergence of this religious revival as a vehicle for addressing social change in the Fuerte valley, yet many Sinaloan Mayo were limited by their belief that their past success in accessing irrigation infrastructure would help them confront new challenges. Though it was not necessarily his intent, Bacosegua's movement offered a vehicle for Mayo farmers to address social change, but while some rallied to his cause, in the Fuerte valley, his home region, there was a significant contingent of Mayo villagers who held that their past success in accessing irrigation infrastructure could, despite all the state's obvious indifference to them, be rekindled again. Meanwhile, in Sonora, where Mayo farmers protested water inequity more directly, Bacosegua's religious revival became a venue to confront the social and cultural fallout of the transformation to commercial agriculture.

The Bacosegua millenarian movement shared characteristics with other native revivals in the Americas. Historian Alfred A. Cave describes how Native American visionaries called for the restoration and preservation of a way of life that was passing for centuries. Indeed, the overarching theme of Indigenous revivals beckoned them to return to traditions which, according to prophets, their people had ignored. God had higher expectations for Native Americans, but if they repented and returned to "right" living, He would turn his anger upon white colonizers. Indigenous visionaries told their disciples that Indians were His chosen people, and by following the teachings of His prophet, they would be rewarded with the restoration of a world that had been lost.[76] In every case, from the eighteenth century to the twentieth century, from North America to South America, participants in native revivals believed that restoring their traditional worlds would fix whatever ailed them.[77] But what exactly were the Mayo followers of Bacosegua asking for in the late 1950s, and what kind of world did they expect to return to?

While native revitalizations in the Americas shared some general characteristics, understanding the specific conditions of the Mayo and Fuerte valleys helps to explain the significance of the Bacosegua movement, especially in terms of hydraulic social mobilization. In analyzing this millenarian movement, N. Ross Crumrine argues, "Societies undergoing change . . . move into a liminal or transition period in which myth and ritual are intensified. . . . Expectations or beliefs concerning the ideal Mayo way of life cannot manifest in the river valley. . . . A society in this impasse tends to become prophet-producing."[78] While both Cave and Crumrine ignore the issue of water availability in revitalization movements, the changing conditions along the river no doubt catalyzed prophecy and intensified religious enthusiasm in the years after 1957. Indigenous villages in the Mayo valley used the Bacosegua movement to call for a return to a time when their lands were not encroached on by Yoris, their natural resources were not disappearing, and most importantly, when they still enjoyed vital, unfettered access to abundant rivers.

Did the process of what David Harvey calls "accumulation by dispossession"—the consolidation of power and wealth by the few at the expense of the masses—occur along the same trajectory in the Fuerte valley as in the Mayo valley?[79] Mayo farmers in both valleys ended up with limited productive farmland and even less irrigation water by the late 1950s, but how each got to this nadir was unique. Both communities employed divergent tactics to voice their disapproval of water availability. It was not a coincidence that Bacosegua (and allegedly God) wanted to revive Mayo identity in Sinaloa at a time when the state had cut off irrigation access to the Indigenous ejidos still using pumps and canals such as La Palma and Jahuara. It appears that his message came as Yoris, with the state's blessing, severed the last, tenuous links Mayo farmers in the Fuerte valley had to the river.

According to anthropologist Charles Erasmus, Mayo villages in the Mayo valley in Sonora used Bacosegua's vision to proactively confront hydraulic inequities. They sincerely believed that God was not only going to provide His Indigenous believers with sufficient rainwater but that He would also punish those who persecuted them with a deluge, flooding dams and destroying canals so that the rivers ran free again. No more would others charge His people for His water. It was a popular message that spread rapidly. Indigenous people both believed it in an immediate, literal sense and—as Erasmus has maintained—used it to express their displeasure with the local Office of Water Resources, which they felt had unjustly favored rich landowners.[80] Curiously, though Bacosegua came from the La Florida ejido of the Fuerte valley in Sinaloa, the prophecy did not have the same effect there.

Unexpectedly, the message received a tepid, even hostile reception in northern Sinaloa. Which begs the question: Why? Did the Office of Water Resources create conditions in the Mayo valley that were more drastically unjust than in Sinaloa? Was water distribution far more equitable in the Fuerte valley, giving farmers less to revolt against? Neither was the case. Both communities suffered under Mexico's developmentalist policies, but how they interacted with government officials and how they suffered differed, and this divergence led to unique outcomes.

Despite some brief glimmers of hope during the Mexican Revolution and the postrevolutionary era, inequality had been a constant and growing theme in the Mayo valley throughout the first half of the twentieth century. When it became a crisis in the 1950s, Mayo people there turned to a millenarian movement. While inequality may not have been the final goal for the Mexican government, it was the unavoidable result of their policies. Geographer Jeffrey Banister makes a case that the history of irrigation development in the Mayo valley from the time of the Porfiriato and well into the 1950s centered on colonization.[81] By the mid-twentieth century various agencies using different approaches had, by controlling access to irrigation and encouraging land grabs, created marginalized ejidatarios in both the Fuerte and Mayo valleys and the entire northwest in general.[82]

While ejidatarios in both valleys shared limited land and water rights in the postwar era, they each had specific, historical landholding patterns that influenced their responses. For example, in the years prior to the Mexican Revolution, the Indigenous people of the Mayo valley endured years of dispossession, reluctantly receiving small plots in exchange for dispossessed ancestral lands.[83] While Fuerte valley Mayo farmers also lost a great deal of land to outsiders in the late nineteenth and early twentieth centuries, the Mexican government rarely distributed small plots to Indigenous groups there. In fact, by the late 1930s when most Sinaloan Mayo villages secured ejidal lands, less than a half dozen, one being Los Goros, actually had titles of private property, a major reason why the majority of Indigenous people of the Fuerte valley supported land reform.[84]

In the years before the revolution, Mayo people in the two regions had shared similar circumstances. Yet they had divergent land tenure preferences after the fighting stopped. An Indigenous leader like Felipe Bachomo, whose forces actually reclaimed some ancestral lands from Fuerte valley hacendados during the revolution, did not exist in the Mayo valley. Instead, Sonoran Mayo soldiers fought alongside the mestizo Álvaro Obregón based on promises that he would reward them with property. While some Mayo veterans received small plots in the Mayo valley after fighting ceased, the majority of Indigenous farmers were forgotten. Nevertheless, the Mayo farmers of Sonora generally continued to support small private property ownership over the ejido system. This choice would have lasting repercussions.[85] Sonoran Mayo smallholders encountered more difficulties attaining water rights than Sinaloan Indigenous ejidatarios who fell back on solidarity and organizational strength.

Felipe Bachomo's revolt from 1913 to 1916 allowed some Indigenous villages in the Fuerte valley to physically regain ancestral properties, but the absence of current, legally recognizable land titles motivated Mayo farmers to support the ejido system in the postrevolutionary era. Because they had few secure titles to their ancestral lands and no Obregón-like figure to help them acquire more, most Indigenous farmers of the Fuerte valley would not be able to hold on to their traditional lands. Most northern Sinaloan Mayo farmers, therefore, supported the state-sponsored agrarian reforms of the 1930s and, in return for forming alliances with state functionaries, dozens of these Mayo communities received dotaciones. In contrast to Mayo villagers in Sonora who were too fractured and isolated on their small, privately held plots, Fuerte valley Indigenous farmers leveraged their political status as ejidatarios to successfully engage in hydraulic social mobilization by navigating the political and social landscape of the postrevolutionary era and securing water rights.[86]

The difference in solidarity and organizational strength between the two valleys went beyond land titles. Farmers in the Mayo valley appear to have been less successful at mobilizing for hydraulic resources. One indication of this is demonstrated by state complaints. In the Mayo valley, state officials protested Indigenous communities' use of weirs and fencerows in the early to mid-twentieth century—but there were no such reports in the Fuerte valley.[87] Oral histories corroborate this difference. Mayo elder Manuel Galindo from La Bajada recalls how some Indigenous farmers drew irrigation water by using weirs and fencerows, yet no other elders from the Fuerte valley share similar recollections. Other sources confirm that these strategies appear to have remained uncommon in northern Sinaloa.[88]

The answer to this hydraulic social mobilization discrepancy is obvious: Sinaloan Mayo farmers had irrigation provided through government agencies or via private (legal and illegal) agreements. By contrast, according to Carla Bacosegua, Sonoran Mayo farmers were forced to depend on traditional technologies such as handmade weirs instead of canals and pumps during the postrevolutionary era.[89] In fact, Francisco Jacinto of Jahuara points out that, unlike the Sonoran Mayo who used reed plants to build weirs and fence rows that diverted river water to their fields, the Indigenous people of the Fuerte valley used such vegetation only to make crafts, such as baskets.[90] In the same sense that the various agencies of the Mexican state were not monolithic and acted differently depending upon circumstance, so too were the lives of various Mayo communities different and dependent upon what was available to them.

One simple explanation for the popularity of the Bacosegua movement in Sonora is that the Mayo valley was a ripe field for such uprisings, having had a series of millenarian movements reaching as far back as the 1890s.[91] Like these earlier iterations—especially the movement of the 1930s—the unrest of the late 1950s and early 1960s predicted that God would use the Mayo River to assist His true believers, flooding the land (a welcome development to farmers who still remembered traditional floodplain farming), washing away Yori hydraulic infrastructure, and drowning the Mayo people's enemies.

Besides the Mayo valley's history of spiritual fertility, there were tangible, profane reasons why Mayo people there would gravitate to the movement. While the Sinaloan Mayo had enjoyed some success in obtaining water through canals, pumps, and dams from the 1920s through mid-1940s, the Sonoran Mayo had no such luck. Their consistent inability to gain irrigation concessions from the 1920s through 1950s had caused them to embrace an outright disdain for the Ministry of Water Resources (SRH).[92] During the difficult years of the 1950s, several Sinaloan Mayo farmers still believed they could negotiate or effect a change in the state bureaucracy—that there still was a practical, political, earthly solution. Sonora Mayo farmers held out no such hope. This difference manifested itself during the Bacosegua millenarian movement. Mayo villagers in Sonora rallied enthusiastically to the message that if they honored and worshiped God with renewed vigor He would champion them, but in Sinaloa the reception was more tepid.

Reflecting the different socioecological reality in the Fuerte valley, a radically different version of Bacosegua's vision emerged there—spurred on by rumors likely spread by Mayo farmers who supported the use of irrigation infrastructure. According to Charles Erasmus, after God spoke to Bacosegua, a strange, unsettling scene unfolded. According to oral sources, the same old man who had appeared before Bacosegua—that is, God—appeared before a group of Mayo men, standing on a Fuerte River dam. The group demanded He get off the dam lest He damage it, and when He defied them, they—apparently unaware of his true identity—began to throw rocks. The old man turned, walked on the river water, and disappeared. Another rumor tied to Bacosegua's vision was that an Indigenous non-follower of the movement in Sinaloa drowned in an irrigation ditch.[93] In a region with a history of Mayo villagers accessing pumps and canals, some Indigenous farmers apparently spread this rumor as a means of defending hydraulic infrastructure, by warning other Mayo people to stay out of irrigation ditches and not interfere with the water. The spread of these rumors also indicates that a group of Sinaloan Mayo farmers—while not as engaged with the movement as their Sonoran Mayo counterparts—nevertheless used the story of God's appearance to convince state functionaries that many of them still supported irrigation infrastructure and would defend its use by any means.[94]

These stories had significant implications in describing the complex views Sinaloan Mayo farmers developed in response to river technology. While Sonoran Mayo farmers used Bacosegua's movement as a means to erase the hydraulic infrastructure and return to an earlier, noninvasive time, Sinaloan Mayo farmers of the Fuerte valley took a more cautious approach. During the postrevolutionary era, dozens of Fuerte valley Indigenous villages had aligned with state agencies in order to receive land and water rights, and despite recent failures, a substantial number of Mayo farmers there still believed government patronage was their best hope. Indeed, the Indigenous farmers of the Fuerte valley who supported the use of dams and canals likely helped spread the rumors about the old man on the dam and the drowning in the ditch in an effort to show functionaries from state agencies like the Fuerte River Commission (CRF) that they understood the value of irrigation infrastructure.

With no legal or economic authority to demand water for their crops, by 1957 some Mayo farmers suggested that cozying up to state functionaries was the only viable option. The issue proved contentious among the Sinaloa Mayo. Carla Bacosegua recollects how, "Yoremes came to disagree on irrigation, some thought the government would let us use it again, but others knew we could not return to those times."[95] By 1957 the CRF had been operating for a little more than five years in the Fuerte valley, and its ascension as ultimate regulators of local river irrigation water caught the imagination of hundreds of Mayo farmers. This faction maintained a hope that the agency, with some prodding, might correct the imbalances plaguing the valley but that outright protest, as in Sonora, might enrage the agency and hurt their chances of procuring water rights.

The apparent support for, or at least toleration of, the CRF by some Mayo farmers does not mean that other Indigenous people of the Fuerte valley did not oppose this agency early on. The SICAE's hold on the Fuerte River in the 1940s had reduced irrigation opportunities for Indigenous farmers not affiliated with the cooperative, but matters grew only worse after the CRF took charge of irrigation distribution in the 1950s. Unlike the SICAE, which provided water for some affiliated Mayo farmers, the CRF uniformly favored corporate development and directed water to the largest private farms at the expense of all Mayo ejidos. Despite these ever-growing difficulties, the Mayo farmers of northern Sinaloa continued to approach the use of irrigation infrastructure in divergent ways. As was the case when any powerful entity or state agency sought to control the Fuerte valley's irrigation resources, some individuals and groups were more prepared than others to cultivate connections and leverage influence. As Carla Bacosegua reminisces, most Mayo villagers did not believe this approach of cozying up to the state would work, but some Indigenous farmers in the Fuerte valley imagined, like a perverse test of faith, that if they shunned the millenarian movement and "defended" dams and canals, the CRF would bestow their blessing upon them. The CRF, however, proved to be an indifferent deity.

Conclusion

Declining Mayo fortunes in the Fuerte valley can only be understood within the context of large landowner control of irrigation water. Previously, Indigenous farmers had made use of canals and pumps. As pressure mounted, they hoped to once again gain access. But though the Fuerte valley had not changed drastically by the late 1940s, attitudes and ideas had. The rains fell, the river ran, and the land still produced, but Mexican politics had shifted under Mayo people's feet.

Behind all the developments of this chapter was the Fuerte River Commission (CRF). Created by the Mexican state in 1951, as it acquired power it also siphoned off irrigation water from the Fuerte River for larger private property owners, believing that they would stimulate commercial agricultural projects and promote economic growth in the region. By design, then, the CRF ignored ejidatario rights and opportunities during this switch to commercial farming. Picking up where the SICAE had begun in the late

1940s, the CRF perfected and streamlined the practice of taking control of water and land out of the hands of independent Mayo farmers. Unlike the postrevolutionary state apparatus that relied on ejidatarios for political patronage, the CRF and the political leaders of the 1950s and 1960s favored commercial farming. In their view, Mayo community autonomy blocked "economic progress."

Analyzing the differences in how the Mayo villagers of the Fuerte and Mayo valleys accessed irrigation water highlights how each community saw widely different opportunities in their hydraulic infrastructure in the 1950s. While Mayo farmers in the Fuerte valley still hoped the state would rectify the irrigation imbalances between the ejidos and private farms, those in the Mayo valley lost hope in secular authorities' ability to ensure canals and dams would ever be equitably shared. Here, instead, they gravitated to a vision of hydraulic infrastructure being wiped away.

Far more literature is dedicated to Mayo valley history than the Fuerte valley, but the Fuerte valley's rejection of Bacosegua is also a part of that millenarian movement. Whether accepting or rejecting the prophecy, the fundamental problem was water, and this work is the first in either region to analyze in-depth the connection between Indigenous people's lack of irrigation water and land theft in the mid-twentieth century. Both communities faced indifferent—if not outright hostile—treatment by the state as demonstrated by stacks of ignored and denied petitions and reduced irrigation access. Mayo farmers in both valleys faced Yori neighbors steeped in a mestizo frontier mentality who took advantage of the state's irrigation policies to pressure Mayo farmers to rent out and finally sell land.

Long before the CRF—or the SICAE—progress in the Fuerte valley meant moving earth and manipulating nature. By the late 1940s and early 1950s that fact had still not changed; what had changed was who would benefit. By then it was large Yori landowners, aligned with the Mexican state, who funded and profited from the construction of irrigation infrastructure. Even when they contributed labor, the smaller, poorer Mayo farmers were still cut out by the Yoris. Far from helping them, when the CRF constructed even larger hydraulic infrastructures such as the Miguel Hidalgo Dam in the mid-1950s and 1960s it raised new obstacles for all Indigenous ejidatarios (regardless of affiliation with the SICAE).[96] The agency's development plans were bold but not foreordained and, by design, relied on both local ecosystems and Indigenous ejidatarios to put up minimal resistance. The fifth and final chapter explores the ways Mayo farmers reacted to their subjugation to state agencies, the elimination of certain fauna, disassociation from a contaminated river, approaches to animals, uses of potable water and other water sources, and substitution of raw materials in their religious ceremonies.

FIVE

From Our River to Theirs

The Effects of Hydraulic Development, 1955 to 1970

> It is certain we viewed the river as an extension of nature. There is a connection between Indians and water. The four elements for us, water, fire, earth, wind, are all a divine gift from God, and they are reflected in the water.
> —CARLA BACOSEGUA

In 1956 the Fuerte River Commission (CRF) placed a statue of the Aztec rain god Tlaloc atop the newly constructed Miguel Hidalgo Dam as a finishing touch. It was a fitting, if ironic, choice. At first blush, the Tlaloc statue appeared to both celebrate the completion of the dam and pay homage to Indigenous culture and knowledge, a token of respect to the region's original inhabitants, the Mayo people. That, however, is not how they saw it. For some Mayo people, finding Tlaloc—the Aztec god of rain—peering out over their homeland was not an unfortunate blunder but a symptom of an endemic problem. Mayo elder Rudolfo Echamea of Borabampo explains the symbolism behind the CRF's choice: "Tlaloc is an Aztec God. Like the Aztecs who controlled Mexico, the government wanted to control us. The dam and the statue showed us that we would no longer receive water and that we better pray for rain."[1] Similar to how their engineers ignored Mayo peoples' needs, the CRF leadership paid so little attention to them that they could not even find a Mayo deity to place upon a dam in their homeland.[2] Mayo farmers like Echamea had spent

10. Tlaloc statue sitting on top of the Miguel Hidalgo Dam. Photograph taken by James Mestaz, June 2019.

decades petitioning the Mexican state for water rights and at times received at least limited support, but the CRF was as foreign and indifferent as the stony face of Tlaloc.

For Echamea and other Mayo elders, Tlaloc was no champion and the dam's completion was no reason to celebrate. Rather, it signaled the culmination of the state's developmentalist program, a crown jewel in a fully centralized hydraulic system that, from the mid-1950s through the 1960s, allowed Yori landowners and state functionaries to collaborate and transform northern Sinaloa and introduce large-scale, commercial agricultural production. Key to this, the CRF knew, was water. Their reasoning was simple: more pressing to farmers than access to arable land was acquiring the water to make it bountiful. Control of the river's flow equated to control of the region.

Yori landowners, however, were not wise river managers. They replaced the symbiosis that had characterized Mayo interactions with the river since before written history with extraction and exploitation, hurting the very asset that was most important to them. First, with the state's blessing, they wrestled away control and access to the river and then cleared out thousands of hectares of natural vegetation along its banks, beginning a decades-long process of defilement. The ultimate indignity was the millions of gallons of chemical and animal waste—the inevitable byproduct of "modern" agriculture and economic development in the 1950s—they dumped directly into the river.

All the while, Mayo ejidatarios with no economic or political capital with which to respond could only bear silent witness. The CRF not only marginalized but assailed them through what can only be called active, engaged neglect. The CRF had detailed, visionary plans for dams and the development of the region but nothing for the actual Mayo farmers who were displaced. They instead would be subject to a series of policies consistent only in their haphazardness and poor funding. Landless Mayo farmers watched as unequal economic development led to startling changes to the Fuerte River, the valley's flora and fauna, the region's economy, and Mayo cultural and religious practices. It was a final assault from which Mayo culture found it difficult to recover.

If a benevolent symbiosis had previously existed between Mayo people and the river, a new, dangerous symbiosis now emerged between Mexico City's desire to see agricultural production increase and Yori farmers' desire to see their profits rise. Previously, following orders from Mexico City, the CRF had privileged Yori farmers with canal access and the right to pump directly from the river, but now the dam ensured that practically all water, the lifeblood of the Fuerte valley, ended up on virtually only non-Mayo fields. Despite some success in the preceding three decades in deploying hydraulic social mobilization tactics to facilitate their physical and cultural survival, Mayo farmers lacked the political capital in the mid-1950s to engage such strategies. A large segment of Mayo elders today believe that their culture began deteriorating in the mid-1950s—not coincidentally the era when irrigation access became systematically unavailable to most Indigenous ejidatarios.

The Fuerte River Commission: Grand Plans but Hidden Schemes

President Miguel Alemán Valdés (1946–52) had high hopes and even greater ambitions when he created the CRF in June 1951. He was so impressed with the achievements of the Tennessee Valley Authority (TVA) in the United States that he wanted to import and replicate the program in key regions of Mexico.[3] The idea that underdeveloped regions could, through careful management, become vibrant contributors to the nation's economy was intoxicating to Alemán, and he was not alone. U.S. historian David Ekbladh argues that by the mid-twentieth century the TVA became "a model for America's governmental efforts to seek to assist in the modernization of agrarian societies in the developing world."[4] Alemán, like others in the developing world, used the TVA as a blueprint for state-sponsored regional economic development agencies that would distribute Mexico's water resources efficiently, boost its agricultural production, and allow it to compete in the global economy. The CRF was to be that agency in the Fuerte valley.

Alemán did not rush into the decision. As early as 1946, his first year in office, he expressed interest in creating local development agencies in Mexico that were similar to the TVA. In one of his first official announcements, Alemán proposed the creation of a decentralized program to solve problems in two regions of Mexico: "Based on the comprehensive regional development and successful resolution of the Tennessee Valley Authority, the Mexican government has decided to design programs to exploit the basins of the rivers El Fuerte in Sinaloa and Papaloapan in Veracruz."[5] The next year, government officials created the first of these regional agencies, known as the Papaloapan Commission, but it took another four years before the CRF came into existence.

According to economists David Barkin and Timothy King, the CRF's stated mission at its creation was simply to "improve, conserve, and expand the Fuerte River irrigation district," but there were deeper ambitions at play.[6] While it was never officially stated, the CRF's creation indicated that the Mexican state had lost faith in the SICAE's ability to maximize the agricultural productivity of the Fuerte valley and that a change needed to be made.[7] However, the political maneuvering required to make this a reality took time, and only in 1955 did President Adolfo Ruiz Cortines strip the SICAE of its four-month monopoly on river water and place the CRF in charge of all river development initiatives. Once the SICAE had been sidelined, state development agencies tasked the CRF with stimulating the economy by increasing the number of profitable commercial agricultural ventures, and by the mid-1950s its administrative tentacles reached into every facet of Fuerte valley economic activity.

The CRF and other regional projects like it turned away from ejidatarios and toward large landowning farmers to both feed the nation's growing population and export crops for cash. Economist Manuel Carlos believes that the federal government invested resources in regions with the capacity to increase irrigated agriculture because, as he asserts, "The object was to end Mexico's reliance on the 'boom or bust' crop cycles that characterize the unpredictable rainfall zones of the country."[8] The state hoped that implementing its developmentalist agenda would achieve what the cooperatives of the 1930s and '40s could not: increase the efficiency of Mexican farmland, prevent the need to import crops, and even produce a surplus for export. Smaller ejidal plots that focused largely on subsistence agriculture, state agencies argued, were too poorly managed to withstand the vagaries of both Mexico's crop cycles and international markets. The trend toward commercial agriculture meant that the ejidatarios of the Fuerte valley no longer received the sort of state backing—in particular, crucial irrigation resources—associated with the postrevolutionary era of the mid-1920s to early 1940s.

The CRF was not the only Mexican river basin project, nor was it the first. In addition to the Papaloapan Commission in 1947, the government undertook the Tecaltepec Project on the Pacific coast that same year and the Grijalva Project in Tabasco and Chiapas in 1951, all of which were intended to boost development in areas where officials determined that agricultural potential had not been reached.[9] In a sense, the earlier basin commissions led to the CRF. Tackling the problem of "developing" the Fuerte River valley was ambitious and would require one of the largest hydraulic projects in Mexico up to that time.

At its inception in 1951, the CRF existed under the jurisdiction of the Ministry of Water Resources (SRH), which was, in turn, responsible for selecting the officials to lead the CRF as it crafted specific plans to develop the valley, known as the Fuerte Basin Project. The people the SRH picked to lead the CRF set for themselves a staggering array of goals, which included

> develop studies and projects for the storage dams and diversion of the Fuerte River and its tributaries; planning, construction, and operation of the areas of irrigation; technical advice through agricultural extension by introducing campesinos to the latest and best techniques of irrigation; help expand and improve the means and ways of communication between producers and consumers or consumer industries for agricultural products; build all works of social benefit in rural areas, and in urban areas contribute to the prosperity and preservation of the health of the user; study

and plan works to prevent and control environmental pollution to air, water, land; and involvement in the planning and construction of works to achieve development under controlled conditions of waterways and in unhealthy coastal lagoons and shorelines.[10]

Even now, these goals read like a list of utopian ideals difficult to attain anywhere, much less the still-developing Mexico of the 1950s! It is unclear if their ambitions rose from earnest hubris or a shrewd calculation that any agency tasked with this much responsibility could command an equal amount of political power. Whatever the case, the commission never achieved these goals.

At first glance, the objectives of the CRF should have benefitted everyone irrespective of race or class in the Fuerte valley, but image did not reflect reality. Ostensibly, the CRF was charged with a noble mission "to assist rural communities" and introduce campesinos to the latest agricultural technologies, but these high-minded goals, which echoed Lázaro Cárdenas's still-popular sentiments in the nation, were actually quite vague. To "assist" rural communities was, for the CRF, to make them into profitable commercial farms where campesinos would be "introduced" to new technologies not as independent farmers but as wage laborers. For whatever criticism the CRF leadership of the time deserves, they proved adept at political obfuscation and understood the need to at least claim that they were mobilizing Indigenous communities while they altered the natural and social landscape of the Fuerte valley to benefit Yori farmers. Mayo people would not be fooled for long, and in less than a decade ejidatarios would routinely equate Yori landowners with state agencies like the CRF.

Just thirteen years after President Lázaro Cárdenas laid the groundwork for the SICAE's political domination by ceding thousands of hectares to newly created ejidos, Fuerte valley farmers again found themselves under the direction of yet another experimental development program. Yet the CRF differed in profound ways from the SICAE. Most notably, the SICAE had been focused on supporting the production of one lucrative crop, sugarcane, but the CRF was given a larger task. It was to spark economic growth by reviving the output of all the crops grown in the Fuerte valley, especially those that had suffered while sugarcane had received preference.

In only one way were the SICAE and the CRF alike: they each had favorites. The SICAE sought to empower affiliated ejidatarios at the expense of local, independent and individualist ejidatarios, while the CRF granted advantages to powerful private landowners over all ejidatarios. Some politically connected (mostly Yori) ejidos did receive some tangible benefits, but this arrangement was nonetheless a difficult pill to swallow since the developmentalist agenda still favored large landowners over ejidal farmers. It was better to be the favorite of the CRF, for the federal government bestowed on it far more financial resources than they ever extended to the SICAE. CRF officials used this money strategically, partnering with private investors who shared their preference to develop commercial farming in the Fuerte valley at the expense of ejidatarios. The only constant in the Fuerte valley was that, despite all the high-minded calls for equity and fairness in distributing resources, there was always an anointed few who benefited at the expense of the many.

The CRF's plans hinged on its ability to disperse benefits—such as potable water, electricity, and schools—to ejidos with access to political power. In turn these ejidos would support the agency in matters of funding or in political battles in Mexico City. But the CRF's agenda was never simply about "efficiently" allocating investments. While the commission apportioned benefits to some ejidos, it relied on an economic system that disproportionately favored large landowners over all ejidal farmers. Money constituted leverage and the CRF used it to transform the culture and social relationships that had dominated the postrevolutionary era in the Fuerte valley.

Even for Mayo ejidatatarios living in mixed ejidos with Yoris—and thus politically connected and enjoying access to the CRF's resources—the social and cultural costs of doing business with the CRF were high. As Mayo elder Mauricio Mejías of Huepaco, a mixed ejido, explains, "The CRF provided potable water, drainage, electricity, schools, housing, and sporting facilities for some Mayo, but only in mixed villages that were no longer strictly Indian. The CRF charged fees to all ejidos but only those with Yoris received benefits. Other ejidos have more vision than us, proposed development projects, and received benefits. Our ejidatarios do not have time for politics, we must work all day to survive, so we received very little from the CRF."[11] Some Mayo ejidatarios like Mejías recall a very real tradeoff between material survival and Indigenous identity. Indigenous ejidatarios often had to weigh the advantages of receiving benefits from the CRF against sacrificing some portion of their identity. As was the case earlier, when some Mayo ejidos were more willing to adapt to changes in the natural landscape than others, after 1953 some ejidos were more willing to align with government agencies like the CRF than others. How many non-Mayo lived in an ejido seems to have been a determining factor in whether or not it aligned with the CRF, but even so, the Mayo members in these communities appear to have agreed to put aside their differences and work with their Yori neighbors.[12]

Most scholarship on the CRF has overlooked the fact that ejidos with a majority Mayo membership have been less successful at aligning with the agency than those in which natives were the minority or completely absent. This was not supposed to be the case, but as in nearly all matters between the CRF and Indigenous communities, there was and remains a chasm between what was supposed to be and what occurred. For example, state functionaries designed the CRF to have a Department of Ejido Affairs, which Manuel Carlos explains, "coordinates all ejido community improvement projects and gives ejidatarios an established channel of access and communication with the agency and its top-level decision-makers."[13] That, at least, was what the department was supposed to do, but it would never achieve these goals. It claimed to work on behalf of all ejidos, but those villages with larger absolute numbers or higher proportions of Yori members had more schooling, fluency in Spanish, and, consequently, the ability to pull political levers. The department was, from the beginning, yet another channel that allowed Yoris to hold the ear of the government.

The elaborate improvement initiatives that local functionaries approved required political clout and the ability to leverage assets within the community, two things Mayo ejidatarios conspicuously lacked. By the mid-1950s the majority of Mayo ejidatarios longed for the decades between the mid-1920s and the early 1940s when the postrevolutionary state helped them access canals and pumps. Ironically, during those years there was no agency specifically looking out for Indigenous community's water needs. Counterintuitively, the less specific an agency's focus upon a village or ejido was, the less discrimination there appears to have been against Indigenous farmers. Agencies such as the SAYF considered irrigation petitions from Mayo villages and ejidos with the same attention and impartiality as those from any other farm. When granted, Mayo leaders distributed resources as they—and the community— thought best. Yet with every layer of bureaucracy dictating how they must distribute these concessions came that much more bias against Mayo farmers and that much less water.[14]

Mayo elders look back upon these earlier years warmly not simply because of the ease in which they secured tangible benefits from the government but because questions of distribution and use were answered communally. In these previous decades, state resources helped facilitate cultural autonomy rather than undermine it, and Mayo leaders decided what was best for their villages based on traditional, Indigenous cultural notions. By the mid-1950s the CRF and other state agencies began to make decisions on behalf of Mayo communities, often with no consultation. It is difficult to discern in the oral histories whether it was the loss of tangible benefits—that is, irrigation—or the loss of cultural autonomy that hurt Mayo farmers the most. Both were absolutely connected to one another and their loss undeniably undermined the community, but the latter eroded the traditions that made up Mayo identity.

To add insult to injury, the growing CRF presence in the area was partly paid for by new charges for irrigation water that all farmers paid but fell unfairly upon ejidatarios. In 1970 Barkin and King clarified that all water users paid an administrative fee of one hundred pesos per year, but ejidatarios also paid "'cuotas de cooperación' of a similar amount for ten years. These quotas are spent through the Commission [CRF] on educational facilities and public facilities and services in the ejidos."[15] Despite being poorer, the CRF made Mayo ejidatarios pay just as much as their private, commercial counterparts and locked them in for longer payments. While some of this money was supposed to be spent on amenities for all ejidos, the CRF, in reality, spent these funds in communities that were either exclusively or majority Yori. In short, the CRF was disproportionately siphoning dwindling Mayo resources and distributing them to their Yori neighbors.

No fee was certain under the CRF. Older methods of paying for irrigation with a portion of the harvest gave way to global market forces that fluctuated, as markets do, more wildly. Worse, while the prices for their crops went up and down, the price for water only increased. In Mayo villages like Los Goros, which—unlike so many others—had maintained irrigation rights into the 1950s, the CRF's demand to be paid in cash led to problems. Even though most Indigenous ejidatarios raised subsistence crops, they still had to find a way to pay irrigation fees with cash or risk losing access. According to Mayo elder Alejandro Inzunza of Los Goros, "We used to trade Yoris a percentage of our crop for water. After the CRF took control, and charged a lot for water, some of us Yoremes established a ten-year contract with them to irrigate ejidal lands. We initially paid twenty pesos annually per hectare, a viable price. But as administrations changed and prices increased, I could not afford it after 1960. Only Yoris could afford irrigation water, so like the other Yoremes, I rented my land to Yoris and worked in the fields for them."[16]

Even Los Goros, which briefly had some political leverage with the CRF, could not avoid paying in cash. The CRF, interested as it was in efficiency and international markets, looked upon barter arrangements as categorically backward and inherently inefficient. Whereas Yori farmers previously accepted a percentage of harvests in exchange for water access, the CRF would do ejidos no favors. Ejidatarios had to compete or forsake their autonomy and slip into the rural labor pool.[17] For those communities not blessed with Los Goros's strengths, the slipping away began even sooner. The CRF did not see any of this as a problem. Rather, commercial farmers gained access to new farmland and secured a reliable labor pool. The suffering of Indigenous ejidatarios was, for the agency, a small price to pay in order to turn the Fuerte valley into a breadbasket for Mexico.

The CRF's Attitudes Made Real: The Miguel Hidalgo Dam as a Case Study

There is no denying that the CRF was economically effective. After it took responsibility for hydraulic construction and irrigation distribution in the Fuerte valley, agricultural production shot up. Between 1955 and 1965 annual profits from crop production increased five-fold from 150 million to 750 million pesos. From the early 1950s to 1970 irrigated farmland increased from 40,000 to 250,000 hectares.[18] These advancements in agricultural output speak to the CRF's success in expanding irrigated properties and creating efficient farmlands, but the numbers hide as much as they reveal.

Fuerte valley farms became vastly profitable but often because water that was supposed to be distributed to all only arrived at large Yori operations. Most Mayo ejidatarios could only make ends meet by taking low-wage jobs at these farms. By the late 1950s Mayo farmers' subordinate status—engineered by the actions of the CRF—had become a recognized fact of life in the region, a sentiment still alive over two generations later. "The CRF did a lot to boost the local economy," says Felicitas Mejía, a Mayo elder from Vinaterias. "But officials lied to us and broke promises, its actions never benefitted the poor. It constructed dams and canals for the rich, but never gave us irrigation water."[19] The CRF could (and did) point to projects that assisted Mayo ejidatarios, but they were limited, token gestures that only benefitted ejidos with large Yori populations and strong political connections.[20]

The best way to analyze the effects of the CRF's hydraulic construction projects on Mayo communities in the 1950s is to focus on its most ambitious structure, the (Miguel) Hidalgo Dam. It was the largest, most celebrated, and most expensive project in the region to that point. Originally known as the El Mahone Dam, the CRF began construction in 1953 near the ejido of El Mahone in the northeastern corner of the municipality of El Fuerte. When completed in 1956, the structure—now known as the Hidalgo Dam—created Sinaloa's largest water reservoir, a massive lake that ran northeast of the dam, swallowing up small farms and twelve ejidos in the municipality of Choix. The CRF boasted that the new dam would irrigate 230,000 hectares of farmland, generate electric energy, control flooding, help develop aquatic fauna, increase water availability for some communities, and be a regional jewel of recreation.[21] As was characteristic for many CRF projects, the dam delivered on few of its promises, yet even those few successes came at the expense of Mayo ejidatarios.

While the construction of the Hidalgo Dam did not start until 1953, this enormous undertaking actually began several years prior. As early as the mid-1940s, the Mexican state dispatched dam experts—many from the United States—to the Fuerte valley to commence the preliminary designs of a massive structure on the upper Fuerte River. The relationship between Mexico's National Irrigation Commission (CNI) and these foreign engineers was beneficial for both parties. The government wanted a rising generation of Mexican hydraulic engineers to learn from the best, so the CNI set its sights on two of the world's foremost experts, Max L. King and Andrew Weiss.[22] Because foreign engineers—especially from the United States—had a reputation as the top specialists in their field, the CNI, and later the CRF, spared no expense in bringing them in to direct the construction of the Hidalgo Dam.

One of the first lessons Mexican engineers had to master was attention to detail, particularly the minutiae of the soil and rock in the region.[23] Finding the most convenient, economically efficient, and structurally sound location upon which to construct a dam was no simple task. The thousands of pages of reports submitted by scientists in the planning of the Hidalgo Dam show the engineers' intense focus on the natural landscape.[24] Dam planners sought a place where they might utilize rock formations and the

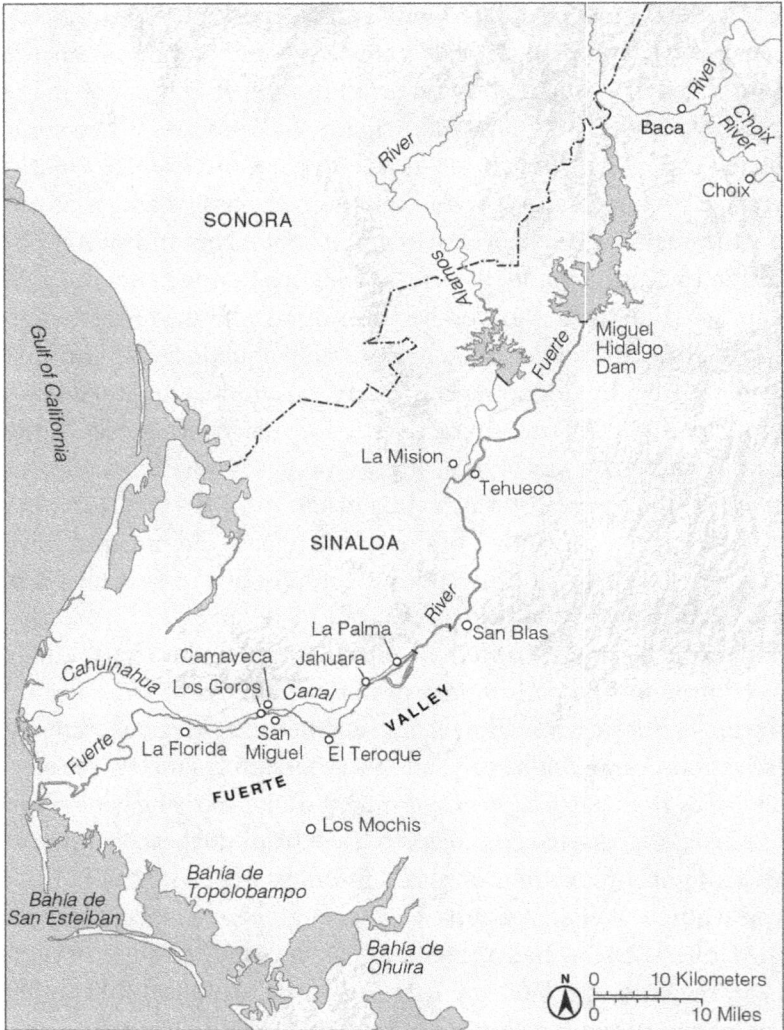

11. Miguel Hidalgo Dam with the Mayo villages of the Fuerte valley. Mapped by Pease Press Cartography.

geological layout of the Fuerte valley to aid in construction. No aspect of the earth along the river was too trivial to escape the geologists' and engineers' attention.

When it came to designing the dam, the level of engagement with the local landscape was admirable. By contrast, the attention paid to local inhabitants was minimal, for far less time went into preparing for how this structure would impact the populations it displaced. In the technical yet vague tone the CRF became quickly adept in, the agency published a pamphlet in 1956 stating that since the dam has misplaced families, the agency "bought the necessary land to provide each family head with a plot to ensure their subsistence. In addition, we paid relocation costs of these villages to new towns and endowed them with water services, medical services, schools, and severance payments for construction."[25] According to the CRF's pamphlet, every "difficult decision" of dispossession was handled fairly and with such care that no one evicted as a result of the dam's construction would be worse off. The truth of that assertion was as thin as the paper the pamphlet was printed on, and the process of relocating and reimbursing these affected farmers was much more complicated than the agency's propaganda suggested.

The CRF may have learned from the CNI's experiences of constructing the Angostura Dam in the neighboring state of Sonora, which caused the subsequent displacement of fifty-nine families from the ejido of Teras in 1941. Sterling Evans illustrates how despite their political mobilization, which included an alliance with the Confederación Nacional Campesina (CNC), ejidatarios still had to succumb to the demand of the CNI and relocate to less fertile lands. In addition to displacing dozens of families, the Angostura Dam project also diverted water from the Yaqui River, limiting the water rights of several Yaqui farmers.[26] Despite some logistical hiccups, the CNI created a blueprint for future state bureaucrats to impose their will on northwest Mexico's small farmers and carry out massive hydraulic projects. Another important question was if Fuerte valley smallholders and ejidatarios also learned from the failures of their neighbor's mobilization tactics.

In 1956, the year its workers placed a statue of Tlaloc on top of the dam and the organization published a pamphlet celebrating its benevolence, the CRF was still settling land issues with displaced communities. The year before, a group of displaced small farmers and ejidatarios joined forces to seek political redress. Their group, the Committee of Ejidatarios and Small Property Farmers Affected by the Vessel of the Miguel Hidalgo Dam, was as long on hope as they were on titles. They sent a letter to none other than the secretary to the president of Mexico in January 1955 explaining that they were representatives of the 1,080 ejidatarios and 1,396 small farmers who lost property due to the dam. The letter added that although the CRF had promised each of these affected farmers ten hectares of land fit for planting, it had only remained true to half its promise. When the committee surveyed the 4,700 hectares the CRF purchased for them, they found the land provided largely consisted of salinated plots, so while there was land for them, it was anything but fit for planting.[27]

While the CRF ostensibly had abided by the letter of the law, it disregarded its spirit, and these farmers were unwilling to accept this offer of new land—even if it was irrigated. Yet the CRF's half-hearted gesture did not really meet the law's requirements. If the agency was prepared to grant ten hectares a piece to the 1,080 ejidatarios, this would have amounted to over ten thousand hectares of farmland, not including lands for displaced small property owners.[28] The slightly less than five thousand hectares offered by the CRF in this petition would not have been nearly enough to distribute ten hectares to each ejidatario. Indeed, it was not even half of what was required.

The relocations were both half-hearted and disruptive. Though the CRF interrupted the Mayo people's physical connection with their ancestral land, they retained their spiritual and symbolic ties to it. Of the twelve ejidos relocated for the Hidalgo Dam, Agua Zarca, Los Picachos, Agua Caliente, Toro, and Baca certainly had Mayo ejidatario majorities, and the remaining seven likely had at least sizable Mayo minorities. There was no cultural explanation for where these communities ended up, only an obtuse bureaucratic logic. For example, the state allocated ejidal plots to displaced Mayo farmers from Toro within the ejidos San Javier and Las Vacas. Some of the displaced Mayo ejidatarios of the Baca ejido received ejidal lands in Juan José Ríos and Bachoco. These ejidatarios adjusted to different surroundings and formed bonds with their new ecosystems, but they never severed their origins in Baca. Two generations later, these Mayo villagers still return to where they once lived to reconnect spiritually with their territory and reaffirm their communal identity by conducting Indigenous religious rituals in Baca.[29]

The Fuerte valley was not unique in any of this; massive dams in other regions of Mexico also displaced Indigenous farmers. The results of the Hidalgo Dam, however, were particularly severe.[30] Like the Mayo ejidatarios of the Fuerte valley, the Mazatec farmers of the Papaloapan Basin, whose lands were inundated by a dam there, were not officially recognized by state bureaucrats as specifically Indigenous. Yet federal bureaucrats assumed that most of those displaced by dam construction were Mazatec people. This presumption reached the Instituto Nacional Indigenista (National Indigenous Institute, INI) who were compelled to step in and design programs to modernize Mazatec people. No similar dynamic or resulting programs came to fruition in the Fuerte valley.[31] The construction of a massive dam in the Papaloapan region led to disastrous consequences for the Mazatec people, as it separated them from the natural landscape vital to the maintenance of their cultural identities, but they found some success in allying with agencies such as the INI. Meanwhile, Mayo farmers had no institutional leverage to fall back upon but instead allied with small, similarly impoverished non-Mayo farmers in their struggle for land rights—again proving that aligning with like-minded Yoris never left their arsenal of mobilization tactics.[32]

Affected farmers of the Fuerte valley saw through the veneer of the CRF's purported compassion and compromise out of a realization that they would have to be willing to accept smaller, less productive plots as compensation. They understood, despite the benevolent tones of the CRF, that the small farmers and ejidatarios whose farms inconveniently lay in the reservoir of the dam were mere obstacles to its completion—obstacles that had to be moved as quickly and with as little fuss as possible. There is scant archival evidence that the CRF saw them as agriculturalists who depended on the land for survival and had a right to continue on as they had. Rather, the true, adversarial relationship between the CRF and the small farmers quickly became clear. Three weeks after the Committee of Ejidatarios and Small Property Farmers sent their first petition to the president's secretary, they followed it with another, more strident message describing the intransigent nature of the CRF. "Up to this date NOT A SINGLE STEP HAS BEEN TAKEN TO SOLVE OUR PROBLEM," their message screamed. "On the contrary, the CRF has caused serious agitation, and we do not understand its purpose, or why they are determined to discredit our government." In the tradition of previous petitions to gain land and water rights, the ejidatarios who submitted this message strategically questioned the allegiance of these state functionaries to the Mexican federal government. If they thought they might drive a wedge between the president and one of his prized projects, they were mistaken.

Even though displaced famers continued to negotiate the terms of relocation, the CRF revealed its immense power by refusing to honor the original, inadequate offer. The CRF promised ten hectares per ejidatario, but when all was said and done it actually disbursed only around 3,343 hectares.[33] Based on the number of ejidatarios (1,080) displaced by the dam's construction, it appears that the number of hectares awarded as compensation (if distributed equally) amounted to roughly three hectares per ejidatario. In fact, it is unclear how many of the 1,080 ejidatarios of the Committee of Ejidatarios and Small Property Farmers received land compensation.

While the Indigenous farmers of the Fuerte valley did not have the institutional allies the Mazatec people did, they still had their fellow Mayo ejidatarios, and after the dam's completion other Mayo ejidos expressed their solidarity with those affected by flooding. The presidents of the executive ejidal committees of the Mayo ejidos Jahuara and Tehueco each submitted complaints via telegram on March 28, 1956, asking the Mexican president to "please grant our request to intervene on behalf of our friends affected by the building of the Miguel Hidalgo Dam."[34] The two ejidos had no other obvious motive to send the message than solidarity. Jahuara and Tehueco lay at least thirty kilometers southwest of the dam, so its construction did not directly flood their lands like other Mayo villages adjacent to the river and closer to the dam (and the leaders of both would have surely complained of flooding if this was the primary reason why they disapproved of the dam). Rather, the receipt of both telegrams on the same day suggests that the messages were both sincere and part of a coordinated effort orchestrated by the leaders of the Committee of Ejidatarios and Small Property Farmers Affected by the Vessel of the Miguel Hidalgo Dam.

The recurrent theme expressed by ejidatarios complaining about the CRF's construction of the Hidalgo Dam was hypocrisy. This state-backed commission consulted numerous experts and dedicated time and energy in planning and executing the physical construction of the dam, yet despite all the effort and hours poured into studying the dam's construction, virtually none was put into addressing the injustices heaped upon dispossessed ejidatarios. It is not too much of an exaggeration to say that the CRF's experts scrutinized the soil composition of nearly every inch of land in the region, so it knew that the land it was securing for displaced farmers was too small and of grossly inferior quality. The only reason it could attempt this (and then stonewall and ignore the complaints that inevitably arose) was because it knew it had the support of the highest reaches of power in Mexico City.

Yori Hubris versus Indigenous Knowledge

While the CRF offered indifference to most ejidatarios—and a particularly cold shoulder to Mayo ejidatarios displaced by the Miguel Hidalgo Dam—through the 1950s and 1960s it offered a warm, encouraging embrace to Yori commercial farmers. This embrace extended past the obvious state-supported investment in expanding commercial farms and the all-important diversion of water to those operations. It extended even to the shared sensibility between Yori landowners and the state that nature could and should be controlled, even dominated. Mayo farmers knew better but could only look on in silence as Yori and state-backed efforts to control nature backfired.

Many Mayo ejidatarios recall how the problems with trying to master nature were apparent in some of the very first, tentative steps the state took, and that these problems only grew worse. For example, Mayo elder Jorge Robles of San Miguel recounts how Yori failures to dominate nature were plain for all to see. "After installing a dam, they said in 1943 that flooding would cease. But one large dam could not prevent the flood that soon came. In 1960 we had two huge dams in place, but it still flooded because the new Hidalgo Dam was about twenty meters too short for it to be truly effective."[35] One of the explicit purposes of the Hidalgo Dam was to limit deluges, yet the erratic flooding of the Fuerte River exposed the hubris of controlling nature. The 1960 flood—a mere four years after the completion of the Hidalgo Dam—revealed that Yori-run state agencies could engineer wealth disparity in the valley. They very effectively created winners and losers by offering and withholding water—but they could not engineer a way to tame the river.

Rather than check flooding, the CRF's hydraulic infrastructure exacerbated it, and Mayo elders could only shake their head in disbelief. "In the years after Yoris created the Hidalgo Dam and canals," Mayo elder Gustavo Aguilar recollects, "it flooded too much when it rained. Villages like ours located by the river, whose ancestors relied on its expected annual overflow for planting crops, suffered the most. Yoris transformed the river from creator to destroyer."[36] In short, the reconfiguration of the Fuerte valley into a major agricultural region made it a perfect target for destructive floods. For centuries, Mayo farmers had relied upon the Fuerte River gently overflowing its banks and creating productive fields for the year ahead, but this was nothing like that. This flooding wiped out crops and stripped soil, leaving fields ruined for the year ahead. One momentous irony to all this was that it was not just the Mayo ejidatarios who suffered.[37] It was no real consolation to Mayo villages, but the fact remained that Yori farmers who had benefited from CRF policies and priorities and gobbled up valuable riverbank land were as likely to be underwater as smaller Mayo ejidatario plots.

As Yoris tried controlling nature, the Fuerte River retaliated through destructive flooding, not discriminating in who it punished. Yet while the river could be indifferent in whose land it washed over, the consequences were not equally shared. Yori farmers had more political support and access to loans and government programs, while Mayo farmers lived with a thinner cushion. One flood could transform a farmer from a secure ejidatario into a wage laborer whose lands were now vulnerable. Mayo elder Oralia Flores of Pochotal reminisces that during a flood, "We saw the river swell and we prayed for the survival of our people, crops, and animals."[38] The destructive flooding that arose from Mexico's developmentalist policies did not break the Mayo people's connection to the river, but it did, inevitably, change it. After the dams were built, Mayo farmers living close to the river's banks spoke less of it as a living being who offered gifts of food, water, and knowledge and with whom they lived in a benevolent relationship. Instead, these river dwellers began to pray to be spared from its wrath. They sought to be removed from its torrents and the dead animals, ruined crops, and contamination that came in its wake. The river remained important, but it had become far more vengeful than benevolent.[39]

In addition to water contamination and crop destruction, the creation of the CRF's dams and canals also directly and indirectly constricted Mayo religious practices. As described above, the CRF devised policies and encouraged Yori farmers to separate Mayo communities away from sacred river sites, but even after it pushed communities away, the hand of the CRF still interfered with religious practices in ways that would be comical if they were not so consistently sad. For example, Mayo elder Carla Bacosegua of La Florida describes, "The CRF constructed a canal near our ejido in the 1960s, but it was not sturdy. Eventually part of the canal burst open and released water, flooding our ejido and destroying a wall of our ceremonial center. The CRF should have at least apologized or helped us fix it."[40] In this particular case the CRF intervened in Mayo religious life not with oppressive policy but negligence, as it literally ruined a religious ceremonial center. The flooding in La Florida is an apt metaphor for the relationship that developed between the CRF and Mayo communities in the 1950s and 1960s: even when it was not trying to, the CRF could hurt Mayo communities.

An additional problem for Mayo ejidatarios arose in the mid-twentieth century and accelerated in the 1960s: contamination. The CRF's policies not only caused the Fuerte River's water to come in devastating inundations or else cut off to a disastrous trickle, what water did arrive was wretchedly toxic. Part of this reflected the fact that expanded commercial farming relied upon heavy use of chemicals that easily found their way to the river. But these chemicals, as dangerous as they were, were also (and still are) largely invisible.

What captured Mayo farmers' attention in the 1960s was the runoff from raising livestock. Mayo elder Carla Bacosegua of La Florida remembers how they used to drink water straight from the river even up to the 1950s. Later on, however, that changed: "Yoris bathed their herds in the river and disrespectfully let animals excrete and urinate in the water. Yoremes did not allow animals into the water because humans consumed it. This changed around the 1960s when more Yoris came. Before then we lived in harmony with the river."[41] It is significant that Bacosegua viewed the 1960s as the turning point in which the river became contaminated, for many elders cite this as the era when Mayo ejidatarios finally lost whatever slim authority or voice they retained over what happened to their river. This popular narrative among elders contends that once the river lost its Indigenous guardians it fell under the complete domination of Yoris who were indifferent to pollution but passionate about profits.

One reason for this narrative of lost Mayo control of the river is that in the 1960s the Mexican state relaxed restrictions on the amount of waste newly established industries in northern Sinaloa could release into the Fuerte River. So, in addition to the large live-stock farms Bacosegua lamented, there were other, new polluters, including meat processing factories that allowed a large part of their refuse to wind up in the river, poisoning it. "Back in the 1960s there were a lot of fish," Mayo elder Mauricio Mejías of Huepaco remembers, "especially mojarra, in the river near our ejido. Poi-sons from the packing plant upstream contaminated the water and killed the fish here. But I saw plenty of mojarra upstream from the packing plant when I fished there."[42] This contamination left Mayo ejidatarios in a bind. Of course, they needed water for their crops, but at the same time they realized that the water they sought was dangerous to their communities. Their deep-rooted connection to the river remained alive, but how close should they physically be to the river was an open question.

These Yori acts of contamination were not limited to physical or chemical defilement; their attitudes toward the river specifi-cally and nature in general leached into the hearts and minds of some Mayo villagers, particularly the younger generations who showed less concern for protecting the river. Mayo elders Nar-ciso Bachomo and Carlos Salcedo of Camajoa explain that their grandparents "used to say *catebamchichahoa*, which means do not throw trash into the river. Our generation of elders respected and took care of the river because it took care of us. New generations believe Yoris own the river, so they have less respect for water and the river."[43] Before the 1960s Mayo elders did not need to articu-late the importance of protecting the river because it was such a common, bonding principle. But as a younger generation—one that had never enjoyed an unimpeded relationship with the river or seen it as anything other than a commodity to be employed and abused—came of age, the older generation had to articulate and make obvious sentiments that had been ubiquitous before. In a sense, this younger generation experienced an inversion of the traditional Mayo relationship with the river: they no longer respected the river with the same deference as their elders because the river no longer took care of them.

Though they were marginalized politically and economically—

and the cultural implications of treating the river so horribly began to manifest in their own communities—Mayo farmers refused to surrender. Life went on and so too did they, even if it meant they had to break the law. Mayo elder Francisco Jacinto of Jahuara used to gather river water for daily use, but after pig farms—and famers using pesticides—contaminated it, he and others stole water from the privately owned Cahuinahua Canal.[44] Apparently the Cahuinahua Canal drew its water further upstream than the Yori industries that contaminated the water flowing by Jahuara. By stealing their water, Mayo farmers demonstrated that they did not recognize the Yori right to monopolize it. For them, the river remained—however many degrees removed—a human right.

Most Mayo ejidatarios today do not rely on water from the Fuerte River like their ancestors. The inability of Mayo people to fulfill their perceived role as river guardians has led some to believe that this is not their river, as it "belongs" to rich Yori farmers. The Mayo youth of the 1960s are the elders of today, and many of them see the Fuerte River as dirty and toxic.[45] In their estimation, the Indigenous ejidatarios who gained land and water rights along the river in the 1930s were the last constituency to genuinely care about the river as a natural phenomenon. They were the last group to appreciate the intrinsic value of the river and not evaluate it in an instrumentalist fashion or appreciate the river only to the degree that it profited them. When the next generations began to lose this perspective, there was no one left to guard the river.

Who Turns On and Off the Tap to Potable Water?

The erosion of Mayo culture had causes that stretched deep into the past and consequences that would reach far into the future, but even more pressing than this dilemma was what the Mayo people would drink. The growing toxicity of the river water beginning in the late 1950s and early 1960s meant that every mouthful they swallowed to quench their thirst put them at risk. This was not true for the Yori population, for they possessed both financial and political resources to combat the issue. Once again, as had been the case for the previous twenty or more years, the Yori population enjoyed a state-sanctioned protection not extended to Mayo communities.

Since the mid-twentieth century, the potable water system in the Fuerte valley's largest city of Los Mochis has been one of the most advanced compared to the rest of Mexico. The Fuerte River Commission set up the city's first water treatment facility in the 1960s and the filtration process has not dramatically changed since. Today the private company Japama purifies the water and sends it through underground pipes to customers in Los Mochis households and to select, well-connected communities of the Fuerte valley.

The drinking water of the Fuerte valley comes directly from the area's three large dams—Huites, Josefa Ortiz de Domínguez, and Miguel Hidalgo—and undergoes roughly the same process most major U.S. cities use to treat their tap water.[46] According to Japama, the first step in the filtration procedure is to run the water through screens to remove large solids such as leaves, tree branches, and garbage. Next, scientists add aluminum sulfate and polymer to eliminate fine particulate matter and prechlorination to kill microorganisms. Water then flows through sedimentation basins to remove clay, silt, and other organic and synthetic matter. The water subsequently passes through sand beds to filter out any remaining matter or particles. The water undergoes one last step of postchlorination where technicians add chlorine to adjust the chemical levels necessary to ensure that during the whole procedure the water stays disinfected.[47]

The purity of the drinking water in Los Mochis has allowed Mochitenses to express a certain sense of pride, bragging about their drinking water as they consume it straight from the tap—an uncommon practice in Mexico—yet their advantage is not shared regionally.[48] Potable water undergoes a much more stringent, expensive, and exhaustive filtration process than piped water does. Because it is less expensive to create, smaller, impoverished communities have generally received piped water that was merely filtered through small screens and treated with only bleach and sodium hypochlorite.[49] It should come as no surprise that for decades piped water has been the only type of filtered water available to most Mayo villages, even though ingesting it directly can cause sicknesses. Ironically, the high cost of a better treatment system forced Indigenous communities to purchase bottled water. While bottled water did not require the outlay of capital that a filtration system would, it was more expensive per liter and, over time, caused these impoverished communities to spend more on drinking water than their wealthier neighbors with filtration systems.[50]

Cheap, short-term fixes—even if they led to higher costs in the long-term—had often been the preferred strategy of the CRF. Residents of the Fuerte valley knew the CRF had a mandate to help them, and when their drinking water became particularly poor they would raise a cry for change. Unless the community possessed immense political power, the CRF generally responded in these cases with relatively cheap forms of "humanitarian relief" rather than systematic investments in water treatment. For instance, a 1963 article in the Los Mochis daily newspaper *El Debate* celebrated the "goodwill of Fuerte River Commission officials, who allowed the [Mayo] village of Capomos to improve its situation in regard to hygiene, by providing its inhabitants potable water."[51] The paternalistic tone of the article, which praises the CRF's goodwill (when it was actually just carrying out one of its organizational mandates), ignores the fact that the filtered water Capomos received was only temporary. Though they could have, the commission did not grant the Mayo ejido permanent access by building a filtration system. The CRF responded to crises and cries with small, token efforts that were enough to relieve any political pressure and allowed it to boast of its concern for communities, yet it never attempted to enact systematic or lasting change in Mayo villages. In that regard the CRF was not much different than the Institutional Revolutionary Party (PRI), of which the commission acted as a bureaucratic arm, in that it monopolized power for decades by co-opting opposition or doing just enough to prevent outright rebellion.

Even Mayo ejidos that cultivated and nurtured political connections found that access to potable or piped water was not easy to come by and difficult to maintain. In the early 1960s, for example,

Jahuara supported a Yori candidate for governor who had delivered water to the ejido in exchange. "By the mid-1960s we had piped, treated water in our ejido," Mayo elder Francisco Jacinto recalls, "but problems persisted. Sometimes the water was scarce and did not reach our houses. We sometimes got sick from drinking it because it was not as filtered as much as potable water."[52] Political patronage was a necessary but insufficient step for communities attempting to secure healthy, clean water. Piped water was never as safe as potable water and required communities to locate a sufficient source, purchase purifying chemicals, and secure a certain level of expertise to make it all happen—all of which required regular amounts of money. Some ejidos like Jahuara might have political resources to spend on water but, being economically underprivileged, lacked the financial resources to secure potable water.

Still Jahuara was lucky in that it had at least episodically safe water. In Mayo ejidos without political allies the drinking water quality could be so consistently dangerous that the health consequences grew dire. Mayo elder Fermín Mopay of Camayeca explains that "in the 1960s we got access to piped water from the river, but it was polluted. Our water was not purified like in some other ejidos, and it was purple. When we took sick children to doctors, they said to stop drinking tap water because that was the cause of illness."[53] The availability of piped water was a technological advancement for some Mayo communities like Jahuara who received somewhat purified, piped water, yet in other villages like Camayeca it only meant that they now had ready access to contaminated, potentially deadly water.[54] Piped water was an especially tricky problem for ejidos to navigate. Without a filtration system, it was ostensibly the best option for poor, small communities. But if these same communities were not on their guard, it might be no better and perhaps—because of its ease of access— even worse than drinking directly from the Fuerte River.[55]

Piped water did not necessarily reflect advancement in Mayo villages, and the quality of water that flowed from the river and through pipes into homes in the Fuerte valley varied. Residents in Los Mochis had some of the best water in North America;

Jahuara had water that oscillated between quaffable and abhorrent; and Camayeca had water that was consistently dangerous. Yet the pipes forced all Mayo villages to share one thing in common: they had less physical interaction with—and consequently less reverence for—the Fuerte River. For Mayo elder Rudolfo Echamea of Borabampo, technological advancement came with unwanted cultural change: "Dams reduce the flow of water running along the bed of the river so we do not see it. Now Yoremes just turn a key and get piped water, eliminating some river practices completely. Women no longer go to the river in the morning to wash clothes and gather water."[56] All across Mexico, women in Indigenous villages routinely labor as water gathers, turning waterways into sites almost exclusively for women. Piped water technology, however, nearly eliminated this vital role that Mayo women played in the maintenance of their village's identity.[57] The CRF and the Mexican state celebrated the arrival of piped water as "progress"—uneven and unequal as it was—but this progress acted to exacerbate a cultural erosion already taking place among Mayo communities.[58]

If unjust irrigation policies and growing toxicity made some Mayo people want to stay away from the river, pipes allowed them to do so. The last spark that encouraged a Mayo tradition of reverence and care for the river—that is, physical interaction with it—had been snuffed out. With the removal of the river from their lives, the most important centripetal force in the Mayo universe disappeared and Indigenous cultural erosion accelerated. This shift also robbed Mayo people of the cohesion that empowered elders to impart wisdom to a new generation—the first generation to ever truly experience a fractured and diminished connection to the river.

Changing Approaches to Religious Ceremonial Materials

In the mid-1940s to mid-1950s, as the dispossession of riverbank land and the shift to commercial agriculture altered Mayo ejidatarios' relationship to the natural landscape, Indigenous villages found innovative ways to adapt, largely (as detailed in chapters 3 and 4) through their use of irrigation infrastructure and political alliances. Yet by the mid-1950s new hydraulic infrastructure and the policies that came with it forced Mayo people to begrudgingly adapt even further. By then ecological changes were having a profoundly negative effect on the local flora and fauna, both of which played an essential role in religious ceremonies.[59] Mayo villages' battle to maintain a connection to their ancestral homeland continued, only now it entailed not only fighting for sacred space but also the religious material that constituted sacred ceremonies. It was as if a Christian congregation had been kicked out of its church and then had all its sacramental objects—crucifix, communion chalice, vestments—taken away too.

The centripetal force of Mayo identity is their care for and connection to the Fuerte River, and their rituals reflect that fact. For example, an integral component to the San Juan ceremony is planting *álamo* (cottonwood) trees along the river.[60] Outside of the demonstrable ecological benefits of having wooded shores along rivers, the Indigenous people of the Fuerte valley believe álamos emit a divine, healing energy and are therefore considered sacred. "In álamo trees," elder Carla Bacosegua of La Florida explains, "we recognize what binds us to the river—the saints and their glory, which is why we planted them and bathed in the river during the San Juan ceremony." However, increasing restrictions on river access in the 1950s and 1960s put an end to the plantings. "Today," she continues, "this connection is missing, as Yoris owned most of that [river shore] property by the 1950s, killing our tradition."[61] Not understanding the spiritual significance of álamo trees, Yoris not only prevented Mayo villages from planting them on river shores but also chopped many of them down.[62]

Álamo trees have several beneficial properties, but Mayo villages used them judiciously. Yori culture, in contrast, celebrated immediate, individual wealth at the expense of the community and local ecosystem. Loreto Coronado, a Mayo cultural expert, describes how "Unlike Yoris who cut down whole trees and do not replant them, Yoremes use álamo tree bark as an herbal remedy and the wood to make *ramadas* [shelters], only cutting enough needed, always asking the tree's permission."[63] Yori pursuit of profit overwhelmed the more sustainable Mayo practices, and in the last half of the twentieth century the trees practically disappeared from the river. They have never fully returned, to the detriment of both Mayo identity and the valley's ecosystem.

The other more obvious use of álamo trees was for lumber, and while both Mayo and Yori communities employed the trees to this end, Mayo culture assured the trees' continued existence in a way Yori culture did not. Mayo ejidatarios used the wood from álamo trees to build ramadas that served as many things to Mayo villagers: meeting places, buildings for food storage, and shelter that allowed them to sleep outside in the warm summer months. Most importantly, ramadas played an integral role in the maintenance of their Indigenous identity, as they acted as sacred sites for dancers, musicians, and holy men to perform religious rituals. The shortage of álamo trees in the 1960s forced Mayo ejidatarios to use alternative materials such as other types of wood to construct ramadas, but elders grew concerned that these new materials—which lacked an origin from along the river—did not possess the same sacred properties and energy as the álamo wood. Worse, they worried that many younger Mayo villagers shared this fear. Enthusiasm for carrying out annual sacred rituals began to flag, for if the material necessary to carry out a "proper" celebration could not be found, would the ceremony even be effective?

The lack of álamo trees was a new and troubling problem that led to growing doubts. Narciso Bachomo and Carlos Salcedo point out, "Yoremes who respected nature knew that the ramada had to be made with álamo wood. If they could not gather enough of this wood to build the ramada, this hurt their relationship with nature."[64] The great irony here is that those who were most religious and committed to carrying out rituals were often those who questioned the substitution of materials. If *they* lost faith, it would take less for other, less religiously committed Mayo villagers to do likewise. Earlier, Indigenous ejidatarios cut off from river access creatively employed artificial apparatuses like canals to gather water so they could conduct rituals such as San Juan. The water in the canals was still water from the Fuerte River, after all, but scraps of wood from other tree species were categorically not álamo wood. Nothing else had the same sacred properties and there was no clever workaround to the problem.

Yori actions undermined Mayo identity piece by piece, first by cutting off their access to river water, then by physically limiting their access to the river, and then by nearly wiping out local álamo trees. The process unfolded over decades, but the results are evident today. Several Mayo elders point out that younger generations are less fluent in the Mayo language. They also accuse younger members of their village of not respecting their natural landscape because they throw trash into the river. While such changing approaches to the river could also be attributed to differences in generational values, elders do not agree. They instead point to the 1950s and 1960s, when raw materials like álamo trees became difficult to access—a cultural crisis for which there was no ready solution.

Injury upon cultural injury piled upon Mayo communities after the mid-1950s. Nothing in nature lives in isolation and the loss of one resource inevitably led to the loss of others. In addition to Yoris cutting down forests for tree branches used in growing crops, they cleared natural vegetation to make room for farmland. The felling of forests had long term effects not only for local ecosystems but also Mayo religious ceremonies, a fact Yoris were either not aware of or simply did not care about. "As Yoris cut trees," Mayo elder Daniel Galaviz of Camajoa recalls, "this eliminated the population of butterflies living in them. Yoremes used butterfly cocoons to make *tenábaris,* rattles traditional dancers attach to their ankles. The decline of butterflies due to deforestation made tenábaris very expensive."[65] Tenábaris were not a load-bearing pillar of Mayo identity like the álamo tree, but it was another piece of their identity chipped away by the Yori fixation on immediate profits. When added to the many other aspects of Mayo identity strained by developmentalist policies, it explains why it became so hard to maintain the rites and rituals that reinforced Mayo villages' most essential asset: their bonds of community.

During this pivotal era of the late 1950s through 1960s, the Fuerte valley ecosystem did not entirely collapse, but key elements of it did, forcing Mayo farmers to make difficult choices that tested their cultural cohesion. Mayo elders believe that respect for the natural landscape and the survival of Indigenous rituals are intertwined. For them, one does not exist without the other. By the late 1960s both the environmental health of the Fuerte valley and the strength of Mayo rituals were strained by Yoris and the CRF, which enabled them, but they were not broken. The region's ecological health was poor but fixable. While the Mayo rituals undoubtedly grew smaller but, having been forged in the crises and doubts of the preceding twenty years, what remained was tempered and more durable. While religious ceremonies were strained, at least some younger people still partook in them. Within the ruins of the last two decades there were seedlings of hope, but in order to see those seedlings sprout into a Mayo revival, a change in circumstances was necessary.

Hydraulic Development, Animal Husbandry, and Hunting

During the mid-twentieth century proliferation of irrigation infrastructure, no aspect of life escaped transformation in the Fuerte valley. Developmentalist policies had targeted the river, land, and plants of the region, so change was expected, but the alterations were so large that even the population of wild animals shifted tremendously. This change, in turn, complicated life for the Indigenous populations dependent upon them. Amid changes to ecosystems, some animal species appeared while others disappeared, limiting Mayo hunting practices. While hunting was a fact of life for Yoremes, an important cultural practice that bonded villagers and a necessary source of vital protein, for Yoris, hunting for food was at best a quaint throwback to an earlier time and at worst a burdensome, vestigial practice that ran directly counter to the goals of expanding agribusiness.

The conflict over animals began, quite literally, close to home. Traditionally, Mayo people had not been large-scale livestock holders, but it was common for ejidatarios to have a few domesticated animals they used to supplement their farm. Often, the most economical way to raise these animals was to let them roam and feed themselves. By the 1950s, after Yoris cleared natural vegetation and replaced it with crops grown with toxic pesticides, Mayo ejidatarios found this option cut off. Compounding the problem, by the 1960s Yoris owned the vast majority of riverbank land, eliminating Mayo ejidatarios' longtime practice of driving livestock to the river to drink. The river water that was available to the animals was increasingly poisoned by the widespread use of pesticides, herbicides, and ammonia fertilizers. As Mayo elder Manuel Galindo of La Bajada recalls, "Yoremes used to raise more animals, but most stopped by the 1960s as it was too hard to sustain them. There were a lot of toxic crops on all sides of us, and no water for the herd."[66] The Fuerte valley's switch to commercial agriculture and the supposed "Green Revolution" had created health risks not only for Mayo villagers but the animals they raised too. By the 1960s these risks, combined with changes in land access and usage, had made raising livestock a poor proposition and many abandoned the practice altogether.

While not as central to Mayo identity as the Fuerte River or their crops, animal husbandry was a vital component of Mayo survival. For generations livestock had provided sustenance for them and were used in trade. But, even more than crops, animals required land, and as Mayo ejidatarios were forced off ejidal plots or to illegally rent properties to Yoris, the ability to keep an animal of any kind diminished. "My family used to eat all-natural food because I raised chickens, turkeys, and ducks," recalls Mayo elder Fermín Mopay of Camayeca. "I sold or bartered with Yoremes and sold eggs to Yoris. But it got harder to raise animals by the 1960s. Yoremes eventually could not afford to buy meat and most did not have land to raise crops to barter."[67] The switch to agribusiness in the Fuerte valley, an effort the federal government believed would make the region into a "bread basket," in fact likely reduced not only the quantity but also the diversity of the foods Mayo ejidatarios ate.

As Yori exploitation of natural resources for profit altered local ecosystems, Mayo ejidatarios scrambled to find new strategies to both maintain a sustainable approach to the natural landscape and raise their own animals. For elder Mauricio Mejías of Huepaco there was real competition for food sources. "Before the 1970s," he contends, "we owned fish and shrimp ponds and raised turtles, letting frogs run wild. But then Yoris collected turtles and frogs to sell to restaurants and stole the fish and shrimp out of our ponds. These animals nearly disappeared because they are worth money."[68] It is easy to blame Yori farmers for their exploitation of animals, but they were only manifesting the Mexican state's call for development in the region. This developmentalist attitude did not limit itself to crops and livestock. Any aspect of the Fuerte region's ecosystem was fair game so long as there was a market from which Yori farmers could profit. The loss of frogs was not just financial; some villages believe them to be sacred and essential to the Yuco Conti ceremony. Here was yet another example of Yori exploitation rippling through the Mayo sacred universe.[69]

Through the 1950s the proliferation of irrigation infrastructure and clearing of natural vegetation in the Fuerte valley led to a decline in the number and variety of some wild animals—including dangerous ones like alligators—and the surfacing of new, invasive species. Some of these new arrivals were more dangerous than the predators they replaced.[70] Eugenia Tico remembers how "in villages like Cahuinahua that saw new artificial bodies of water appear, we started seeing more mosquitos and water snakes in the 1950s. A lot of these snakes were poisonous and dangerous. We had to be more careful when we walked near the river."[71] "Progress" along the Fuerte River brought water that was not only poisonous in and of itself (because of runoff) but also due to the animals it introduced.

Then as now, the clearing of forests and grasslands for agriculture and livestock production in the mid-twentieth century constituted the greatest threat to the conservation of terrestrial wildlife and ecosystems in Mexico.[72] The erasure of forests and vegetation led to a reduction in wild game such as deer and rabbit in northern Sinaloa, making hunting more difficult for Indigenous villages. Mayo people hunted, of course, to secure food, but the hunt itself was about more than securing protein; it reinforced relationships within the village. As Ralph Beals, who studied Mayo communities in the 1930s, observed, "Large animals were generally hunted cooperatively. . . . On the return of the hunters the chief divided the meat among all the villagers."[73] As Yoris cleared scrub brush and forests to make way for farmland and irrigation projects, the number of wild game species Mayo hunters had depended on for generations declined. "We used to hunt deer, iguanas, rabbit, armadillo, and snakes," Mayo elder Roberto Escalante reminisced, "but human populations, irrigation development, and agricultural expansion reduced the number of these animals. Yoris cleared the animals' natural habitat, trees and scrub brush, forcing them to flee to the hills to survive."[74] Yoris treated wild brush and trees as just another obstacle to development, rather than as a home for animals that had been integral to Mayo diets and communal hunting practices. The loss of farmland was devastating, but Mayo communities may have held out the hope that nature, beyond the surveyed lines of the field, had remained resilient.

By the mid to late 1960s, when Mayo hopes of ecological resilience were nearly dashed, the first federal agencies tasked specifically with controlling forestry, hunting, and fishing emerged.[75] The fact that the Mexican state put resources behind such bureaus suggests that wildlife extraction had become as excessive as Mayo elders suggest. It is unclear who was responsible for overhunting. Mayo villages tried to carry on their communal hunts even while numbers declined. They claim, however, that it was the non-Indigenous newcomers who engaged in excessive hunting as animal populations fell. It is likely that Mayo elders are right. First, only Yoris had the political leverage and sense of empowerment to break the law and ignore government restrictions on hunting. Second, in every other interaction with nature, Yoris demonstrated their cultural norms of extracting and exploiting resources for immediate gain—even if they went past the point of sustainability.

With the disappearance of some animals, Indigenous ejidatarios shifted to new sources of necessary animal protein. For instance, Mayo elder Daniel Galaviz of Camajoa recalls a jarring change that his family had to embrace. "My family owned a small portion of land that we lost. The irrigation waters made the animals we used to eat like deer and rabbits disappear. The only animal that remained was a rat, but it was healthy to eat because it only ingested leaves high up in trees."[76] While the Mayo people of the Fuerte valley were not the first population to alter their diets due to the implementation of national economic policies, they are the first documented Indigenous group in the mid-twentieth century forced to alter their diets as a consequence of Mexican development initiatives centered upon hydraulic infrastructure.[77]

But even with the shift to rat as a protein, the CRF's policies played out in complicated ways. The proliferation of canals and dams resulted in the growth of snake populations, which changed the balance of the food chain. Mayo elder Sabás Ynustrosa of La Mojonera remembers, "Canals and irrigation structures brought mosquitos, flies, and insects like tarantulas, centipedes, and scorpions. But it also brought the *cabeza prieta* [ground snake] that ate all of these pests and went into the water and ate rats. We saw less rats after the snake appeared."[78] The fact that some Mayo ejidatarios had to eat rats instead of venison and rabbit—and then compete against invasive snakes for them—serves as a salient reminder that the alterations in local ecosystems unfolded in ways no one could have predicted. While rats disappeared near La Mojonera, near Camajoa they became a source of food. The type of fauna available within particular Mayo villages helped each to determine their coping strategies, for there could be no one, single response.

Indigenous Fishing Adaptations in the Fuerte Valley

The center of the Mayo world was always the Fuerte River, and for centuries the river provided not only water but also food. Yet, as was the case in so many other examples, the influx of Yoris into the Fuerte valley strained local ecological resources. No matter to what degree each Mayo ejido or individual depended on fishing, Yori overfishing affected everyone in the Fuerte valley.

Until the 1940s fishing was a communal enterprise for the Indigenous people of the region, largely carried out by Mayo villages poisoning fish that came to spawn at the mouth of the Fuerte

River with herbs and then collecting the catch.[79] Similar to hunting, the head of a village distributed the entirety of a daily catch among all the villagers. It was both a means of ensuring that the larger community was well-fed and establishing harmony and peace among the various Mayo villages. But such a communal endeavor depended on the availability of large amounts of fish, a condition that became jeopardized by outsiders.

For decades outsiders and newcomers had been extracting fish and shrimp from the Fuerte River. In the early 1920s a California-based company set up a shrimp-packing plant in the town of Topolobambo. By 1941 fishing had grown so contentious that local Mayo and Yori fishermen put aside their cultural and economic differences to form a fishing cooperative to protect their shared interest in keeping out better capitalized foreign operators. The Fish Production Cooperative Society of the Fuerte River sought to ensure fair prices for the sale of their products, maximize the potential of the river, and protect against outside competition and overfishing. According to the cooperative's constitution, any Mayo or Yori fisherman who had lived in the Fuerte valley for more than five years could join.[80] From this first effort, other cooperatives spread out through northern Sinaloa in the mid-1950s and 1960s. While the state supported these cooperatives' attempts to monitor and restrict fishing, their efforts were not enough to prevent the overexploitation of local waterways and fish harvests from the river plummeted.

As was the case with farming in the Fuerte valley, Mayo fishermen/women attempting to protect resources became overwhelmed and pushed aside by ambitious individuals and companies with more resources. According to Mayo elder Manuel Galindo, who was both a farmer and fisherman in La Bajada, "Yoremes did not overfish our resources like Yoris, who also broke the law by fishing out of season. By the 1970s there were less shrimp, octopus, and bass. The *caguama* [loggerhead turtle] are almost extinct."[81] Knowing state officials would turn a blind eye, some Yori fishermen/women not affiliated with the collective extracted staggering numbers of aquatic animals from Fuerte valley waterways, while their Indigenous counterparts—who had the state's official approval to fish and could have taken advantage of the minimal government oversight on overfishing—largely did not. The simple fact was that Mayo fishermen/women did not have access to markets large enough to justify overfishing. For them, these animals were a local, cheap, reliable food source to fall back on, and they had a strong interest in ensuring the animals' survival.[82]

In addition to overfishing, lower water levels in the river and increased contamination made it hard for aquatic life to flourish in the Fuerte River. But, as Mayo villagers had proven with the Yuco Conti ceremony, water was fluid, and as canals became part of the larger aquatic infrastructure, fish came with them.[83] "At first," elder Carla Bacosegua recounted, "there were few fish or other edible creatures in the canals, but soon fish, shrimp, and even *cauque* (small lobster) began to appear. Yoremes continued to fish in the Fuerte River but were less successful. We adapted to the changing environment by fishing in canals."[84] The proliferation of new water sources sometimes even changed the occupations of entire Indigenous communities. As elder Laura Apodaca of La Misión explains, "We lost most of our ejidal land and did not have space to grow enough crops to feed ourselves. We were forced to learn how to fish in canals or the dam reservoir. We have limited food resources, so like Yoremes in nearby ejidos, we spend our days fishing. Over the years we became a fishing community."[85] The appearance of aquatic animals in canals must have been a welcome site for Mayo ejidatarios, especially after their near disappearance in rivers and other natural bodies of water.

The state and its Yori representatives might have sought to grind Mayo people down and turn them into a hydraulic army, but nature, while never favoring these Indigenous people, never entirely turned her back upon them. Life blossomed in new and unexpected ways, and some Mayo people, always attuned to the ebb and flow of life in the Fuerte valley, kept a keen eye out for these changes. If they could not farm, then they would fish, but, above all, they would attempt to stay on the land and near the river.

Conclusion: Mayo Identity in a Time of Fracturing

After 1940 the dominant theme to Mayo life was adaptation to unwanted and unwarranted change. No years between 1940 and today saw changes come as quickly and fiercely than the mid-1950s through 1960s. In those years the developmentalist agenda of the Mexican government acted like an anvil, hammering Mayo communities to conform to Yori standards and be part of a "modern" Mexico. Whether consciously or not, "progress" came at the expense of more ancient, sustainable Mayo traditions.

The historical changes present in this chapter are categorically different from the first four chapters. Until the 1950s Mayo hydraulic social mobilization had varied depending upon the natural landscape, the type and placement of hydraulic infrastructure, and the political power of individual communities. There had been no monolithic, universal Mayo response, but after the 1950s, that variance among Mayo communities diminished and responses became more uniform as all became marginalized economically and politically. Some remained wealthier or more well-connected than others, but the differences between Mayo villages paled in comparison to the difference between Yoris and any Indigenous community. It was this latter difference that defined this period.

Mayo farmers had previously used pumps, canals, and other hydraulic technologies in similar ways to Yoris, but even so, they still held to practices involving the natural landscape and a reciprocal approach to the Fuerte River that distinguished them from non-Mayo farmers. Some Mayo elders consider the mid-1950s and 1960s as the time when those practices and that approach began to weaken and the reduced role of the river and natural landscape in their lives rapidly deteriorated their culture. As riverine development became more centralized and irrigation rights placed in the hands of private entities, only some access to Fuerte River water—such as the use of canals for fishing—remained a possibility. Yet this limited access was somehow enough for Mayo villages to remain intact and for their culture to survive.

The developmentalist attitude that unified the disparate and often conflicting Mexican state agencies that arose in the 1950s allowed for minimal Indigenous agency. State functionaries in the CRF made decisions that impacted Indigenous communities with virtually no ejidatario consultation. Before the 1950s Indigenous people may have been junior partners to the state, but they commanded at least some respect and enjoyed some say in policies that affected them. By the mid-1950s the actions and policies of the state revealed that not only did it no longer see the Mayo ejidatarios as worthy constituencies with useful knowledge to be trusted in local decisions, but it also looked upon them as an obstacle to development that had to be removed. That shift still impacts both the ecology of the Fuerte valley as well as Mayo culture.

Epilogue

Remaining Strong

The ceremony of San Juan fell on a particularly hot day in June 2019. Even at nine in the morning the sun beat down, and though it was warm enough to swim, the last thing Gabriel Valenzuela wanted to do was wade in the pungent Fuerte River. His cousin Roberto, however, had different plans. As Gabriel stood at the edge of the river and watched participants dunk the statues of Jesus and San Juan in the water (as depicted in figure 12) near the town of San Miguel Zapotitlán, Roberto came from behind and pushed him in. Although in years past practically the whole village would have been in the river with him celebrating, by 2019 the monumental level of pollution in the water meant that only a few dozen entered the river while everyone else watched from the banks. The San Juan ceremony was still central to the people of San Miguel and nearby villages, and prayers—in both Spanish and the Mayo language—to God, Jesus, and a host of saints sang out over the river as they had for centuries, one part of the event had changed. Gabriel had not gotten dunked by chance, for local elders had not only allowed but encouraged people to throw and push others into the water in order to—in a playful way—reconnect with and affirm their traditions and communal bonds.[1]

The changes to the San Juan ceremony are a microcosm of the malleability the Mayo people have demonstrated in their relationship with the river between 1927 and 1970. Yori alterations to the

12. San Miguel participants dunking Jesus and San Juan statues into the Fuerte River. Photograph taken by James Mestaz, June 2019.

13. San Miguel participants begin gathering at the banks of the Fuerte River near San Miguel. Photograph taken by James Mestaz, June 2019.

Fuerte valley's political and physical landscape during this period threatened both the Mayo homeland and their way of life but only because of a vicious cycle the Mexican government engineered. In this arid region irrigation manifested as political power and political power manifested as irrigation, but—except for a brief period in the 1930s—state and federal agencies routinely denied Mayo villages irrigation because they lacked political connections. These villages, in turn, could not cultivate lasting political connections because they could never secure irrigation.[2] Yet, as *Strength from the Waters* shows, this was not a situation to which Mayo farmers simply acquiesced. Rather, they bended but did not break, adapting traditions and notions so that they could guard what was most precious to them: remaining physically and spiritually close to their sacred river. Even when they were bested on politi-

cal and economic fronts by Yoris and the local and federal officials
that favored them, Mayo villages shifted their efforts to cultural
realms, as in the case of the San Juan ceremony that Gabriel unintentionally participated in so directly.

Like the valley that shares its name, the Fuerte River runs right
through the heart of this book, and the most important change
to the river from the 1920s through the 1960s was the intensive
use of hydraulic technology. Hydraulic technology was the driving force of both continuity and change in Mayo society from the
1920s to the 1960s, for Mayo farmers' historic embrace of pumps,
canals, and aqueducts during this period were acts of resistance
more than investments in productivity. They had to embrace technology, but how they embraced it and what it meant to them was
entirely of their own making.[3] In much the same way that they
did not spurn pumps or canals in order to hold true to some ossi-
fied, timeless notion of what it meant to be Mayo, they also did not
employ them in order to become modern, profit-maximizing farmers. Narciso Bachomo and Carlos Salcedo explain that for all their
deep attunement to supernatural forces, Mayo farmers remained
firmly rooted in the reality of twentieth-century Mexico and that
their employment of technology was "neither resistance nor complicity, but rather adaptation. It was the acceptance of this technology and they accomplished more by using it."[4] That is, technical
adaptation—the integration of non-Indigenous technologies and
practices with their own—allowed Mayo communities to maintain and defend their identity and even change tradition in ways
that served them best.[5]

It is easy, given their place in the hierarchy of the region, to
underestimate the Mayo people's ability to adapt. At midcentury
it was not obvious, even to sympathetic observers, that Yoremes
could adapt fast enough to keep up with the wave of changes around
them. Even sympathetic scholars have been guilty of making this
assumption.[6] Charles Erasmus studied Mayo villages along the
Fuerte River from the 1930s to the 1950s, but toward the end of his
studies he predicted that Mayo culture would eventually disappear,
fractured by mobility, economic opportunities elsewhere, and the

growing presence of Yori culture.[7] He was, of course, wrong, and the root of his mistake was in underestimating the Mayo people's ability and even willingness to change. The reciprocal connection between Yoremes and the Fuerte River was never predicated upon fixed, immutable practices. It was never merely ritualistic, but rather a living, evolving attachment rooted in genuine sentiment and in practices that could change form but at heart still allowed Mayo people to manifest their reverence for the sacred. We would do well to learn from his mistake and to not only appreciate the Mayo people's ability to adapt but to see the adaptations uncovered in this book as recent manifestations of a longstanding theme in Mayo history.

Post-1970 Mayo Hydraulic Social Mobilization

Despite challenges, the Fuerte River still remains at the heart of Mayo identity. After 1970 Mayo water activists not only learned from the successes and failures of their predecessors but also, as all Mayo generations have, adapted and tried new strategies. One of the more revolutionary of these approaches was looking out beyond their region.

In June 1996 a group of Mayo ejidatarios from the northern Fuerte valley calling themselves the "Defense of the Mayo Culture of Huites" met in Choix, Sinaloa, with delegates from five other Mexican Indigenous groups from regions in Chiapas, Oaxaca, and Guerrero where dams were interfering with their cultural practices.[8] The conference, entitled the "First Meeting of Indigenous People Displaced and Affected by the Construction of Dams," allowed the delegates to discuss their respective situations, compile a report, and draft a petition demanding two things from the Mexican state. First, they asked the National Water Commission (CNA) to immediately return agricultural land to the Mayo people of the Huites ejido and to allow them access to the Luis Donaldo Colosio dam. Second, they requested that the state resolve problems generated by dams in the other regions of Chiapas, Oaxaca, and Guerrero and cancel projects that violated the rights of Indigenous people.[9]

In addition to these demands, the delegates also collaborated to define what they collectively meant by territory and natural resources and how the two could secure the particular rights they held as Indigenous people. Territory, they determined, included not only their villages, sacred spaces, and the surrounding flora and fauna, but also the resources supporting life, most notably water. The delegates also asserted their right to develop their culture, demanding that the state recognize traditional governments and customs and consult Indigenous communities and defer to their judgment on development proposals that might impact public spaces or natural resources within their villages.[10]

Here was one of the Mayo people's most daring assertions of Indigenous rights since Bachomo's Revolution (1913–16), but little came of it. The CNA responded that the petitioners had rights as farmers who might be impacted by the dam but not as Indigenous communities. A sympathetic report from the National Indigenous Institute (INI) acknowledged Indigenous people's cultural rights to sacred land and rivers, but there was little new in this.[11] The INI had bestowed similar recognition to Indigenous groups in regions such as Oaxaca a few years before, but the INI could never go toe-to-toe with the CNA. When the question of whether or not to build a dam came up, everyone knew who had the ear of the highest powers in Mexico.[12] The acknowledgment that Mayo activists and their allies had secured from the CNA as farmers and their cultural rights as asserted by the INI in principle had changed little in practice. Irrigation water was still too expensive for Mayo farmers, and most riverbank land remained in the hands of more powerful Yoris.

Yet some good came of the Choix delegates' efforts. Mayo farmers were still poor and could not compete economically with their neighbors, but with their new recognition from the INI in hand, they could carry on the fight culturally. In the twenty-five years since the conference, Mayo activists have leveraged their government-endorsed recognition as the native people of the Fuerte valley in order to secure the right to practice religious ceremonies, opening a new front in the struggle for access to scared river locations.

Mayo elders Narciso Bachomo and Carlos Salcedo point out that Mayo activists today "attempt to rescue sacred locations vital to Indigenous religious ceremonies. Some ceremonies can only be practiced in the river or on riverbanks, and activists repeatedly inform the Indian Affairs Commission and Commission of Ecology that we lack access to both. Some government officials support granting these rights, but the government shows minimal will to make necessary changes. Activists' methodical process is to first appeal to Mexican officials, laying a foundation to eventually petition the Inter-American Court of Human Rights."[13] The Mayo struggle now centers on political mobilization to energize riverine ceremonies in locations where they previously could not be held.[14] Even though Mayo participants converge on Indigenous ejidos that still have access to their riverbanks such as Pochotal, a rising generation of Mayo leaders want to conduct riverine rituals closer to home. Mayo leaders hope that as their people assert themselves and the old traditions spread out through the ancestral homeland, other Yoremes will flock in greater numbers to the rituals and ceremonies that make up the core of their identity. With this strategy, Mayo hydraulic social mobilization adaptation remains on full display today, as activists exploit political rights in order to keep their social and cultural connection to the river.

Contemporary Mayo Cultural Survival

Obstacles remain, however, and how Mayo people should respond spurs as much debate among today's elders as adaptations did in the past. The most obvious problem is the cost of carrying out traditional ceremonies and rituals. *Strength from the Waters* is a recording and even celebration of the Mayo people's ability to adapt and survive in the face of challenges that might have overwhelmed others. Yet while change has been a constant for Yoremes in the twentieth century, there was, especially in the latter half of the century, a nagging question of whether too much adaptation brought on too quickly could bring more harm than good. Mayo participants of every generation since at least the 1950s, for example, have reportedly complained about the rising costs of ceremonies, and the current generation is no different.[15] As Mayo elder Flor Escalante of Jahuara contends:

> The ingredients to make traditional food used in festivities are expensive. The *tenábaris* [leg rattles used by dancers] cost between 800 and 1,500 pesos [60–115 U.S. dollars], who can afford that? Some Yoremes make their outfits, but to construct a pair of tenábaris [they] must travel to the mountain many times to find particular buds of plants that have become rare. Some use synthetic materials like aluminum or plastic to make them. These fake materials do not produce the same sound and perhaps detract from Yoreme culture.[16]

While the decline of butterfly cocoons in the 1960s made it difficult to construct tenábaris, the issue today is compounded by the disappearance of certain plant buds from the natural landscape. While adaptation has worked in the past in some cases—changing diets and the types of animals Yoremes consumed, for instance—the substitution of synthetic materials to build ramadas is still not accepted by many. Some Mayo elders worry that changing yet another sacred material might be stretching adaptation into an invention of something wholly new.[17]

Could too much change sever the bonds of continuity with the sacred Fuerte River? As much as Mayo leaders have shown a willingness to experiment and adapt, they often hint at an aspiration to return to older traditions. In the same way that elders encourage the growth of álamo trees to provide material for traditional ramadas, there is also hope of planting and encouraging the growth of the plants that produce the buds used in making tenábaris.[18] While many await the day that traditional materials return in quantities enough for everyone, the prospects for this are far off. Until then, it is probable that use of synthetic materials will continue to increase. Or, like so many other aspects of Mayo life, subtle differences between villages will emerge, with some embracing synthetic materials, others rejecting them, and still others turning a blind eye when plastic tenábaris show up among traditional materials at a festival.

Not all changes can be so easily excused. In the last few decades, the growing number of Yoris who participate in Yoreme celebrations has become particularly polarizing. Whether Yoris are attempting to prove their deep roots in the local community, show off to single Mayo of the opposite sex, or claim their Indigenous roots, Mayo elders approach this new, unexpected dilemma in different ways. There are Mayo alive today who remember their grandparents being driven off sacred sites with whips, belts, and even the threat of guns who cannot reconcile themselves to the recent interest that Yoris have shown to Mayo traditions. This group generally expresses concern for cultural disintegration and Yori appropriation. Yet there are others who see a chance to make the traditions genuinely popular or to at least cultivate allies as Mayo leaders seek greater influence. This group takes a more nuanced approach and, though cautious as to the Yoris' motives, teaches the dances and traditions to outsiders.[19] In exchange for teaching Yoris the true meaning of their old ways, these elders expect non-Mayo allies to pass traditions on to new generations of Mayo people and culturally sensitive Yoris, ensuring the survival of these practices.[20] Yoris participating in ceremonies and appropriating Mayo traditions—a practice that has only become popular in the past two decades—is one of the costs of cultural survival in the twenty-first century, but there is no clear consensus as to what extent, if any, this dilutes Mayo culture. The ability of Mayo elders to both regulate which Yoris participate in sacred ceremonies and ensure that those who are selected grasp the larger, cosmological significance of the traditions they are participating in will likely determine how future Mayo generations judge this new outsider interest in their culture.

While not all changes to Mayo life in the fifty years after 1970 have escaped controversy, there is one development that has been uniformly welcome. As a careful reading will show, all the official ejido leaders in this book have been men, and before that—as mentioned in the introduction—the same has been true of the position of cobanaro. This does not mean that Mayo women were silent in their villages—just the opposite. Mayo elder Juanita Buimena of El Teroque explains, "Decades ago only men were ejidal leaders and cobanaros, but they consulted us women—who usually had the best ideas—before any large decisions. Some traditional female roles disappeared, so we started becoming cobanaros, dancers, and musicians; this keeps our culture alive."[21] Irrigation infrastructure nearly eliminated some of the chores that women traditionally carried out, such as fetching water from the river, but they have gradually created new and more important roles for themselves over the years. As the power of ejidal committee members deteriorated over time, the position of cobanaro reemerged in Mayo communities. In recent decades women like Juanita Buimena have shouldered this vital role. On the one hand, this change is not so radical as it first appears. After all, Mayo culture does not subscribe to rigid gender norms nearly as much as their neighboring Yoris. Yet, on the other hand, this change was momentous. First, a once-dormant Mayo institution had returned to prominence. Second, not only had it returned but now women leaders were officially as highly respected as their male counterparts. For a young Mayo girl aspiring to accomplish a great deal for herself and her village, this no doubt meant a great deal.[22]

Over the last two decades the reassertion of Indigenous identity in Mexico in the wake of the 1994 Zapatista uprising coupled with more proactive Mayo mobilization tactics has resulted in the popularization of Yoreme ceremonies in the Fuerte valley.[23] Perhaps outside curiosity in Mayo culture and the expansion of women's roles will help the broader society better understand the symbolic connection between Indigenous people and the Fuerte River. Female Yoris in particular could become more interested in Mayo ceremonies after viewing more female traditional dancers and musicians. The popularity of Indigenous religious ceremonies indicates that Mayo traditions have indeed become a vital component of Fuerte valley culture in general, something the famous Mayo general Felipe Bachomo could not have imagined when he launched his bloody revolt more than a century ago.

Mayo Adaptation and the Future

Mayo culture is much like the river at its center: strong, fluid, and perennially returning. It moves through time, always changing and yet always remaining. But this imagery may not go far enough. Perhaps Mayo culture is like the larger ecosystem of the Fuerte valley. After all, Yori farmers' attempts to clear thousands of hectares of scrub brush, trees, and other natural vegetation and replace them with large-scale farms proved more difficult than they expected— the native flora and fauna kept coming back. When Mayo elder Felicitas Mejía of Vinaterrias explains Yori alterations to the land, her words could be describing the Mayo people: "It was not easy to get rid of these plants, as the roots are very strong. Yoris dug deep within the earth to remove them. Often when they completely removed the plant and the root, the seed fell to the earth and the plant was born again."[24] There is something poetic in this view of the Mayo experience. Some of the native seeds Mejia refers to are smaller than a speck and yet they take root, struggle in the arid, inhospitable climate, and still burst back. Likening the Mayo people to a small seed is no insult, for in the Juyya Annia, all are considered equal.

Yoris in the twentieth century did not understand, let alone embrace, the Mayo conception of Juyya Annia. The Fuerte River was a resource available for their exploitation, and the Mayo people— like the native scrub along the river's bank—were an easily removed obstacle. But Yoris miscalculated the Mayo people's bond with and how far they would go to preserve Juyya Annia. Mayo hydraulic social mobilization efforts are just the most obvious demonstration of their commitment to the stewardship of Juyya Annia. Securing irrigation was always a means to an end and not, as was the case for their Yori neighbors, an end unto itself. The consistent underestimation of Mayo people and the lengths to which they would mobilize and adapt explains why Yoris in the Fuerte valley were never completely successful in preventing Indigenous people from acting as stewards of their vital ecosystems. Even as Mayo farmers lost their lands and could no longer grow their sacred corn, beans, and squash as before, becoming laborers and working for Yori landowners still fulfilled their longstanding role of tilling the soil and facilitating life within the local ecosystem.[25] Through all the changes detailed in this book, Indigenous culture survived.

The future of the Mayo people, especially through the lens of their current economic circumstances and rights to land and the river, appears somewhat bleak. For instance, multinational corporations like Monsanto and Dupont have moved into the area and, like Benjamin Johnston one hundred years before, seek to monopolize local land and water rights and introduce new crops—in this case transgenic corn. While this may seem like a depressing example of historical continuity, much has changed. For one, since the 1990s the Mayo people are less likely to fight alone and are mobilizing with other Indigenous groups. The past few decades have seen an increase in Mayo activists attending national and international conferences where Indigenous and campesino groups learn successful strategies of how to navigate the current political and economic climate.

By reaching out, this generation of Mayo villagers has shown a great willingness to learn from others, but they have just as much to teach other water protectors and grassroots environment organizations across the globe. Their history is a veritable playbook of liberating hydraulic social mobilization tactics. Native activists in such places as the Standing Rock Reservation in North and South Dakota could benefit from the knowledge of how Mayo farmers satisfied both economic and cultural needs by embracing the petitions process, new technologies, and political alliances. There are definitely parallels between the two, and each can learn from the other. The Mayo experience proves that modern states must understand that providing native communities even minimal political space can result in three mutually reinforcing goals: increased inclusion into mainstream society, self-sufficiency, and autonomy. Environmental activists undoubtably would appreciate the basic tenets of Juyya Annia and the notion that all elements of an ecosystem rely upon one another. Yet activists, politicians, and especially corporations have to be routinely reminded that water remains the centerpiece of these natural environments. Given that all productive actions require water, we should follow the lead of Mayo activists and treat it as a living entity to be protected at all costs.

Time will tell if younger generations of Mayo people will listen to the voices of elders and let their ancestors' mobilization strategies inspire them to find their own means of engaging the Fuerte River in a way that conserves their culture in the face of shifting physical and political landscapes. In economic terms the future of the Mayo people looks difficult, but on more than one occasion in the past century it seemed positively dire, and it would be a mistake to count them out. Despite Charles Erasmus's prediction of their cultural decline and disappearance, Mayo identity remains strong now and shows all signs of staying that way in the future. This is largely due to the fact that Mayo people still reside close to their sacred river, guarding it, honoring it, and drawing strength from it.

ampliación: Ejidal land extension.

campesino: Rural farmers, especially those who shared an understanding of their rights to land and water in the postrevolutionary and postwar period.

cobanaro: Traditional Mayo village governor.

collectivists: Members of the SICAE sugarcane cooperative.

cooperative: An organization of ejidos producing a commodity collectively. This book considers the Sociedad de Interés Colectivo Agrícola Ejidal (Agricultural Society of the Collective Ejidal Interest, SICAE) both a collective and a cooperative, and therefore uses the terms interchangeably.

dotación: A federal grant of communally managed land. The federal government could also bestow a separate water dotación or attach water rights to a land dotación.

ejidatarios: Land reform beneficiaries and members of an ejido.

ejido: Land reform parcel.

hacienda: Large estate or even plantation whose owners were known as hacendados.

hydraulic cultural mobilization: Use of water rights/technology to protect cultural practices such as ceremonies. Also refers to the modification of cultural practices to maintain access to the water necessary to perform them. A more specific category of hydraulic social mobilization employed largely but not exclusively by Indigenous villages intent on protecting their identity.

hydraulic infrastructure: Canals, pumps, aqueducts, and any technology that promoted irrigation.

hydraulic social mobilization: A popular movement to acquire water rights. This term is not specific to Indigenous groups such as the Mayo, who did in fact use political alliances, petitions, and new laws in the same way as Yoris, while also employing more particular tactics of hydraulic cultural mobilization to protect cultural practices vital to their Indigenous identity.

independents: Mayo ejidatarios who were not members of ejidos affiliated with the sicae.

individualists: Ejidatarios who were not members of the sicae sugarcane cooperative, but were members of ejidos in which some ejidatarios were members of the cooperative.

Juyya Annia: Mayo term describing the natural world, or Mother Nature.

loggers: Members of the Ejidal Forestry Cooperative, or scfe in Jahuara.

mestizo: Most scholars use this term to describe mixed-race people. This book uses it to describe non-Indigenous people and uses Mestizo and Yoreme interchangeably.

milpa agriculture: Traditional Indigenous farming technique in which corn, beans, and squash are grown together, usually for subsistence purposes.

non-loggers: Ejidatarios of Jahuara who were not members of the scfe cooperative.

postrevolutionary: Period following the Mexican Revolution, generally understood as occurring between 1917 and the early 1940s. This book defines the time period as spanning from 1917 to 1942.

río Zuaque: Word combining Spanish and Mayo languages that Mayo villagers use to describe the Fuerte River.

Yoreme: A term Mayo people use to describe other Indigenous people, and within the context of this book, this term is usually used to describe other Mayo people in particular.

Yori: A term used by Mayo people to describe non-Indigenous people.

All translations from Spanish—including oral histories, archival documents, and secondary sources—were completed by the author.

Introduction

1. These fiestas consisted of dancers, musicians, and prayers that integrated Mayo practices with a folk Catholicism.

2. Word also spread to Mayo people in the Mayo valley and Yaqui people in the Yaqui valley.

3. Mayo people in the Mayo valley believed God would flood the region. While the story of the appearance of God eventually subsided, it regenerated Indigenous rituals that continue to unify Mayo people today. Erasmus, *Man Takes Control*, 288.

4. The Fuerte valley is unique in that Indigenous farmers integrated canals, pumps, and dams into their worldviews and practices in order to defend their cultural autonomy. This differed from their Indigenous brethren in the Mayo valley, where they flouted and destroyed such technologies because they could never gain such access. The several previously published works regarding Mayo culture in the Mayo valley include Banister, "Río Revuelto"; O'Connor, *Descendants of Totoliguoqui*.

5. At times hydraulic cultural mobilization is a more appropriate term to use when discussing Mayo cultural survival in the context of Indigenous cultural practices such as the San Juan ceremony. Yet, while hydraulic social mobilization and hydraulic cultural mobilization are two sides of the same coin, the latter is merely a function of the former. Use of hydraulic social mobilization first appeared in Mestaz, "Sweetness and Water Power," 1–25.

6. This book gains inspiration from Mikael Wolfe's regional analysis of the state's difficulties in distributing water equitably in the postrevolutionary period and the political, economic, and environmental consequences. Wolfe, *Watering the Revolution*.

7. Mayo villages had a longstanding connection with agriculture based on a reciprocal agreement in which they combined water, earth, and seed to create plant life that in turn helped sustain them.

8. Mestaz, "Sweetness and Water Power." Hydraulic histories of northwest Mexico alone include Aboites, *La irrigación revolucionaria*; Banister, "Río Revuelto"; Muehlmann, *Where the River Ends*; Evans, "La angustia de La Angostura"; Doolittle, "Intermittent Use and Agricultural Change on Marginal Lands," 255–66. Another pivotal hydraulic history of Mexico is Wolfe, *Watering the Revolution*. Northwest Mexican ethnohistories include McGuire, *Politics and Ethnicity on the Río Yaqui*; Erasmus, *Contemporary Change in Traditional Societies*, vol. 3; O'Connor, *Descendants of Totoliguoqui*; Radding, *Wandering Peoples*; Spicer, *The Yaquis*.

9. Chapter 1 discusses the impact Felipe Bachomo's 1913 revolt had on future mobilization strategies.

10. This book uses the more specific term "campesino" rather than "peasant" to describe rural farmers. Both Mayo and non-Mayo farmers of the Fuerte valley adopted the ideals of the postrevolutionary state initiatives that granted them rights to land and water, allowing them to understand their shared interests. Christopher Boyer defined campesinos as a social group with shared political and economic interests and recognized history of oppression. Boyer, *Becoming Campesinos*, 3. Chapter 2 discusses Mayo farmer's ability to join non-Mayo organizations to fight for their rights. See also Mestaz, "Sweetness and Water Power."

11. Other recent works highlighting peasant mobilization in the mid-twentieth century include McCormick, *The Logic of Compromise*; Gillingham and Smith, *Dictablanda*.

12. Mestaz, "Sweetness and Water Power."

13. While other authors have effectively documented Indigenous people's water mobilization strategies, none have connected the fight for water to Indigenous cultural survival as thoroughly as this book. Examples of other recent works describing native hydraulic social mobilization include Matsui, *Native Peoples and Water Rights*; López, "In Hidden View," 188–202.

14. Oral history expert Alessandro Portelli argues that the discrepancy between fact and memory increases the value of oral sources as historical documents. These sources tell us less about events than about their meaning, revealing unknown aspects of known events. Portelli, *The Death of Luigi Trastulli and Other Stories*.

15. Privott, "An Ethos of Responsibility and Indigenous Women Water Protectors in the #NoDAPL Movement," 74–100; Dean, "The Violence of Collection," 29–51; Adams-Campbella, Glassburn Falzetti, and Rivard, "Introduction," 109–16.

16. Russell, "Indigenous Knowledge and Archives," 161–71; Flavier, "The Regional Program for the Promotion of Indigenous Knowledge in Asia," 479.

17. Garcia Canclini, *Hybrid Cultures*.

18. Chapter 4 discusses this case in more detail.

19. Radding, *Wandering Peoples*, 17.

20. Liffman, *Huichol Territory and the Mexican Nation*; Collier, *Fields of the Tzotzil*; Boyer, *Political Landscapes*.

21. Muehlmann focuses on the Cucapá people of Baja California. Muehlmann, *Where the River Ends*.

22. Wolfe's study is based in the Bajío region of Mexico. Wolfe, *Watering the Revolution*.

23. Some of the revisionist literature that this book builds on includes Gillingham and Smith, *Dictablanda*, and Boyer, *Political Landscapes*.

24. Gill, *La conquista*, 5.

25. Secretaria de Agricultura y Recursos Hidraulicos, *Memoria de la comisión del río Fuerte*, 31.

26. Secretaria de Agricultura y Recursos Hidraulicos, *Memoria de la comisión del río Fuerte*, 34.

27. Olmsted, *Report on the Properties of the United Sugar Companies*, 13.

28. Barkin and King, *Regional Economic Development*.

29. Mayo people also consider Yaquis to be Yoremes (siblings). Mayo villages have always contested these categories and membership criteria within their communities.

30. Census data and scholars have historically had different opinions on what constituted a "Mayo" or "Indigenous" person throughout the twentieth century. The best estimates for the current Indigenous population in the Fuerte valley range from ten thousand to twenty thousand, roughly the same number that existed throughout the twentieth century.

31. In his dissertation "Río Revuelto," Jeff Banister makes this assertion about Mayos in the Mayo valley, but the same is true for Mayos in the Fuerte valley, and in fact the same could be said for many Indigenous people and their lands throughout Mexico during this time. Mayo people in that region use the term "Yorem" instead of "Yoreme." Banister, "Río Revuelto," 243.

32. Banister, "Patria Fugáz," 103–44.

33. Quintero, *Historia integral de la región del río Fuerte*, 579–610.

34. The next few chapters will analyze some of these laws.

35. The following chapter discusses this law and how Mayo villages used this legislation, as well as land reform policies to defend their identity.

36. Ejidos were not established in the Fuerte valley until the late 1930s.

37. A handful of other ejidos formed in the few years before and after this time. Much of the land was confiscated from large landowners such as Johnston.

38. Outsiders, usually schoolteachers, often helped Indigenous communities with these applications.

39. Yoris were often more politically connected, formally educated, or at least Spanish speaking, any or all of which helped an ejido acquire resources from the Mexican state.

40. Beals, *The Contemporary Culture of the Cáhita Indians*, 84, 91.

41. Article 27 of the Constitution stated that only male heads of the household could be ejidatarios. Article 27, Constitution of Mexico 1917.

42. Juanita Buimena and Carla Bacosegua are among several Mayo interview participants who attest to the history of reciprocal gender roles and claim that women were vital in the decision-making process in Mayo villages throughout the twentieth century. Yet they also downplay the category of gender in Mayo people's hydraulic liberation. This reflects the idea that all gender roles were equally vital in the struggle to secure such rights. Carla Bacosegua, interview by James Mestaz, La Florida, Municip. Ahome, Sinaloa, Mexico, March 14, 2014; Juanita Buimena, interview by James Mestaz, El Teroque Viejo, Municip. El Fuerte, February 14, 2014.

43. Chapter 2 discusses how Cárdenas promoted collective farming through the creation of the SICAE sugarcane cooperative and the ways in which it later succumbed to corruption and developmentalist policies in the 1940s and 1950s.

1. Their Technology, Our Way

1. Margarito Aguilar to the SAYF, May 13, 1931, AHA, Aguas Nacionales, Caja 1008, Expediente 14157.

2. The federal government claimed ultimate authority on surface water while corporations, communities, and individuals alike were required to petition the SAYF for water concessions. After the intense fighting of the Mexican Revolution, a very progressive 1917 Constitution laid the framework for social change. Moderate presidents generally held back these changes, including land reform, until the mid-1930s. 1926 Mexican Law of Irrigation with Federal Waters.

3. Various Mayo villages in the Fuerte valley applied for irrigation concessions between 1927 and 1942, such as Bamoa and La Palma, but Los Goros had the largest number of applications and therefore produced far more documents than other villages.

4. Large landowners and even communities attempted to convince state functionaries that Mayo lands were not fully cultivated and that they should be annexed and redistributed. Chapters 2 and 4 discuss these cases in more detail.

5. Several Indigenous groups throughout Mexico similarly conducted river rituals that tied water to their cultural and physical survival. Gálvez and Embriz Osorio, "Los pueblos indígenas de México y el agua," 12.

6. López Aceves, "Los mayos de Sinaloa," 19.

7. López Carrera, Atlas yoreme del municipio de Ahome, 12.

8. Environmental stewardship plays an essential role in several other Indigenous cultures, such as the Mixtec of Oaxaca whose practices regulate the conservation of natural resources. López Ramírez, "Los Ñuu Savii," 71–82.

9. This Mayo approach to water as spiritual and utilitarian rather than profitable is shared by other Indigenous groups throughout Mexico, as these Indigenous societies do not give water an economic valuation. Such Indigenous groups also similarly conduct religious ceremonies in order to reciprocate. Gálvez and Embriz Osorio, "Los pueblos indígenas," 12, 17.

10. Other Mexican Indigenous groups, such as the Teenek of the Huasteca region, rely on their oral traditions to express the centrality of waterways in their identity. Ochoa Ávila and Arias, "Cuando Maamlaab y Junkil aab despiertan," 59–70.

11. Daniel Galaviz, interview by James Mestaz, Camajoa, Municip. El Fuerte, Sinaloa, Mexico, March 6, 2014.

12. Among other similar studies, environmental scholar Cassandra Brooks discussed the reciprocal connection the Wabanaki people of the northeastern United States established with their river based on exchange between humans and nonhumans. Their cultural practices were built on the knowledge that overexploiting the river jeopardized their existence. Brooks and Brooks, "The Reciprocity Principle and Traditional Ecological Knowledge," 11–28.

13. The fact that a woman was charged with defending waterways reflects Mayo beliefs in gender reciprocity. Some Mayo elders consider old water woman the same entity as the river god Bawahamjuna. Beals, *The Aboriginal Culture of the Cáhita Indians*.

14. Librado Cuadros, interview by James Mestaz, La Palma, Municip. El Fuerte, Sinaloa, Mexico, February 29, 2014.

15. As mentioned in the book's introduction, Mayo people refer to the Fuerte River as río Zuaque. Narciso Bachomo and Carlos Salcedo, interview by James Mestaz, Camajoa, Municip. El Fuerte, Sinaloa, Mexico, March 21, 2014.

16. Technically the term *mestizo* means mixed-race people. Mayo people sometimes used the term mestizo to refer to non-Indigenous people, but it is more commonly used by scholars. Mayo people generally used the term Yori to refer to non-Indigenous people, therefore this book uses the terms Yori and mestizo interchangeably.

17. Other scholars who see language as the largest distinguishing Mayo trait include Uriarte, *Sinaloa yoreme*, 11. Crumrine also reveals the following differences: Mestizos are generally submissive to Catholicism or lack interest in god, while Mayo believe they have a contractual obligation to enact ceremonies that appease their syncretic god and save humanity from catastrophic natural disaster; Mayo hold a past-present time orientation and mestizos a present-future one; the Mayo modality of relationship is lineal and collateral, while mestizos are individualistic; Mayo believe innate human nature is power-seeking, whereas mestizos view humans as good but corruptible. Crumrine, "Mechanisms of Enclavement Maintenance and Sociocultural Blocking of Modernization," 25–29.

18. Several Indigenous groups throughout the world, and particularly in Mexico, view water as vital to both cultural and physical survival. For a more detailed explanation of these beliefs, see Martínez Ruiz and Murillo Licea, *Agua en la cosmovisión de los pueblos indígenas en México*.

19. Figueroa and López Alaniz, *Encuentros con la historia, Choix, tomo 1*, 146.

20. Ochoa Zazueta, *Los mayos*, 80. Other scholars have discussed this notion of religious syncretism in Mexico, including Taylor, *Magistrates of the Sacred*.

21. Uriarte, *Sinaloa yoreme*, 8.

22. Figueroa and López, *Encuentros con la historia, Sinaloa*, 146.

23. Uriarte, *Sinaloa yoreme*, 12.

24. Juan Valenzuela, interview by James Mestaz, Camajoa, Municip. El Fuerte, Sinaloa, Mexico, July 13, 2014; Carlos Salcedo, interview by James Mestaz, Cama-

joa, Municip. El Fuerte, Sinaloa, Mexico, March 21, 2014; Jorge Robles, interview by James Mestaz, San Miguel, Municip. El Fuerte, Sinaloa, Mexico, May 25, 2014.

25. The "Mayo community" in this work are the Indigenous people of the Fuerte valley who became bound together through historical experiences and cultural beliefs—and the practices (religious, social, economic) that supported this belief system. According to anthropologists Martin Robards and Lilian Alessa, community resilience refers to the adaptive capacity to evolve alongside social and environmental changes. Robards and Alessa, "Timescapes of Community Resilience," 415–27.

26. Gill, *La conquista*, 6.

27. José Figueroa explains that in contrast to Yaqui villages, Mayo people did not recognize communal property that exceeded the boundaries of a community within its small villages. This worldview led Mayo people to focus first and foremost on their immediate locality with the consequence that their political voice became fragmented and dispersed as early as the sixteenth century. Figueroa and López Alaniz, *Encuentros con la historia, Sinaloa*, 52.

28. Craig Cipolla explains ethnogenesis as a common process among Native American groups, and particularly among the Brothertown Natives of the East Coast. Cipolla, *Becoming Brothertown*.

29. As mentioned in the introduction, Mayo people refer to each other as Yoremes and to non-Indigenous people as Yoris.

30. Ochoa Zazueta, *Bachomo*, 284.

31. Similar to other Indigenous groups in the Americas, such as the Teenek people of the Huasteca area of Mexico, the Mayo people's resistance was tied to their ability to assert their identity in modern times. Ochoa Ávila and Arias, "Cuando Maamlaab y Junkil," 62; Ariel de Vidas, *El trueno ya no vive aquí*.

32. Mario Gill and Filiberto Quintero are among the many scholars that give this estimate, Ochoa Zazueta gives a more conservative estimate of 3,500 Mayo soldiers. Ochoa Zazueta, *Bachomo*, 225; Gill, *La conquista*; Quintero, *Historia integral*.

33. Jorge Robles, interview by James Mestaz.

34. Ochoa Zazueta, *Bachomo*, 264.

35. Beals, *The Contemporary Culture*, 50.

36. Near the end of Bachomo's campaign, his forces were armed with seven-millimeter Mausers, and Winchester and Remington 30-30 rifles. Ochoa Zazueta, *Bachomo*, 293.

37. Barth, *Ethnic Groups and Boundaries*.

38. Soldiers of the Moderate Constitutionalist faction that soon gained control of the country after the Mexican Revolution defeated and executed Bachomo in 1916. The introduction discusses this cycle of Mayo history in more depth.

39. Díaz was not technically president from 1880–84, but he installed a puppet president who did his bidding.

40. Olmsted, *Report on the Properties*. 65.

41. In 1917 one dollar equaled roughly one hundred Mexican pesos. Internal memo of Ministry of Development, January 16, 1918, AHA, Aprovechamientos Superficiales, Caja 4728, Expediente 65446.

42. United Sugar owned roughly the same amount of property in both 1917 and in 1924.

43. Olmstead, *Report on the Properties*, 87.

44. While the federal government did not proportion all of the water from the river to farmers, favoritism for USCOS compelled functionaries to act like there was only enough water for the conglomerate, and therefore farmers such as Zakany were left with limited access. José Zakany to the Ministry of Agriculture and Development, December 31, 1920, AHA, Aprovechamientos Superficiales, Caja 891, Expediente 12763.

45. As mentioned in the introduction, Article 27 of the 1917 Constitution made water property of the federal government. The intent was for the government to grant water rights to peasants. Yet moderate postrevolutionary presidents used vague language of "public interest" in the constitution to transfer this ownership to private parties.

46. Banister, "Patria Fugáz." Sterling Evans also points out that between 1926 and 1940, the CNI funded thirty-three massive irrigation projects. Most of these were designed to bring water to small and medium sized farmers. Evans, "La angustia de La Angostura," 57.

47. Wolfe, *Watering the Revolution*, 203; Aboites Aguilar, "The Transnational Dimensions of Mexican Irrigation," 72.

48. Wolfe, *Watering the Revolution*, 72–73.

49. Mikael Wolfe's work thoroughly interrogates the efficacy of hydraulic technology, or lack thereof, in postrevolutionary Mexico. Wolfe, *Watering the Revolution*.

50. These protests were in vain. Julio Zapata to Ministry of Agriculture and Development, July 8, 1926, AHA, Aprovechamientos Superficiales, Caja 499, Expediente 14040.

51. Figueroa and López Alaniz, *Encuentros con la historia, Sinaloa*, 25–26.

52. Public schooling was not available to most Indigenous rural people when Aguilar was a youth.

53. The Fuerte River's waters were indeed calmer during the dry months out of the year. Margarito Aguilar to SAYF, January 28, 1927, AHA, Aguas Nacionales, Caja 1008, Expediente 14157.

54. The initial cost for water pumps was very expensive, between 20,000 and 40,000 pesos per unit. Adding the cost of fuel to run the pumps and repairs, it was nearly impossible for small farmers to afford. Wolfe, *Watering the Revolution*, 80. Irrigation access was particularly difficult for Mayo farmers to attain, since most did not produce a massive crop surplus, and the average daily wage for laborers at this time was approximately one peso a day.

55. The rough waters, formed as a result of the annual flooding from the rainy seasons, June through September and December through February, were easier to obtain since there was more water for state agencies to proportion.

56. SAYF to Margarito Aguilar, January 28, 1927, AHA, Aguas Nacionales, Caja 1008, Expediente 14157.

57. While the amount requested was higher, 320,000 annual cubic meters, the fact that he asked for the rough waters made the request more attainable. Margarito Aguilar to the SAYF, November 4, 1927, AHA, Aguas Nacionales, Caja 1008, Expediente 14157.

58. Mikael Wolfe offers a detailed explanation of this paradox, in particular, the obstacles small farmers faced in attaining access to water in the postrevolutionary period in Mexico. Wolfe, *Watering the Revolution.*

59. There is no evidence that these particular farmers formed such a cooperative in the 1920s. This suggestion to form a cooperative could also be seen as foretelling the formation of the SICAE sugarcane cooperative that did in fact pull their resources and construct irrigation infrastructure starting in the late 1930s. I detail these developments in chapter 2.

60. Several petitions filed by small farmers explaining exploitative practices from other companies attest to this.

61. Valdés and Company to the SAYF, February 24, 1928, AHA, Aguas Nacionales, Caja 1008, Expediente 14157.

62. Margarito Aguilar to the SAYF, May 13, 1931, AHA, Aguas Nacionales, Caja 1008, Expediente 14157. One hectare is 2.47 acres.

63. Margarito Aguilar to the SAYF, May 13, 1931, AHA, Aprovechamientos Superficiales, Caja 1631, Expediente 14045.

64. Juan Kelly to the SAYF, January 9, 1931, AHA, Aprovechamientos Superficiales, Caja 1631, Expediente 14045.

65. Boyer, *Political Landscapes,* 169.

66. Mayo elder Alejandro Inzunza explained that they were all natives in Los Goros and Camayeca and wanted to gain rights as Indians to show that their connection to land and water was different from Yoris. This memory and corresponding documents suggest that Mayo farmers strategically used this label to their benefit. Alejandro Inzunza, interview by James Mestaz, Los Goros, Municip. Ahome, Sinaloa, Mexico, February 14, 2014.

67. Margarito Aguilar to Pascual Ortiz Rubio, May 13, 1931, AHA, Aprovechamientos Superficiales, Caja 1631, Expediente 14045.

68. Pascual Ortiz Rubio's office to SAYF, May 23, 1931, AHA, Aprovechamientos Superficiales, Caja 1631, Expediente 14045.

69. Both communal and individual properties were under attack under the Díaz regime, and tactics varied regionally and by village, and included *reparto de tierras* (land distribution). Discussion of some of these strategies can be found in Ohmstede and Butler, *Mexico in Transition.*

70. SAYF to Margarito Aguilar, May 26, 1931, AHA, Aprovechamientos Superficiales, Caja 1631, Expediente 14045.

71. Villages generally formed these types of committees when they applied for a dotación.

72. Margarito Aguilar to Pascual Ortiz Rubio, August 30, 1931, AHA, Aprovechamientos Superficiales, Caja 1631, Expediente 14045.

73. 1931 Mexican Federal Labor Law.

74. Margarito Aguilar to Pascual Ortiz Rubio, August 30, 1931, AHA.

75. Campesino and Indigenous groups often overlapped as several Indigenous farmers joined Yori campesinos in order to struggle for water and land rights. Yet Mayo villagers definitely distinguished between campesino indígenas and campesino Yoris.

76. As explained in the introduction, moderate constitutionalist presidents were not ready to fully implement the radical concepts of the constitution, enacting for instance, only minimal land reform. Article 27, Constitution of Mexico 1917.

77. Alejandro Inzunza, interview by James Mestaz.

78. We do not know for sure if Inzuna in fact saw Kelly in his village at this exact moment but remembering certain details such as a non-Mayo man's smile shows that a Yori was present in their village around this time period and that they did celebrate having access to water.

79. Mayo and Yori farmers did share some solidarity during the SICAE's reign of power in the early 1940s through late 1950s, as discussed in chapters 2, 3, and 4. Yet ethnic divisions also intensified in this time period and grew exponentially worse after the mid-1950s.

80. Alejandro Inzunza, interview by James Mestaz.

81. The several petitions Mayo villages/ejidos submitted to state agencies from 1927 to 1942 in a quest to attain water rights include Bamoa ejidal commission to the SAYF, May 11, 1935, AHA, Aguas Nacionales, Expediente 14227, Caja 1013; Victor Ontiveros to the SAYF, January 20, 1937, AHA, Aguas Nacionales, Expediente 64579, Caja 7749.

82. An example of such a document is Margarito Aguilar to SAYF, March 14, 1932, Archivo General Agrario (hereafter AGA), Dotación y Accesión de Aguas, Expediente 2466, Legajo 1, Asunto Toca, Los Goros, Municipio Ahome.

83. As mentioned in the previous section, Margarito Aguilar illegally received water in the 1920s.

84. Margarito Aguilar to SAYF, March 14, 1932, AGA.

85. Although some Mayo leaders understood the new laws, the majority were illiterate and most did not speak Spanish. The fact that the villagers invoked federal water laws suggests that they used the services of a schoolteacher, lawyer, or other educated individual who understood the nuances of irrigation legislation. Secretaria de Agricultura y Fomento, *Ley de aguas de propiedad nacional y su reglamento*, Paragraph 1, Article 34, 16.

86. Margarito Aguilar to SAYF, August 14, 1932, AGA, Dotación y Accesión de Aguas, Expediente 2466, Legajo 1, Asunto Toca, Los Goros, Municipio Ahome.

87. Margarito Aguilar to SAYF, August 24, 1932, AGA, Dotación y Accesión de Aguas, Expediente 2466, Legajo 1, Asunto Toca, Los Goros, Municipio Ahome.

88. Archival documents do not clarify Aguilar's success in this particular case, nor do Mayo elders remember exactly what happened. What is most important is that this case exemplified his tenacity and the value he placed on water rights.

89. While Aguilar sent this land reform petition on behalf of only Los Goros, he continued to make requests on behalf of both Los Goros and Camayeca for water concessions.

90. The SAYF did not grant Los Goros an ejido at this time. Margarito Aguilar to SAYF, July 21, 1931, AGA, Dotación, Expediente 23/1362, Legajo 1, Asunto Local, Los Goros, Municipio Ahome.

91. Chapter 2 delves deeper into such policies. Particularly, as other studies do, it shows how his initiatives empowered state functionaries after 1940 to encroach on the rights of the Indigenous and peasant communities these programs purportedly attempted to help. See also, Mestaz, "Sweetness and Water Power"; McCormick, "The Logic of Compromise"; Knight, "Cardenismo," 73–107.

92. Scott and Banister, "The Dilemma of Water Management," 66.

93. Aboites, *El agua de la nación*, 142; Scott and Banister, "The Dilemma of Water Management," 66.

94. At the point Los Goros received its dotación, it stopped partnering with its neighboring village Camayeca in its petitions.

95. It is unclear if Los Goros purchased these pumps from the previous owners, acquired other pumps, relied on gravity to propel water through canals, or found another way to draw water from the river. Two-hundred eight hectares were uncleared thorn scrub labeled as susceptible to farming. Four hundred hectares were mountainous areas that were formerly classified as national property. SAYF Official Report, September 21, 1938, AGA, Dotación y Accesión de Aguas, Expediente 33/5655, Legajo 1, Asunto Toca de Dotacion, Los Goros, Municipio Ahome.

96. Some of this ampliación land was dedicated to growing sugarcane collectively, which presented challenges to communal harmony that Los Goros and other Mayo villages faced as a result of joining a sugarcane cooperative; the topic of the next chapter. SAYF Official Report, September 21, 1938, AGA.

97. The Los Goros ejido therefore extended the Los Goros village, which now included ejidatario plots as well as those of small property owners.

98. Alejandro Inzunza, interview by James Mestaz.

99. Nabhan, *Enduring Seeds*, 71.

100. Los Goros small property owners to SAYF, January 31, 1938, AHA, Aprovechamientos Superficiales, Caja 1929, Expediente 29006.

101. The letter included a list with the size of the tracts of the forty-two small property holders, ranging from one hectare to eight hectares. Los Goros small property owners to SAYF, January 31, 1938, AHA.

102. Aguilar always covered his own personal interests. In October 1937, as Los Goros received a dotación, Aguilar was listed as one of the outgoing officers of the executive committee but later turned up in the official record as president of the ejidal commission in 1946. This evidence points to the idea that some small property owners

of Los Goros—such as Margarito Aguilar, Isidiro Aguilar, and Sotero Yocupicio—had received a portion of the ejidal land and may have leveraged their privilege into gaining leadership positions within the ejidal structure. These other small property owners were also listed as ejidatarios in petitions to the state from the 1930s through the 1950s. October 14, 1937; April 27, 1946; October 31, 1937; October 31, 1955, AGA, Ampliación de ejidos, Expediente 25/11427, Legajo 8, Ejecución, Los Goros, Municipio Ahome.

103. Los Goros small property owners to SAYF, October 24, 1942, AHA, Aprovechamientos Superficiales, Caja 1929, Expediente 29006.

104. Los Goros small property owners to SAYF, October 24, 1942, AHA.

105. Los Goros small property owners to SAYF, October 24, 1942, AHA.

106. Los Goros small property owners to SAYF, October 24, 1942, AHA.

107. Los Goros small property owners to SAYF, October 24, 1942, AHA.

108. Mayo people indeed made less of a distinction between canals and rivers as time passed. Chapter 4 describes how, when some Mayo villages lost access to their river shores in the 1950s, they began to perform the San Juan ceremony in the canals themselves.

109. SAYF internal memo, November 5, 1942, AHA, Aprovechamientos Superficiales, Caja 1929, Expediente 29006.

110. SAYF internal memo, November 5, 1942, AHA.

111. Other factors—for example, a lack of funds to continue with construction, since this was wartime and supplies were scarce—may have influenced this decision. Government functionaries may have also been concerned that Mayo farmers could protest or rebel if they did not come to their defense.

112. The fact that many Yori farmers had migrated to the Fuerte valley within a generation or less speaks to this limited attachment to the land.

113. The percentage invested, not the total sum, was unprecedented. Under President Manuel Ávila Camacho, the CNI directed nineteen massive irrigation projects. Evans, "La angustia de La Angostura," 57.

2. Sweetness and Water Power

1. Rufino López to the Agrarian Department, April 8, 1956, AGA, División, Fusión y Permutas, Expediente 231.3/138, Legajo 2, Asunto Local, El Teroque, Municipio El Fuerte.

2. The term "individualist" is pejorative because it makes it sound as if these farmers only cared about their individual needs, when in fact their actions were often inspired by the well-being of the entire village. The ability of the SICAE officials to set the discourse by assigning the term "individualist" exhibited its power and highlights the obstacles Mayo nonmembers faced.

3. Rufino López to the Agrarian Department, April 8, 1956, AGA.

4. Other recent scholarship ties Indigenous autonomy to water access, such as Mendoza García, "El manantial La Taza de San Gabriel Chilac (Puebla)," 225–58.

5. Collectivists were cooperative members, and I use the terms interchangeably throughout this chapter.

6. A work that discusses other examples of this is Boyer, *Political Landscapes*.

7. Collectivist leaders knew that individualist complaints to state officials regarding land dispossession were stronger if the lands in dispute were being cultivated. As long as an ejidatario held onto ejidal lands, they still enjoyed such rights as voting in ejidal meetings.

8. Mayo villages became ejidos by this point, so I use the terms "village" and "ejido" interchangeably.

9. This affirms recent scholarship that argues that the Mexican federal government's authoritarianism in the mid-twentieth century depended on both negotiation and compromise with the ruled. Recent works on state formation in the mid-twentieth century include McCormick, *The Logic of Compromise*; Gillingham and Smith, *Dictablanda*.

10. This era in the Fuerte valley resembled the early twentieth century in Veracruz, which saw similar changes. Myrna Santiago describes how a shift to the oil economy in the Huasteca region caused the displacement of Indigenous people, the alteration of the natural landscape, and the formation of new social groups. Santiago, *The Ecology of Oil*.

11. While Article 27 of the 1917 Constitution states that both land and water will be redistributed, recent scholarship on the importance of peasant movements in postrevolution and postwar Mexican state formation has tended to overlook the importance of water. Recent scholarship includes Boyer, *Political Landscapes*; Padilla, *Rural Resistance in the Land of Zapata*; McCormick, *The Logic of Compromise*; Gillingham and Smith, *Dictablanda*. To be fair, some recent scholarship does express the importance of campesino hydraulic mobilization, such as Wolfe, *Watering the Revolution*; Vitz, *A City on a Lake*; Graham, "A Tale of Two Valleys," 31–80.

12. Eckstein, *El ejido colectivo*, 1.

13. Collectivists in the Fuerte valley had their own personal lots in addition to sharing fields where they produced sugarcane.

14. This chapter refers to the SICAE as both a collective and cooperative. Mexico was the first to practice this type of agriculture in the Western Hemisphere, and Israel was the only other country in the world that used this system as much as Mexico. Eckstein, *El ejido colectivo*, 1.

15. Knight, "Cardenismo," 90.

16. Among several works discussing Cárdenas's use of clientelism is Vaughan, *Cultural Politics in Revolution*.

17. Boyer and Wakild, "Social Landscaping in the Forests of Mexico," 185; Boyer, *A Land between Waters*, 11.

18. Development expertise was not yet the norm in the 1930s. It was mostly engineers who created ejidos, and they staffed the Agrarian Department, the Ejido Bank, the CNI, and other state organizations.

19. Boyer, *Becoming Campesinos*, 226.

20. Cárdenas did give cooperative members' chosen leaders at least partial control, yet the state heavily regulated operations. Eckstein, *El ejido colectivo*, 1.

21. Articles 139 and 148, 1934 Agrarian Code.

22. Romero-Ibarra, "La reforma agraria de Cárdenas," 107.

23. There was also a disconnect between state bureaucrats and peasants. Emily Wakild points out that starting in the Cárdenas era, the distance between those receiving state-based benefits and those administering them mirrored class distinctions and cultural differences the revolution had hoped to end. Wakild, *Revolutionary Parks*, 9–10.

24. Some works that focus on the collectives include Schobert, *Historia de una gesta obrero campesina*; Fallaw, *Cárdenas Compromised*; Glantz, *El ejido colectivo de Nueva Italia*; Gledhill, *Casi Nada*; Restrepo and Eckstein, *La agricultura colectiva en México*; Wolfe, *Watering the Revolution*; Bantjes, *As if Jesus Walked on Earth*; Banister, "Río Revuelto"; Boyer, *Political Landscapes*.

25. Cárdenas also believed in regulated capitalist development, with the state intervening to ensure more equitable distribution of wealth. His successors trended more toward unfettered capitalism.

26. Gladys McCormick also discusses the connection between rural authoritarianism and the shift to industrialization that started during the Cárdenas era. See McCormick, *The Logic of Compromise*. Recent scholarship on the subject argues that Cárdenas was much more of a capitalist reformer than a socialist.

27. Schobert, *Historia de una gesta obrero campesina*, 13.

28. Romero-Ibarra, "La reforma agraria de Cárdenas," 109.

29. USCOS owned the local telephone and electric companies and exerted its political influence. Romero-Ibarra, "La sociedad colectivo agrícola industrial," 4, 9, 12.

30. Schobert, *Historia de una gesta obrero campesina*, 71–75.

31. Most Mayo villages did not have valid land grants, receiving title for the first time under the Mexican government, whose functionaries provided more resources to one faction than another, creating privileged ejidatarios.

32. Romero-Ibarra, "La reforma agraria de Cárdenas," 116.

33. Romero-Ibarra, "La reforma agraria de Cárdenas," 117.

34. The Cárdenas regime created the bank in 1935. Schobert, *Historia de una gesta obrero campesina*, 3.

35. The total value, including the USCOS property, was three million pesos. The bank also lent another two and a half million pesos to the SICAE for new sugarcane farming equipment. Romero-Ibarra, "La reforma agraria de Cárdenas," 117.

36. Tensions between the two countries still ran high at this point despite FDR's Good Neighbor policy.

37. Mintz, *Sweetness and Power*, 47.

38. Several reports support these figures, including Delegate Luis Llanes to the Agrarian Department, November 13, 1934, AGA, Dotación, Expediente 23/1362, Legajo 8, Asunto Toca, Los Goros, Municipio Ahome; Alfonso Ruenes to Jesús Benitez of the Agrarian Department, November 21, 1954, AGA, Privación de Derechos Agrarios y Nuevas Adjudicaciones, Expediente 271.71/35, Legajo 2, Los Goros, Municipio Ahome.

39. Padilla, *Rural Resistance in the Land of Zapata*, 59.

40. Oral histories suggest that the majority of individualists preferred growing traditional subsistence crops. Yet the guaranteed wages and access to irrigation water given to collectivist sugarcane farmers would have been difficult for individualists to turn down. Individualists would have at least preferred a choice.

41. Although there is a dearth in the number of complaints collectivists leveled against the SICAE, the fact that some exist suggest that many grew frustrated with the collective. One example of this includes Los Goros Ejidal Commission to President Ruiz Cortines, June 28, 1953, AGN, Adolfo Ruiz Cortines, 521.7/17.

42. 1942 Mexican Census, Population of Municipalities in Sinaloa, 43.

43. Bernabé López, interview by James Mestaz, Los Mochis, Ahome, June 17, 2014.

44. Mayo ejidal leaders filling collectivist ranks could have also been fiesteros—those covering the costs of religious fiestas—as their economic devotion to Indigenous identity earned them respect in their villages. Yet Indigenous collectivists likely did not use their daily wage of six pesos to fund fiestas, as these events declined at a dramatic rate from the mid-1940s to late 1950s. Six pesos was significantly higher than the one to two pesos most laborers earned at that time. Charles Erasmus argues that nine fiestas disappeared in that time period. Erasmus, *Man Takes Control*, 281.

45. These terms of membership and leadership did not always turn out to be the case. For instance, most of the members of Los Goros's first ejidal committee in 1937—before the split between factions—were still individualist ejidal committee members in 1948, meaning they had not become collectivists. Acta de Elección, October 14, 1937, AGA, Ampliación, Expediente 25/11427, Legajo 8, Asunto Ejecución, Los Goros, Municipio Ahome; Ejidal Committee to Secretariat of Agriculture and Livestock, June 10, 1948, AGA, Dotación, Expediente 23/89, Legajo 1, Asunto Trabajos Técnicos, Los Goros, Municipio Ahome.

46. Bernabé López, interview by James Mestaz. Kinship networks existed in these Mayo villages and also played a role in separation between the two factions.

47. Lázaro Cárdenas to the Agrarian Department, January 11, 1939, Archivo General de la Nación (hereafter AGN), Lázaro Cárdenas, Expediente 404.1/1593. Cárdenas enacted Article 91 of the Agrarian Code to ensure that irrigation rights were included in the ejidal expropriation.

48. While gaining access to the water concessions of USCOS and other sugarcane properties gave the SICAE control over huge amounts of water from the Fuerte River, the 1943 water monopoly solidified this control.

49. August 11, 1943, AHA, Aguas Nacionales, Expediente 17668, Caja 1314.

50. U.S. sugarcane production and German beet sugar production declined slightly after 1943, while Mexico's sugarcane production increased steadily in the same time period. Banco de Mexico, *Industria, Tomo 1*, 364–66.

51. Eckstein, *El ejido colectivo en México*, 66.

52. Lorena Schobert specifically justified the water monopoly by arguing that Ávila Camacho had interest in the production of sugar and food in general, given the context of the war. Schobert, *Historia de una gesta obrero campesina*, 138.

53. Eckstein, *El ejido colectivo en México*, 65.

54. Tanalis Padilla discusses the unfair advantage the sugarcane industry held over ejidatarios in mid-twentieth century Morelos in *Rural Resistance in the Land of Zapata*.

55. Max Weber describes power as "the chance of a person or a group to enforce their own will even against the resistance of others involved." Weber, "The Distribution of Power within the Community," 137.

56. Tensions indeed existed, for instance, between farmers of the Colonized Lands of Los Mochis and the ejidatarios of these fifty-two ejidos, as the two sides had been fighting over land and water rights since the late nineteenth century.

57. The names of the fifty-two ejidos were not identified in the flyer. Leaflet created by several protest groups, n.d., AGN, Manuel Ávila Camacho, 404.2/310.

58. Ejidal Land Defense Committee to President Ávila Camacho, February 14, 1955, AGN, Manuel Ávila Camacho, 404.2/310.

59. Since this letter also did not specify which thirty-two ejidos were members of their group, it is impossible to know if any were affiliated with the SICAE or were part of the fifty-two ejidos that allegedly participated in the creation of the previous flyer.

60. Ejidal leaders to SAYF, October 11, 1943, AHA, Aguas Nacionales, Expediente 17668, Caja 1312.

61. The SICAE's enforcement of the river monopoly during selected times of the year helped Mayo collectivists, but there were many more Mayo individualists than collectivists.

62. Chapters 3 and 4 discuss the actions of "independent" Mayo farmers in more detail.

63. Act of census clearance, José Manuel Flores, Agrarian Department, March 16, 1945, AGA, Privación de Derechos Agrarios y Nuevas Adjudicaciones, Expediente 271.71/35.

64. Act of census clearance, José Manuel Flores, Agrarian Department, March 16, 1945, AGA.

65. It is unclear how General Cruz gained control of the pumping plant. After falling out of favor with former president Calles, he went into exile for six years but returned when his good friend Cárdenas assumed the presidency. Most likely Cárdenas granted him these lands and water rights in order to retain a trusted friend and ally. Cruz, *Roberto Cruz en la Revolución Mexicana*; Ynocente Montiel to Manuel Ávila Camacho, November 8, 1944, AGA, Dotación, Expediente 23/89, Legajo 3, Asunto Ejecución, Los Goros, Municipio Ahome.

66. Antonio Velásquez to Agrarian Department, January 5, 1945, AGA, Privación de Derechos Agrarios y Nuevas Adjudicaciones, Expediente 271.71/35, Legajo 1, Asunto Toca, Los Goros, Municipio El Fuerte.

67. Ynocente Montiel to Manuel Ávila Camacho, November 8, 1944, AGA.

68. We can infer that the Montiels did not sign. Antonio Velásquez to Agrarian Department, January 5, 1945, AGA.

69. It is likely the ejidal committee enticed individualists into voting for the confiscation by promising them access to irrigation water from the confiscated lands. All

documents referring to the 1944 meeting agree that the individualist sector passed this resolution by popular ejidal vote.

70. Collectivists sometimes annexed individualists' lands even if they were not fallow, but agricultural production at least justified individualist land claims.

71. Had the ejidal leaders confiscated this land, they would have by law offered Montiel other lands but not necessarily access to irrigation rights, which were absolutely pivotal.

72. Certificate of Agrarian Rights, April 14, 1947, AGA, Privación de Derechos Agrarios y Nuevas Adjudicaciones, Expediente 271.71/35, Legajo 1, Asunto Toca, Los Goros, Municipio El Fuerte.

73. Mayo people refer to each other as "Yoreme." Alejandro Inzunza, interview by James Mestaz, Los Goros, Municipio Ahome, Sinaloa, Mexico, February 14, 2014.

74. Such patterns were also reported by other Mayo individualists in ejidos such as Zapotillo.

75. San Miguel Zapotitlán continues to act as a regional Mayo ceremonial center. Carlos Moroyoqui, interview by James Mestaz, Los Goros Uno, Municipio Ahome, Sinaloa, Mexico, April 10, 2014.

76. Most of this land was confiscated from Streeter and Company. Agrarian Department to Director of Agrarian Rights, October 16, 1948, AGA, Privación de Derechos Agrarios y Nuevas Adjudicaciones, Expediente 271.71/10717, Legajo 7, Asunto Trabajos de Depuración Censal, El Teroque, Municipio El Fuerte.

77. It is difficult to say if the individualist assertion was correct, for the 1948 census omitted the exact number of hectares each side held. National Peasant Confederation to Agricultural Department, September 19, 1955, AGA, Dotación, Expediente 23/3684, Legajo 1, Asunto Ejecución, El Teroque, Municipio El Fuerte.

78. José López to Agrarian Department, November 5, 1954, AGA, Dotación, Expediente 23/3684, Legajo 1, Asunto Ejecución, El Teroque, Municipio El Fuerte.

79. Unlike with other rivers, it did not matter that El Teroque was downriver. Several collectivist communities were located downriver from El Teroque but still received access, unlike individualist communities upriver.

80. Rufino López to Ejidal Agrarian Organization, October 14, 1955, AGA, División, Fusión y Permutas, Expediente 231.3/138, Legajo 2, Asunto Local, El Teroque, Municipio El Fuerte.

81. The CRF was roughly modelled around the Tennessee Valley Authority. Chapter 5 discusses the CRF in more detail. See Barkin and King, *Regional Economic Development*.

82. While the CRF did take over control of the Fuerte River in 1955, the collectivists still maintained their water rights for a few more years.

83. Schobert, *Historia de una gesta obrero campesina*, 208.

84. Rufino López to Adolfo Ruiz Cortines, October 14, 1955, AGN, Adolfo Ruiz Cortines, Expediente 404.1/5375.

85. Buimena's parents were individualists. Felipe Buimena, interview by James Mestaz, El Teroque Viejo, El Fuerte, February 14, 2014.

86. Both Indigenous and Yori ejidatarios depended on river water to grow crops but, since Mayo farmers also used it to conduct traditional ceremonies such as that of San Juan, the communal use of the river was at the heart of their identity. Chapter 4 discusses San Juan in detail.

87. The term Yori usually referred to mestizos, but since El Teroque consisted entirely of Mayo ejidatarios, individualists were claiming their fellow Mayo had lost their Indigenous identity and became "Yoris." Request to activate the division of the ejido, November 8, 1958, AGA, Privación de Derechos Agrarios y Nuevas Adjudicaciones, Expediente 271.71/10717, Legajo 7, Asunto Trabajos de Depuración Censal, El Teroque, Municipio El Fuerte.

88. It is possible that this term "white" was also an indictment of the SICAE itself for not following through on its promises to provide proper resources to the collectivists and for the entire ejido.

89. The individualists had never grown sugarcane but were willing to try if it meant receiving irrigation water. Rufino López to Banco Nacional de Crédito Ejidal, August 31, 1955, AGA, Privación de Derechos Agrarios y Nuevas Adjudicaciones, Expediente 271.71/10717, Legajo 7, Asunto Trabajos de Depuración Censal, El Teroque, Municipio El Fuerte.

90. In the late 1950s the cost of planting and harvesting a hectare of sugarcane was around MX$1,400, compared to the cost to grow a hectare of maize, which was around MX$350. Economic Agricultural Study, March 12, 1958, AGA, División, Fusión y Permutas, Expediente 231.3/94, Legajo 1, Asunto Ejecución, Camajoa, Municipio El Fuerte.

91. Several collectivists also began to align with the CNC's rival, the Confederación de Trabajadores de México (Confederation of Mexican Workers), which supported the SICAE. The rivalry between the CNC and CTM in the Fuerte valley mirrored a nationwide political struggle between the two groups to win the hearts and minds of rural campesinos.

92. Several Indigenous groups found ways to align with the CNC in order to advance their political agendas and protect their cultural practices throughout the twentieth century. María Muñoz details how Indigenous activists in the late twentieth century expertly used the CNC's political power for their own benefit while still maintaining their Indigenous identity separate from the CNC's peasant identity. Muñoz, *Stand Up and Fight*.

93. Arturo Luna Lugo to Agrarian Department, September 19, 1955, AGA, Dotación, Expediente 23/3684, Legajo 1, Asunto Ejecución, El Teroque, Municipio El Fuerte.

94. Arturo Luna Lugo to the Agrarian Department, October 3, 1955, AGA, División, Fusión y Permutas, Expediente 231.3/138, Legajo 2, Asunto Local, El Teroque, Municipio El Fuerte.

95. As noted in the introduction, *milpa* refers to corn, bean, and squash subsistence crops.

96. Agrarian Department to Eliseo Galaviz Bernal, June 14, 1956, AGA, División, Fusión y Permutas, Expediente 231.3/138, Legajo 2, Asunto Local, El Teroque, Municipio El Fuerte.

97. The inability to arrange a deal with the CRF was just one example of collectivists and the SICAE continually preventing individualists from securing irrigation agreements with third parties.

98. Agreement between the ejidatarios of El Teroque, July 23, 1956, AGA, División, Fusión y Permutas, Expediente 231.3/138, Legajo 2, Asunto Local, El Teroque, Municipio El Fuerte.

99. September 21, 1938, AGA, Dotación, Expediente 23/990, Legajo 3, Asunto Toca, Huepaco, Municipio El Fuerte.

100. September 21, 1938, AGA.

101. Agrarian Department to the office of Agricultural Certificates, October 14, 1948, AGA, Privación de Derechos Agrarios y Nuevas Adjudicaciones, Expediente 271.71/7208, Legajo 1, Asunto Investigación de Usufructo Parcelario, Camajoa, Municipio El Fuerte.

102. Adolfo Orive Alba to President Miguel Alemán Valdés, September 17, 1947, AGN, Miguel Alemán Valdés, 508.1/250.

103. Schobert, *Historia de una gesta obrero campesina*, 182. Other than the mention of Camajoa's and El Teroque's concessions, there were very few documents that detailed how much water ejidos received from the SICAE Canal, bringing into question the cooperative's transparency. These documents must have existed because they were necessary for water management.

104. In 1950 collectivist sugarcane cutters accused the SICAE of fraud in the amount of thirty billion pesos for the illegal sale of water from its irrigation system. It would have been no surprise if the allegations of corruption against SICAE officials were true, as was the case with most state-backed agencies placed in charge of distributing valuable resources in Mexico. Schobert, *Historia de una gesta obrero campesina*, 193.

105. October 14, 1948, AGA, Privación de Derechos Agrarios y Nuevas Adjudicaciones, Expediente 271.71/7208, Legajo 1, Asunto Investigación de Usufructo Parcelario, Camajoa, Municipio El Fuerte.

106. Schobert, *Historia de una gesta obrero campesina*, 145.

107. Daniel Galaviz, interview by James Mestaz, Camajoa, Municip. El Fuerte, Sinaloa, Mexico, March 6, 2014.

108. Los Goros Ejidal Commission to President Ruiz Cortines, June 28, 1953, AGN.

109. June 2, 1955, AGA, Privación de Derechos Agrarios y Nuevas Adjudicaciones, Expediente 271.71/7208, Legajo 1, Asunto Investigación de Usufructo Parcelario, Camajoa, Municipio El Fuerte.

110. *La Palabra*, June 7 and 21, 1956, Culiacán, Sinaloa; Schobert, *Historia de una gesta obrero campesina*, 210.

111. Refugio Aquí to Agrarian Department, August 23, 1956, AGA, División, Fusión y Permutas, Expediente 231.3/152, Legajo 1, Asunto Ejecución, Camajoa, Municipio El Fuerte.

112. Aqui family to Agrarian Department, October 8, 1956, AGA, División, Fusión y Permutas, Expediente 231.3/152, Legajo 1, Asunto Ejecución, Camajoa, Municipio El Fuerte.

113. Engineer Leon Garduno Gautier to C. Augustin Cristerna Beltran of the Agrarian Department, May 21, 1957, AGA, División, Fusión y Permutas, Expediente 231.3/94, Legajo 1, Asunto Ejecución, Camajoa, Municipio El Fuerte.

114. Engineer José Luis Torres Espinosa to the Agrarian Department, March 10, 1958, AGA, División, Fusión y Permutas, Expediente 231.3/94, Legajo 1, Asunto Ejecución, Camajoa, Municipio El Fuerte.

115. Engineer José Luis Torres Espinosa to the Agrarian Department, March 10, 1958, AGA.

116. Chapter 5 discusses the Fuerte River Commission and its developmentalist tactics in detail.

117. Daniel Galaviz, interview by James Mestaz.

118. Pueblos America, accessed May 21, 2021, https://mexico.pueblosamerica.com /i/cinco-de-mayo-32/; https://mexico.pueblosamerica.com/i/teroque-viejo/; https:// mexico.pueblosamerica.com/i/oro-pinto-goros-uno/; https://mexico.pueblosamerica .com/i/goros-numero-dos/; https://mexico.pueblosamerica.com/i/camajoa/.

119. The epilogue to this book discusses this local pride and the maintenance of Mayo ceremonies.

120. This adaptive ability underscores the growing influence and power of state officials, especially those who controlled water. Schobert, *Historia de una gesta obrero campesina*, 208.

3. When the State Fails

1. Ejidatarios were members of the ejido. Julian Valenzuela, interview by James Mestaz, La Misión, Municip. El Fuerte, Sinaloa, Mexico, July 29, 2014.

2. Independent Mayo are those who are members of villages that were never affiliated with the SICAE.

3. This belief came from personal observation, but it also likely reflected outside theories. More discussion of this follows in a later section.

4. Julian Valenzuela, interview by James Mestaz.

5. Chapter 2 discusses individualist Mayo and their hydraulic social mobilization tactics (a popular movement to secure water rights).

6. A small number of Mayo farmers were also not members of ejidos, but with no known sources that detail their experiences, an analysis of this group falls beyond the scope of this book.

7. As mentioned previously, this book defines the postrevolutionary period as 1927–42, which differs from how other scholars have characterized it.

8. This appears to be the same Cecilio Román mentioned in chapter 2. Paulino Tapia to Department of Waters, May 13, 1943, AHA, Aguas Nacionales, Caja 1312, Expediente 17668.

9. The collectivists' power in Jahuara shows that huge incentives were attached to membership in a state-backed cooperative, one of which was self-defining as collectivists and referring to their adversaries as individualists when neither term was completely accurate.

10. Boyer, *Political Landscapes*, 106.

11. Chapter 2 describes how the Mexican state created the Ejidal Bank to extend credit and knowledge to ejidal farmers. Jose M. Racho memo to Department of Agrarian Affairs and Colonization, January 13, 1970, AGA, Dotación, Expediente 23/13154, Legajo 1, Asunto Toca, Jahuara, Municipio El Fuerte.

12. Ejidal Bank to SAYF, June 16, 1943, AHA, Aguas Nacionales, Caja 1312, Expediente 17668.

13. Heriberto Valdes Romero to Ejidal Bank, May 27, 1948, AHA, Aguas Nacionales, Caja 1314, Expediente 17668.

14. Agrarian Department to SAYF, August 24, 1945, AHA, Aguas Nacionales, Caja 1313, Expediente 17668.

15. The fact that loggers buried some of the canal shows that the non-loggers had already started constructing some of the proposed project. Guillermo Escamilla Leon to Humberto Alatorre, September 5, 1944, AHA, Aguas Nacionales, Caja 1312, Expediente 17668.

16. Groups as remote as Andean shamans also embraced modern technology, welcoming the incorporation of antibiotics into traditional healing practices because they held the attitude that they should aspire "to know more, not to know better." De La Cadena, *Earth Beings*, xxii.

17. Guillermo Escamilla Leon to Humberto Alatorre, September 5, 1944, AHA.

18. Timothy Mitchell explains how these conflicting logics were particularly apparent when it came to water governance in Egypt. Mitchell, *Rule of Experts*.

19. It is not perfectly clear as to why non-loggers did not report the loggers, but most likely they held out hope that they would gain access to this pump eventually.

20. Chapter 2 provides an in-depth analysis of the SICAE's control of the Fuerte River, which included a four-month official monopoly on irrigation water from the river.

21. Gustavo Aguilar, interview by James Mestaz, Los Goros, Municip. Ahome, Sinaloa, Mexico, April 4, 2014. Francisco Jacinto, interview by James Mestaz, Jahuara, Municip. El Fuerte, Sinaloa, Mexico, July 13, 2014.

22. Ejidal Bank to SAYF, January 13, 1945, AHA, Aguas Nacionales, Caja 1312, Expediente 17668.

23. Raymundo Enríquez Cruz to Alfonso Gonzales Gallardo, March 23, 1945, AHA, Aguas Nacionales, Caja 1312, Expediente 17668.

24. Agrarian Department to SAYF, August 24, 1945, AHA.

25. The blueprint did not include an image of the SICAE Canal, which ran parallel to the Fuerte River and would have been positioned between the river and the irrigation canal.

26. Raymond Pierotti used the term "traditional ecological knowledge" to describe Indigenous people's changing views of nature, suggesting that their ability to incorporate new observations and information has contributed to the longevity of Indigenous tradition by keeping it fresh and relevant. He also pointed out that Indigenous

people contend that the attitude and philosophy involved, rather than the technology, are what make a practice traditional. Pierotti, *Indigenous Knowledge, Ecology, and Evolutionary Biology*.

27. Champagne, "Rethinking Native Relations," 3–23.

28. Scholars championing this assimilationist approach in the postrevolutionary period included Carlos Basauri and Manuel Gamio, whose ideas gained more prominence in the postwar era.

29. While the Mexican state continually chose modernization over Indigenous knowledge, particularly in this time period, such decisions reflected a longstanding tradition that persists even today of native communities adapting to interaction with outsiders by invoking traditional practices and state functionaries undervaluing these local approaches. Romero Navarrete et al., "La autogestión del agua de riego en comunidades indígenas de México," 235–52.

30. Memo, head of SAYF, October 25, 1945, AHA, Aguas Nacionales, Caja 1313, Expediente 17668.

31. Mottier, "Calculating Pragmatism," 331–63.

32. Flor Escalante, interview by James Mestaz, Jahuara, Municip. El Fuerte, Sinaloa, Mexico, July 13, 2014.

33. As noted in previous chapters, Mayo people referred to non-Indigenous people as Yoris, and other Mayo people as Yoremes. In this context I use Yori and mestizo interchangeably.

34. Heriberto Valdez to Samuel Castro, June 9, 1948, AHA, Aguas Nacionales, Expediente 17668, Caja 1314.

35. Chapter 2 discusses this shift.

36. SAYF to Bartolo and Marcelino Valenzuela, July 22, 1942, AHA, Aguas Nacionales, Expediente 6140, Caja 555; Memo, Head of Department of Waters, October 16, 1944, AHA, Aguas Nacionales, Expediente 17668, Caja 1312.

37. SICAE to SAYF, May 7, 1947, AHA, Aprovechamientos Superficiales, Expediente 8176, Caja 553.

38. Several large landowners were able to maintain their properties despite the massive land reform program of the 1930s, and even added to their holdings in the 1940s and 1950s.

39. The fact that the Ejidal Bank lent money for this project was ironic, since ejidal farmers never had access to the structure.

40. "Será construido el canal de Cahuinahua," *El Debate*, May 19, 1948.

41. Alfonso Velázquez to Miguel Alemán Valdés, July 6, 1948, AGN, Expediente 508.1/18, Miguel Alemán Valdés; Alfonso Velázquez to Federal Treasury, July 6, 1948, AGN, Expediente 508.1/18, Miguel Alemán Valdés.

42. María Muñoz provides a detailed analysis of how Indigenous groups in postwar Mexico were forced to work both within and outside the system in order to attain their political goals. Muñoz, *Stand Up and Fight*.

43. Augusta de Yta to the Director of the Ministry of Hydraulic Resources, July 29, 1948, AHA, Aguas Nacionales, Expediente 27590, Caja 1961.

44. This protest was part of a long history of Latin American Indigenous mobilization centered around water. While such protests were common in the twentieth century, they have become even more frequent in the twenty-first century. Bolivia's "Water Wars" are an example of such recent mobilization. Assies, "David versus Goliath in Cochabamba," 14–36.

45. Librado Cuadros, interview by James Mestaz, La Palma, Municip. El Fuerte, Sinaloa, Mexico, February 29, 2014.

46. If other Mayo in both the Fuerte and Mayo valleys heard of these protests it could potentially create widespread Indigenous unrest and halt hydraulic development. Chapter 1 details Bachomo's revolt in the Fuerte valley from 1913 to 1916, as well as detailing the opposition of the widening of a canal in Los Goros because it would have meant the dispossession of both the canal and their plots.

47. Antonio Caballero to Miguel Alemán Valdés, April 12, 1948, AGN, Expediente 508.1/360, Miguel Alemán Valdés.

48. Lorenzo Robles to Miguel Alemán Valdés, March 16, 1949, AGN, Expediente 508.1/250, Miguel Alemán Valdés.

49. Lorenzo Robles to Miguel Alemán Valdés, March 16, 1949, AGN.

50. Fiege, *Irrigated Eden*, 41.

51. Some ejidatarios hoped for the government to engage in house cleaning operations, essentially removing the canal that caused such destruction.

52. Meliton Castro to President Miguel Alemán Valdés, March 22, 1949, AGN, Expediente 508.1/250, Miguel Alemán Valdés.

53. La Palma had received a dotación in 1937.

54. The petitions to fix the problem and/or provide financial compensation had ended in 1949, meaning that the state had likely at least fixed the flooding problem by then. Lining it with concrete, which is how it sits in its current state, would have prevented water from overflowing the sandy banks and flooding La Palma. Heriberto Valdes Romero to Antonio Rodríguez, January 26, 1951, AHA, Aguas Nacionales, Expediente 6151, Caja 555.

55. Antonio Rodríguez to Heriberto Valdes Romero, July 28, 1951, AHA, Aguas Nacionales, Expediente 6151, Caja 555.

56. Sabás Ynustrosa, interview by James Mestaz, La Mojonera, Municip. El Fuerte, Sinaloa, Mexico, August 2, 2014.

57. Sara Herrán Viuda de la Vega was one of the few women who owned property in the Fuerte valley in the mid-twentieth century. Mexican law allowed women to own property, but most did not have the economic means to do so. The land rights afforded to widowers in particular was one of the ways that women came to own property. Chapter 4 will expand on the de la Vega case and the connection between Mayo land loss and their lack of irrigation rights. Heriberto Valdes Romero Memo to Ministry of of Hydraulic Resources, June 29, 1951, AHA, Aguas Nacionales, Expediente 66858, Caja 4830.

58. Roberto Escalante, interview by James Mestaz, La Palma, Municip. El Fuerte, Sinaloa, Mexico, February 29, 2014.

59. Juan Valenzuela, interview by James Mestaz, Camajoa, Municip. El Fuerte, Sinaloa, Mexico, July 13, 2014.

60. Chapter 2 details a similar process in which individualists cleared their lots in response to the SICAE's expansion tactics.

61. Sheil et al., "How Forests Attract Rain," 341–47.

62. Some of these elders include Jorge Robles and Alejandro Inzunza. Jorge Robles interview by James Mestaz, San Miguel, Municip. El Fuerte, Sinaloa, Mexico, May 25, 2014; and Alejandro Inzunza, interview by James Mestaz, Los Goros, Municip. Ahome, Sinaloa, Mexico, February 14, 2014.

63. Matthews, *Instituting Nature*, 101.

64. Comisión del Río Fuerte, *Datos hidrométricos*, 17.

65. Comisión del Río Fuerte, *Datos hidrométricos*, 17; Instituto Nacional Estadística y Geografía, *Anuario Estadístico de Sinaloa*. 1930 and 1952 ranged between the lowest annual rainfall of 377 millimeters (1940 being the driest year), and 906 millimeters (1943 being the wettest year). The most recent dry year was in 2005, which measured 306 millimeters. The wettest recent year was in 2004, which measured 951 millimeters. July and August remained the months with the most precipitation by far, while January through May recorded very limited rainfall in every year.

66. One reason they would have remembered this prior era as bountiful is because many Mayo villages had access to pumps and canals.

67. Wolfe, *Watering the Revolution*, 182.

68. Peppler, "'Old Indian Ways' of Predicting the Weather," 200–209.

69. Mauricio Mejías, interview by James Mestaz, Huepaco, Municip. El Fuerte, Sinaloa, Mexico, July 21, 2014.

70. Jorge Robles, interview by James Mestaz, San Miguel, Municip. El Fuerte, Sinaloa, Mexico, May 25, 2014.

71. Other Latin American Indigenous groups in both ancient and modern eras also used methods to predict rain and changes to the weather. Rivero-Romero et al., "Traditional Climate Knowledge," 1–11; Orlove et al., "Ethnoclimatology in the Andes," 428–35.

72. Peppler, "Old Indian Ways," 203.

73. Indigenous farmers throughout Mexico, such as the Chontal Maya of Tabasco, continue to depend on their observations of nature to give them an advantage in productive activities involving water such as agriculture, fishing, and flood management. Martínez Ruiz, "Los verdaderos dueños del agua y el monte," 139.

74. Several Indigenous Mexican groups, such as Nahua of Guerrero, Mixe of Oaxaca, and Maya of several southern states, continue to perform similar rain requesting ceremonies. Gálvez and Embriz Osorio, "Los pueblos indígenas," 17. A specific example is the Hikuri Neixa ceremony the Wixaritari, or Huichol, people enact, which marks the start of the rainy season. Neurath, "El agua en la cosmovisión wixarika," 57.

75. Most, and some argue all, Indigenous groups in Mexico practice syncretic rituals. Nahua people of Guerrero for instance practice a syncretic rain requesting

ceremony named Santa Cruz, invoking both Catholic saints and Indigenous dieties. Martínez Ruiz, "Zitlala," 83–100.

76. Yoremes include Yaquis of the Yaqui valley and Mayo people of both the Mayo and Fuerte valleys. This is one example among many of the Indigenous people of Mexico appropriating aspects of Catholicism. Erasmus, *Man Takes Control*, 270.

77. Water is an important element in the practice of traditional religion, as the tenachi conducts certain practices with water, such as leading the San Juan ceremony. Loreto Coronado, interview by James Mestaz, Los Mochis, Municip. Ahome, Sinaloa, Mexico, August 7, 2014.

78. Charles Erasmus describes the role of the tenachi, or the *maestro* as he refers to these holy men, in great detail. See Erasmus, *Man Takes Control*.

79. Neighbors to the Mayo, the Rarámuri or Tarahumara, located mostly in Chihuahua, carry out a similar ritual named the Yúmari. Similar to the Mayo tradition, the Rarámuri usually perform this dance in the driest months of the year, April and May. Martínez, "Aguas que nacen en el cielo y en la tierra," 29–44.

80. Several Mayo elders consider this river god the same entity as "Old Water Woman." Horacio Pitahaya, interview by James Mestaz, Boca de Arroyo, Municip. El Fuerte, Sinaloa, Mexico, July 29, 2014.

81. It is important to note here that the Yuco Conti ceremony is indeed another example of hydraulic social mobilization. Yet because Mayo villagers used strategies to protect their Indigenous culture, it falls under the more specific category of hydraulic cultural mobilization. In such instances where cultural aspects asserted themselves, Mayo activists were fundamentally addressing "social" needs. Hence cultural leverage was yet another aspect of hydraulic social mobilization.

82. Narciso Bachomo and Carlos Salcedo, interview by James Mestaz, Camajoa, Municip. El Fuerte, Sinaloa, Mexico, March 21, 2014.

83. Uriarte, *Sinaloa yoreme*, 44.

84. Laura Apodaca, interview by James Mestaz, La Misión, Municip. El Fuerte, Sinaloa, Mexico, July 29, 2014.

85. Chapter 2 gives an in-depth analysis of El Teroque's hydraulic social mobilization strategies in the 1950s.

4. The Inward Turn

1. As stated throughout the book, the terms "mestizo" and "Yori" are used interchangeably and refer to non-Mayo individuals.

2. Mauricio Mejías, interview by James Mestaz, Huepaco, Municip. El Fuerte, Sinaloa, Mexico, July 21, 2014.

3. As mentioned in chapter 3, independent ejidatarios are those whose ejido remained independent from the SICAE sugarcane cooperative. The actions of individualists and collectivists involved in the cooperative are covered extensively in chapter 2.

4. Carlos, "Enclavement Processes, State Policies, and Cultural Identity," 33.

5. Sanderson, *The Transformation of Mexican Agriculture*, 155.

6. Ironically the SICAE was oppressive to nonaffiliated farmers but generally acted as a check upon aggressive state policies and private practices.

7. Chapter 5 discusses the CRF in more detail and the epilogue documents the INI's involvement in the Fuerte valley in the 1990s.

8. Messerli et al., "From Nature Dominated to Human Dominated," 459–79. Endfield, *Climate and Society in Colonial Mexico*, 5.

9. Cáhitas were the predecessors to Mayo culture. Messerli et al., "From Nature Dominated to Human Dominated."

10. Messerli et al., "From Nature Dominated to Human Dominated," discusses this concept of a buffer.

11. Messerli et al., "From Nature Dominated to Human Dominated."

12. Roberto Escalante, interview by James Mestaz, La Palma, Municip. El Fuerte, Sinaloa, Mexico, February 29, 2014.

13. Mateo Quintero, interview by James Mestaz, Tehueco, Municip. El Fuerte, Sinaloa, Mexico, July 27, 2014.

14. Figueroa, *Por la tierra y por los santos*, 120.

15. In neighboring Sonora, the amount of irrigated land nearly doubled between 1950 and 1970. Nabhan and Holdsworth, *State of the Sonoran Desert Biome*, 34; Evans, "La angustia de La Angostura," 72.

16. Secretariat of Industry and Commerce, *1960 Ejidal Census*, Mexican Agricultural, Livestock.

17. Secretariat of Industry and Commerce, *1960 Ejidal Census*, Mexican Agricultural, Livestock.

18. Roberto Escalante, interview by James Mestaz.

19. June 17, 1952, AHA, Aprovechamientos Superficiales, Expediente 65544, Caja 4782.

20. March 14, 1952, AHA, Aprovechamientos Superficiales, Expediente 67381, Caja 4852.

21. While some ejidatarios complained that their lands had been annexed illegally, the state began to side with non-ejidatarios more and more. Engineer Heriberto Valdez Romero Memo to CRF, October 23, 1951, AHA, Aprovechamientos Superficiales, Expediente 66858, Caja 4830; Apolonio Aqui to CRF, December 18, 1952, AHA, Aprovechamientos Superficiales, Expediente 64401, Caja 4742.

22. Agrarian Department Memorandum, November 5, 1936, AGA, Dotación, Expediente 23/3641, Legajo 4, Asunto Ejecución, La Palma, Municipio El Fuerte.

23. Engineer Heriberto Valdez Romero Memo to CRF, October 23, 1951, AHA.

24. Numerous petitions Sara Herran Viuda de la Vega filed in the 1940s exhibit her resolve in regaining some of her lands, an example of which is Juan B. Rojo in representation of Sara Herran Viuda de la Vega to the Agrarian Department, May 10, 1944, AGA, Dotación, Expediente 23/3641, Legajo 4, Asunto Ejecución, La Palma, Municipio El Fuerte.

25. Engineer Heriberto Valdez Romero Memo to CRF, October 23, 1951, AHA.

26. It is possible that some of these original Indigenous ejidatarios and their descendants lost touch with ancient traditions over time and stopped speaking the language or identifying as Mayo. Consequently, others ceased from recognizing them as Indigenous. But Indigenous elders suggest that La Palma's changing demographics within the last sixty years are best explained by legal and economic forces rather than a decline in cultural practices and weakened Mayo identity. Roberto Escalante, interview by James Mestaz; Librado Cuadros, interview by James Mestaz, La Palma, Municip. El Fuerte, Sinaloa, Mexico, February 29, 2014.

27. The engineer actually claimed the majority of inhabitants were "Mayan." July 13, 1936, AGA, Dotación, Expediente 23/3641, Legajo 4, Asunto Ejecución, La Palma, Municipio El Fuerte.

28. The website PueblosAmerica.com asserts that 55 percent of the population of La Palma is Indigenous, yet Mayo expert Loreto Coronado asserts that the university he works for Universidad Autónoma Indígena de México considers Indigenous residents as the minority in this ejido. Additionally, Mayo elders Roberto Escalante and Librado Cuadros both contend that Yoris now constitute the majority in La Palma, and Mayo people are the minority. Pueblos America, accessed May 21, 2021, https://mexico.pueblosamerica.com/i/la-palma-202/.

29. Among a number of such denials in the postrevolutionary and postwar period include Office of the General Agency to the Ejidal Committee of Guayabo, November 13, 1941, AHA, Aprovechamientos Superficiales, Expediente 2611, Caja 4749.

30. Jorge Robles, interview by James Mestaz, San Miguel, Municip. El Fuerte, Sinaloa, Mexico, May 25, 2014.

31. Several documents show the state's refusal to grant riverbank lands to ejidatarios, for example: J. J. Islas Leon to Victor Ontiveros, February 12, 1940, AHA, Aprovechamientos Superficiales, Expediente 64579, Caja 4749.

32. Article 27, Constitution of Mexico 1917.

33. Laura Apodaca, interview by James Mestaz, La Misión, Municip. El Fuerte, Sinaloa, Mexico, July 29, 2014.

34. Crumrine, "Mechanisms of Enclavement Maintenance and Sociocultural Blocking of Modernization," 49, 143.

35. Librado Cuadros, interview by James Mestaz.

36. In 1965 wage earners made up 46.1 percent of the labor force in northwest Mexico, compared to just 24.1 percent nationally. Sanderson, *The Transformation of Mexican Agriculture*, 160, Secretariat of Agriculture and Cattle Raising and Bank of Mexico, S.A. Projections of Supply and Demand for Agricultural Products in Mexico to 1970 and 1975.

37. Bantjes, *As if Jesus Walked on Earth*, 93.

38. Escalante omitted the name of the hydraulic project he worked on. However, by the years and location indicated, he likely helped build the Álvaro Obregón Dam on the Yaqui River, which was started in 1947 and completed in 1952. Roberto Escalante, interview by James Mestaz.

39. Sabás Ynustrosa, interview by James Mestaz, La Mojonera, Municip. El Fuerte, Sinaloa, Mexico, August 2, 2014.

40. Indigenous laborers of the Fuerte valley, on the other hand, were generally contracted by private entities who did share some similarities with the tyrants described by Wittfogel but fell under a whole different economic system and used alternative tactics of coercion. Wittfogel, *Oriental Despotism*.

41. Among several examples of scholars refining Wittfogel's ideas is Jeffrey Banister, who questions his notions of materialism, power, and the social dynamics of water. Banister, "Are You Wittfogel or against Him?" 205–14.

42. Worster, *Rivers of Empire*, 40; Several scholars have also critiqued and/or built on Worster's ideas, such as Pisani, *Water, Land, and Law in the West*.

43. Mateo Quintero, interview by James Mestaz.

44. Gill, *La conquista*, 92. Some works detailing the history of the Fuerte valley, such as Gill's, give a very one-sided view without accounting for the dispossession of Mayo properties.

45. Banister, "Río Revuelto," 36.

46. O'Connor, *Descendants of Totoliguoqui*, 38.

47. Guss, "The Selling of San Juan," 452.

48. Like the first Catholics to celebrate San Juan, each used the festival to protect their own traditions. The result was a mélange of San Juan celebrations throughout the new world, such as an Indigenous drinking festival in Ecuador focusing on reciprocity or an Afro-Venezuelan equivalent where participants use African drumming and dancing to question their marginalization within that country. Guss, "The Selling of San Juan," 452–73; Barlett, "Reciprocity and the San Juan Fiesta," 116–30.

49. Chapter 1 discusses this symbiotic relationship in more detail. Narciso Bachomo and Carlos Salcedo, interview by James Mestaz, Camajoa, Municip. El Fuerte, Sinaloa, Mexico, March 21, 2014.

50. Oralia Flores, interview by James Mestaz, Pochotal, Municipio El Fuerte, March 25, 2014.

51. The Otomi of the central Mexican Plateau also recognize both the Catholic and Indigenous roots of San Juan. At first glance it appears that the Otomi understand their gods' role in water as a more gender reciprocal act, as San Juan is a turbulent water god, but only on June 24. The feminine version, San Juanita, is in charge of water for the rest of the year. Yet while Mayo people do not recognize San Juanita, they do believe, as mentioned in chapter 1, that their waterways are protected by Old Water Woman or Bawahamjuna. Lazcarro Salgado, "Las venas del cerro," 99.

52. Beals, *The Contemporary Culture*, 144.

53. In San Miguel Zapotitlán today, the ceremony starts at the town square on the evening of June 23. Musicians and dancers enact the matachin and deer dances the entire night. The next morning, participants start a procession to the river, continuing the music and dance. The procession stops at intersections to bless the four directions, performers offer a few songs at the Indigenous church, and then they proceed to the river. Many Yoremes enter the river carrying statues of Jesus Christ and

San Juan, dipping them in the water and offering prayers in Spanish and the Mayo language that ask for water in the coming year and thank the river for its blessings. I viewed these San Juan rituals in San Miguel in June 2019, and other informants such as Narciso Bachomo and Carlos Salcedo verified that similar practices take place in such ceremonial centers as Mochicahui.

54. The first anthropological work that ties this Christian ritual with precontact rituals is Beals, *The Contemporary Culture*, 66.

55. The immense scholarship on the Mayo people of Sonora has shed further light onto the cultural traditions of Sinaloan Mayo people.

56. The river could inflict punishment by flooding those who did not pay it homage. Crumrine, *The Mayo Indians of Sonora*, 116.

57. Crumrine, *The Mayo Indians of Sonora*, 27.

58. Other Indigenous groups of Mexico, such as the Nahuas of Chicontepec, Veracruz, recognize the link between this Catholic saint, San Juan, and the importance of water in their cultural practices. These Nahua people also believe that water has healing properties, as evident through such ceremonies as achihualotl and moaltiliztli. Gómez Martínez, "El agua en la cosmovisión de los nahuas de Chicontepec," 105.

59. Such Mayo participants as Carla Bacosegua, Narciso Bachomo, and Laura Apodaca attest to this universal participation, although they also point out that each village today practices the ceremony in different ways.

60. Oral interviews of Carla Bacosegua, Narciso Bachomo, and Laura Apodaca.

61. The Mayo people continue to unwittingly repeat a longstanding anti-Semitic trope created by a Medieval Catholic Church and used to persecute millions of innocent Jewish people for centuries. Carla Bacosegua, interview by James Mestaz, La Florida, Municip. Ahome, Sinaloa, Mexico, March 14, 2014.

62. Laura Apodaca, interview by James Mestaz.

63. Felicitas Mejía, interview by James Mestaz, Vinaterrias, Municip. El Fuerte, Sinaloa, Mexico, July 17, 2014.

64. Horacio Pitahaya, interview by James Mestaz, Boca de Arroyo, Municip. El Fuerte, Sinaloa, Mexico, July 29, 2014.

65. Indigenous elders such as Laura Apodaca recalled times when she was a young girl, in which several Mayo people owned canoes and visited each other by navigating up and down the Fuerte River.

66. Arturo Escobar discusses in depth the importance of rivers as territory in Colombia. Escobar, *Territories of Difference*, 146.

67. Mauricio Mejías, interview by James Mestaz.

68. These actions could be construed as cultural genocide.

69. Ronaldo Baisegua, interview by James Mestaz, San Miguel, Municip. Ahome, Sinaloa, Mexico, June 24, 2018.

70. Narciso Bachomo and Carlos Salcedo, interview by James Mestaz.

71. Librado Cuadros, interview by James Mestaz.

72. Oralia Flores, interview by James Mestaz.

73. In addition to Erasmus's study, N. Ross Crumrine referred to Bacosegua as Damian Bohoroqui. Crumrine, *The Mayo Indians of Sonora*; Erasmus, *Contemporary Change*.

74. Carla Bacosegua, interview by James Mestaz.

75. Erasmus, *Contemporary Change*; Crumrine, *The Mayo Indians of Sonora*. Both Crumrine and Erasmus confirm that Mayo natives of Sonora and Sinaloa believed Bacosegua (or Bohoroqui) healed their brethren.

76. Cave, *Prophets of the Great Spirit*, 2.

77. Other millenarian movements include that of Jack Wilson (Wavoka), a member of the Paiute tribe, which came to be known as the Ghost Dance across the American West and Great Plains in the late nineteenth century, as well as several Mayo millenarian movements in the late nineteenth and twentieth centuries. The most recent before this event occurred in the late 1930s. Rahal, "The Ghost Dance as a Millenarian Phenomenon," 171–81. Bantjes, *As if Jesus Walked on Earth*, 33–34.

78. Crumrine, *The Mayo Indians of Sonora*, 31, 142.

79. Harvey, *The New Imperialism*.

80. Erasmus, *Contemporary Change in Traditional Societies*.

81. Banister, "Río Revuelto," 243.

82. The theft of Indigenous lands was a common theme in northwestern Mexico more broadly, especially in the Yaqui valley where the Yaqui people had fought off outsiders from conquest into the twentieth century. Hu-Dehart, *Yaqui Resistance and Survival*; Banister, "Patria Fugáz."

83. Jeffrey Banister points out that Mayo veterans after the revolution in particular demanded the restitution of their pueblos, lands, and waters, yet Mayo people generally ended up with small plots and in less rare cases in the twentieth century received ejidos consisting of portions of these pueblos, lands, and waters. Banister, "Patria Fugáz," 116, 133; Banister, "Río Revuelto."

84. Chapter 1 details Los Goros's land rights. Official property records found in such locations as the General Agrarian Archive show few records of Mayo villages actually owning plots of private property.

85. While the Mayo population of Sonora doubled from the mid-1930s to mid-1950s, the amount of land they held remained stagnant. Approximately 5,000 ejidatarios resided in the Mayo River valley by 1955, but only 2,700 private property holders controlled the majority of harvestable acreage and irrigation resources. Crumrine, *The Mayo Indians of Sonora*, 143.

86. Chapter 1 provides more details on the link between irrigation rights and ejidatarios during the 1930s and early 1940s. Environmental historian Mikael Wolfe points out that other peasant groups—such as those in the Laguna region—found value in hydraulic infrastructure in the postrevolutionary period and used it to liberate themselves from existing power structures. Wolfe, *Watering the Revolution*, 60.

87. Jeffrey Banister relates that such uses became so prevalent within the Mayo valley that landowners and government officials (who sometimes were one in the same) lodged several complaints against Mayo communities. Banister, "Patria Fugáz."

88. Manuel Galindo, interview by James Mestaz, La Bajada, Municip. El Fuerte, Sinaloa, Mexico, April 11, 2014.

89. Bacosegua is likely referring to the fact that the Mayo River has a smaller hydraulic flow than the Fuerte River. Carla Bacosegua, interview by James Mestaz.

90. Francisco Jacinto, interview by James Mestaz, Jahuara, Municip. El Fuerte, Sinaloa, Mexico, July 13, 2014.

91. Bantjes, *As if Jesus Walked on Earth*, 33–34.

92. Erasmus refers to this agency as the Office of Water Resources, when he likely means the SRH.

93. Erasmus, *Contemporary Change*, 286.

94. Some Mayo elders such as Carla Bacosegua and Manuel Galindo corroborate these findings, even claiming that Mayo farmers supporting the use of irrigation infrastructure indeed spread these rumors. Carla Bacosegua, interview by James Mestaz; Manuel Galindo, interview by James Mestaz.

95. Carla Bacosegua, interview by James Mestaz.

96. Because the SICAE was defunct by the late 1950s, independent, collectivist, and individualist Mayo people began to face increasingly similar negative circumstances.

5. From Our River to Theirs

Epigraph: Carla Bacosegua, interview by James Mestaz, La Florida, Municip. Ahome, Sinaloa, Mexico, March 14, 2014.

1. Rudolfo Echamea, interview by James Mestaz, Borabampo, Municip. El Fuerte, Sinaloa, Mexico, June 23, 2019.

2. Aztec-influenced artifacts found by archaeologists, such as petroglyphs and pottery, and language similarities are still unexplained. Yet there are far more differences between the ancient Mexica and Cáhita cultures, and Mayo people do not recognize Tlaloc as their own God. Nakayama, *Sinaloa*; Quintero, *Historia integral*.

3. Torre C. Olsson provides a thorough analysis of the communication between U.S. and Mexican state functionaries and in particular of how Mexican politicians such as Alemán integrated the Tennessee Valley Authority's framework into that of their own development plans. Olsson, *Agrarian Crossings*.

4. Ekbladh, "Mr. TVA," 335–74.

5. Presidential Declaration, December 10, 1946, AGN, Miguel Alemán Valdés, 508.1/18.

6. Barkin and King, *Regional Economic Development*, 110.

7. This change represented a national trend in which the Mexican state moved away from supporting collectives in favor of development initiatives favoring large-scale agricultural operations.

8. Carlos, *Politics and Development in Rural Mexico*, 21.

9. Barkin and King, *Regional Economic Development*, 93.

10. Secretaria de Agricultura y Recursos Hidraulicos, *Memoria de la comision del río Fuerte*, 76.

11. Mauricio Mejías, interview by James Mestaz, Huepaco, Municip. El Fuerte, Sinaloa, Mexico, July 21, 2014.

12. The demographics of the ejidos of the Fuerte valley have changed over the decades, usually pointing to a decline in Indigenous populations. For Huepaco the percentage of Indigenous inhabitants declined from 47 percent to 27 percent from 2010 to 2020, and elders such as Mauricio Mejias argue that there has been an even sharper decline since the 1960s. Pueblos America, accessed May 21, 2021, https://en.mexico .pueblosamerica.com/i/huepaco-2/; Mauricio Mejías, interview by James Mestaz.

13. Carlos, *Politics and Development*, 19.

14. Of course, as discussed in chapter 2, the SICAE did have their hands in deciding the fate of irrigation resources in the 1940s and looked out for the needs of their own members.

15. Barkin and King, *Regional Economic Development*, 113.

16. Alejandro Inzunza, interview by James Mestaz, Los Goros, Municip. Ahome, Sinaloa, Mexico, February, 14, 2014.

17. Records from the Ministry of Water Management confirm that Los Goros and some other mixed ejidos still had access to water from the Camayeca aqueduct in 1949. If some of the ejidatarios of Los Goros were able to maintain access to this aqueduct by the mid-1950s, as Inzunza confirms, this explains how they simply just bought the water from the CRF without having to apply for a new concession. Engineer Juan Guerrero Alcolcer to Engineer Heriberto Valdez Romero of the Ministry of Water Management, March 28, 1949, AHA, Aguas Nacionales, Expediente 17668, Caja 1314.

18. Carlos, *Politics and Development*, 13, 18.

19. Felicitas Mejía, interview by James Mestaz, Vinaterrias, Municip. El Fuerte, Sinaloa, Mexico, July 17, 2014.

20. The example provided by Mauricio Mejías, in describing benefits some Mayo ejidatarios received in ejidos such as Constancia and Charay reflects this point.

21. 1956, AHA, Consultivo Técnico, Expediente 6799, Caja 702.

22. The pair oversaw the construction of the Conchos project. Aboites, "The Transnational dimensions," 75. Weiss also appears prominently in other recent scholarship on Mexican water governance and construction, such as Wolfe, *Watering the Revolution*.

23. Mikael Wolfe discusses in great depth how Mexican hydraulic engineers or *técnicos* negotiated technology and the physical landscape. Wolfe, *Watering the Revolution*.

24. An example of such a report includes the following language: "We have resting on the fast dipping surface of the formation strongly folded sericitic slates and therefore by itself propensed to slidings even in sound state a cover of detritus material of the same slates." Report on the Construction of the Hidalgo Dam, March 20, 1947, AHA, Consultivo Técnico, Expediente 7237, Caja 751.

25. CRF Pamphlet, 1956, AHA, Consultivo Técnico, Expediente 6799, Caja 702.

26. Evans, "La angustia de La Angostura," 64–66, 69–70.

27. The number of ejidatarios and small property owners affected by the dam's construction were agreed upon by various state agencies including the CRF and the committee of farmers. Committee of Ejidatarios and Small Property Farmers Affected by the Vessel of the Miguel Hidalgo Dam to the Secretary of the President of Mexico, January 31, 1955, AGN, Adolfo Ruiz Cortines, 508.1/207.

28. A chart showing the amounts of land affected by the dam's construction indicate that there was a lot of crossover between those designated as ejidatarios and small property owners, but there were some small property owners who were not ejidatarios. Committee of Ejidatarios and Small Property Farmers to the Secretary of the President of Mexico, January 31, 1955, AGN, Adolfo Ruiz Cortines, 508.1/207.

29. Guadalupe Espinoza Sauceda, "Los yoremes mayo de Choix." *Río Doce*, May 15, 2018.

30. Since the 1940s dams have displaced several Indigenous groups in Mexico, including Mazatecs, Chinantecs, Tzotziles, Tzetzales, Zoques, Pames, and Otomíes. Most Indigenous people's success in defending their territory against dam construction has come in recent years, such as the Nahuas of Guerrero, whose political mobilization prevented the construction of the San Juan Tetelcingo hydroelectric dam. Gálvez and Embriz Osorio, "Los pueblos indígenas," 20, 21.

31. Schwartz, "Displacement, Development, and the Creation of a Modern Indígena," 222–43.

32. It took until 1996 for the INI to acknowledge the cultural rights of Indigenous people in respect to the land and river in the Fuerte valley. This came after the Mayo people of the Huites valley, who protested the construction of the Huites Dam, organized a conference of Mexican Indigenous people who had been negatively affected by dams. López et al., *Los mayos de huites desplazados por la presa*.

33. Most of the details of the land disbursement actually came out two decades later. Engineer Jesús García Santacruz, Ministry of Agriculture and Hydraulic Resources to Angel Sandoval Romero, Chamber of Deputies, November 21, 1983, AHA Infraestructura Hidraulica, Expediente 1969, Caja 96.

34. Presidents of the executive ejidal committees of Jahuara and Tehueco to President Adolfo Ruiz Cortines, March 28, 1957, AGN, Adolfo Ruiz Cortines, 508.1/207.

35. Jorge Robles, interview by James Mestaz, San Miguel, Municip. El Fuerte, Sinaloa, Mexico, May 25, 2014.

36. Gustavo Aguilar, interview by James Mestaz, Los Goros, Municip. Ahome, Sinaloa, Mexico, April 4, 2014.

37. Despite the danger of flooding, some Mayo farmers continued to ask God for precipitation through their performance of religious rituals such as the Yuco Conti, described in chapter 4. The explanation for this is relatively simple: rain water in the valley is only partially responsible for causing floods. The larger cause of overflowed banks is the heavy precipitation in the Sierra Madre Mountains of Chihuahua, where the river begins. Farmers cut off from irrigation still needed rain to see their crops harvested. After the building of the Hidalgo Dam, the villages that continued to pay dancers, musicians, and holy men to conduct such rituals were those

less negatively affected by flooding because they were located either in the lower river area or further away from the banks of the river.

38. Oralia Flores, interview by James Mestaz, Pochotal, Municipio El Fuerte, March 25, 2014.

39. Within Indigenous cosmogony, water has the power to both create life and take it away. Other Mexican Indigenous groups embraced this duality, such as the Nahuas of Chicontepec, Veracruz, who believed that water's ambivalent behavior allowed it to fertilize, heal, and vivify while at other times causing disease, death, and disaster. Gómez Martínez, "El agua en la cosmovisión," 102.

40. Chapter 3 discusses a similar problem with a canal's faulty construction in the 1940s, highlighting how such issues persisted into the 1960s. Carla Bacosegua, interview by James Mestaz.

41. Carla Bacosegua, interview by James Mestaz.

42. Mauricio Mejías, interview by James Mestaz.

43. The word "Catebamchichahoa" comes from the Mayo language. Narciso Bachomo and Carlos Salcedo, interview by James Mestaz, Camajoa, Municip. El Fuerte, Sinaloa, Mexico, March 21, 2014.

44. Francisco Jacinto, interview by James Mestaz, Jahuara, Municip. El Fuerte, Sinaloa, Mexico, July 13, 2014.

45. This toxicity is why (as discussed in chapter 4) large numbers of Mayo people began to refuse to bathe in the river during the San Juan ritual.

46. The one major difference with this process is that U.S. cities treat their water by adding fluoride, while Los Mochis does not.

47. Japama, "Proceso de potabilización," video, 6:45, 2011.

48. Not all people in Los Mochis drink water from the tap—many prefer bottled water.

49. José Infante, interview by James Mestaz, Los Mochis, Municip. Ahome, Sinaloa, Mexico, March 9, 2014.

50. Another recent issue is that this also invited extra waste from the plastic bottles, which has become more of a problem in some Mayo villages than others.

51. "Gestiones para llevar el agua a Capomos" El Debate, October 6, 1963.

52. Francisco Jacinto, interview by James Mestaz.

53. Fermín Mopay, interview by James Mestaz, Camayeca, Municip. Ahome, Sinaloa, Mexico, February 27, 2014.

54. Lack of water treatment has caused diseases in other Indigenous groups throughout Mexico, such as gastrointestinal infections among Pimas, Yaquis, Tepehuanes, and Mixes, amebiasis and ascariasis among Purépechas, as well as trachoma among Kikapús, Zotziles, and Mixtecs. Gálvez and Embriz Osorio, "Los pueblos indígenas," 21.

55. Piped, untreated water has been common throughout rural Mexico since the mid-twentieth century and still continues to be a major health issue in some communities. Only recently have changes addressed this problem. Silva Rodríguez de San Miguel, "Rural Water Supply in Mexico," 129.

56. Rudolfo Echamea, interview by James Mestaz, Borabampo, Municip. El Fuerte, Sinaloa, Mexico, July 23, 2014.

57. Such spaces for female water gatherers helps explain reciprocal relations in Indigenous communities. Gálvez and Embriz Osorio, "Los pueblos indígenas," 17. While the near disappearance of water gathering roles filled by Mayo women may have led to cultural decline, it also opened up opportunities for some women. As piped water proliferated in Mayo villages over the last six decades, this has allowed women to pursue roles such as cobanaro, dancers, or musicians over time. The epilogue discusses this in more detail.

58. As pipes brought sacred water into their homes, Mayo people, as well other Indigenous groups such as Maya Tzotziles of Chiapas, pondered its effect on the culture and organization of their community. Murillo Licea, "Manejo y organización comunitaria del agua en los Altos de Chiapas," 35.

59. Emily Wakild points out that in the postrevolutionary period in particular, compromises were forged between economic development and environmental protection, which led to the creation of national parks. In regions such as the Fuerte valley, designated for crop production, such environmental protections were practically nonexistent in the postrevolutionary period, and by the postwar era the economy took absolute precedence. Wakild, *Revolutionary Parks*, 5.

60. Chapter 4 provides an in-depth analysis of the importance of the San Juan ceremony.

61. These trees are endemic to the landscape and were not introduced from elsewhere. Mayo elders such as Carla Bacosegua claim that this treeplanting ceremony has been a tradition even before the arrival of Spaniards. Carla Bacosegua, interview by James Mestaz.

62. Mayo people are among several Indigenous groups of the Americas who find spiritual qualities in álamo/cottonwood trees. For instance, the Tewa Indians named clans, such as sacred dancer clans, after particular cottonwood trees. Robins, *Ethnobotany of the Tewa Indians*, 42. Omahas used also their wood for the poles of the buffalo tent, where they held a ceremony that ensured the souls of hunted buffalo lived on. Havasupai made sacred drums from hollow legs of cottonwoods. Navajo made cradles and ceremonial cravings from cottonwood. Sioux construct a hoop from the cottonwood and perform the Sundance underneath it. Thus it becomes the tree of life. Hageneder, *The Meaning of Trees*, 160–62.

63. Loreto Coronado, interview by James Mestaz, Los Mochis, Municip. Ahome, Sinaloa, Mexico, August 7, 2014.

64. Narciso Bachomo and Carlos Salcedo, interview by James Mestaz.

65. Yoris cut trees to not only clear space to plant crops but also to form sticks used to cultivate crops such as tomatoes. While they indiscriminately removed all species of trees, the most popular ones used to create rods for crops were acacia and hawthorn trees. Sterling Evans provides more details on the demand for tomato poles in northwest Mexico in Evans, "Baja and Beyond," 148–66; García Becerra, "La pena de muerte en la legislación del estado de Sinaloa," 35. Daniel

Galaviz, interview by James Mestaz, Camajoa, Municip. El Fuerte, Sinaloa, Mexico, March 6, 2014.

66. Manuel Galindo, interview by James Mestaz, La Bajada, Municip. El Fuerte, Sinaloa, Mexico, April 11, 2014.

67. Fermín Mopay, interview by James Mestaz.

68. Mauricio Mejías, interview by James Mestaz.

69. Yoris increasingly harvested and hunted frogs for food, animals that are essential for some villages to perform the Yuco Conti ceremony. Those villages that relied upon frogs found that enthusiasm for the ceremony waned. Chapter 4 details the importance of this ceremony and its use of frogs.

70. Indigenous populations in other regions of Latin America, such as Peruvian Amazonian Ribereños, adapted to similar ecological disruptions by using their familiarity with local ecosystems to adjust their traditional practices. Hiraoka, "Aquatic and Land Fauna Management among the Floodplain Ribereños of the Peruvian Amazon," 202.

71. Tico was likely referring to the *cabeza prieta* (ground snake). Eugenia Tico, interview by James Mestaz, Cahuinahua, Municip. El Fuerte, Sinaloa, Mexico, March 3, 2014.

72. Valdez et al., "Wildlife Conservation," 276.

73. Beals, *The Aboriginal Culture of the Cáhita*, 14.

74. Roberto Escalante, interview by James Mestaz, La Palma, Municip. El Fuerte, Sinaloa, Mexico, February 29, 2014.

75. While a postrevolutionary forestry ministry that did in fact have regulations on hunting existed in the 1920s, such restrictions were rarely enforced or obeyed. The federal government technically created the Office of Forestry, Hunting, and Fishing in the early 1950s, but with few resources. In 1964 it was elevated to the Office of Wildlife and given more resources, enabling it to enforce more restrictions. Valdez et al., "Wildlife Conservation," 274; Simonian, *Defending the Land of the Jaguar*.

76. Daniel Galaviz, interview by James Mestaz.

77. Several communities through different eras and geographic regions of the world were forced to change their diets as a consequence of new policies, usually tied to federal guidelines influenced by global economic priorities taking precedence over local concerns. Langa Herrero and Marcos, "La aplicación del derecho a la alimentación en las crisis humanitarias," 149–62.

78. Sabás Ynustrosa, interview by James Mestaz, La Mojonera, Municip. El Fuerte, Sinaloa, Mexico, August 2, 2014.

79. Beals, *The Aboriginal Culture of the Cáhita*, 18.

80. Fish Production Cooperative Society Charter, August 11, 1941, AGN, Manuel Ávila Camacho, 623.2/723.1.

81. Manuel Galindo, interview by James Mestaz.

82. As development transformed the natural landscape of northwestern Mexico, Indigenous groups such as the Mayo and their neighbors the Rarámuri of Chihuahua had to curtail such practices as fishing, hunting, and gathering plants. Yet in

sticking with their cosmogony, they continue such activities in a manner that regulates the relationship between humans and the natural environment. Martínez, "El agua en la cultura Rarámuri?" 147.

83. Water contamination has left negative consequences for Indigenous fishing practices throughout Mexico. For example, fishing has almost completely disappeared for the Chinantec people of Oaxaca, who have not seen a resurgence of aquatic animals in canals. Gálvez and Embriz Osorio, "Los pueblos indígenas," 22.

84. It is unclear if Bacosegua referred to earthen canals or those lined with concrete, but she probably meant both. It would have been easier, however, for aquatic animals to live in earthen canals. Mayo experiences with canals stand in direct contrast to those in the western United States discussed by environmental historian Donald Worster, who points out that modern canals are not an ecosystem, but abstracted water separated from the earth and used for profit. Worster, *Rivers of Empire*, 5. Carla Bacosegua, interview by James Mestaz.

85. Laura Apodaca, interview by James Mestaz, La Misión, Municip. El Fuerte, Sinaloa, Mexico, July 29, 2014.

Epilogue

1. Roberto Valenzuela and Gabriel Valenzuela, interview by James Mestaz, San Miguel Zapotitlán, Municip. Ahome, Sinaloa, Mexico, June 24, 2019.

2. The Mayo people were never completely powerless, as their strategies of resistance often mirrored those of other marginalized peasants as noted in Scott, *Weapons of the Weak*.

3. Some of the respondents that believed it was resistance included Carla Bacosegua of La Florida and Alejandro Inzunza of Los Goros.

4. Narciso Bachomo and Carlos Salcedo, interview by James Mestaz, Camajoa, Municip. El Fuerte, Sinaloa, Mexico, March 21, 2014.

5. These adaptations could also be viewed as "envirotechnical," as noted in Wolfe, *Watering the Revolution*. What was new here was the scale and scope of hydraulic technology, an adaptation that made it qualitatively different from the colonial and national periods through the 1920s.

6. Beals, *The Contemporary Culture of the Cáhita Indians*; Beals, *The Aboriginal Culture of the Cáhita Indians*; Erasmus, *Contemporary Change*; Erasmus, *Man Takes Control*.

7. Erasmus's faulty and borderline racist analysis was not an aberration, but rather typical of that discipline in that time period. Erasmus, *Man Takes Control*.

8. The Mayo people of the Fuerte valley continued to mobilize from 1970 to 1996, but the details of these hydraulic social mobilization tactics fall beyond the scope of this book.

9. Comité para la Defensa, *Primer encuentro*, 20–21.

10. Like many Indigenous groups in Mexico at the time, this committee was undoubtedly inspired by the EZLN (Zapatista) uprising of 1994. Comité para la Defensa, *Primer encuentro*, 12.

11. López et al., *Los mayos de huites.*

12. The state of Oaxaca officially recognized Indigenous peoples' rights to uses and customs in 1995. See Eisenstadt, "Usos y Costumbres and Postelectoral Conflicts in Oaxaca," 52–77.

13. Narciso Bachomo and Carlos Salcedo, interview by James Mestaz.

14. Some Mayo elders have recently considered attempts to convince the Mexican government to declare the Fuerte River a legal being, following New Zealand Maori people's success at changing the legal designation of the Whanganui River, yet no efforts have, as of yet, been set in motion. Salmond, "Tears of Rangi," 285–309.

15. In chapter 5 I pointed out that some elders complained about the rising costs of these ceremonies in the 1960s. Charles Erasmus also related such complaints by Mayo people in the 1950s. Erasmus, *Man Takes Control,* 279.

16. Currency conversion was based roughly on July 2014 rates. Flor Escalante, interview by James Mestaz, Jahuara, Municip. El Fuerte, Sinaloa, Mexico, July 13, 2014.

17. Chapter 5 discusses the problem of substituting synthetic materials for both *ramadas* and *tenábaris.*

18. Some Mayo elders discussing these possibilities include Laura Apodaca and Flor Escalante.

19. Jorge Robles, interview by James Mestaz, San Miguel, Municip. El Fuerte, Sinaloa, Mexico, May 25, 2014.

20. An example of such a Yori learning traditions from Indigenous elders is Oralia Inzunza, who approaches these dances and traditions with respect. While men usually filled the role as dancers, the fact that her instructor is teaching a woman also shows that more elders don't consider gender a factor in who learns. Oralia Inzunza, interview by James Mestaz, Zapotillo, Municip. Ahome, Sinaloa, Mexico, January 20, 2014.

21. Juanita Buimena is an exception in discussing gender roles, as most Mayo elders, both male and female, continue to deflect or ignore questions regarding this topic. Juanita is an expert on this transition in gender roles, as she became El Teroque's *cobanaro/a* in 2007. I have also personally noticed an increase in female traditional dancers and musicians from 2013 to 2020. Juanita Buimena, interview by James Mestaz, El Teroque Viejo, Municip. El Fuerte, February 14, 2014.

22. Scholarship in the past two decades has more fully analyzed Latin American women's growing political roles, especially their hydraulic social mobilization tactics. For example, see Bennett et al., *Opposing Currents.*

23. Several Mayo elders point to these explanations to account for the growing popularity of Mayo ceremonies, which include Felicitas Mejía, interview by James Mestaz, Vinaterrias, Municip. El Fuerte, Sinaloa, Mexico, July 17, 2014; Sabás Ynustrosa, interview by James Mestaz, La Mojonera, Municip. El Fuerte, Sinaloa, Mexico, August 2, 2014; Alejandro Inzunza, interview by James Mestaz, Los Goros, Municip. Ahome, Sinaloa, Mexico, February 14, 2014.

24. Felicitas Mejía, interview by James Mestaz.

25. Beals, *The Contemporary Culture of the Cáhita Indians,* 207. See also the introduction to this book.

BIBLIOGRAPHY

Manuscripts/Archives

1917 Mexican Constitution
1926 Mexican Law of Irrigation with Federal Waters
1931 Mexican Labor Law
1934 Agrarian Code
1942 Mexican Census, Population of Municipalities in Sinaloa
AGA. Archivo General Agrario (Agrarian Archives)
AGN. Archivo General de la Nación (Mexican General National Archive)
AHA. Archivo Histórico del Agua (Historical Water Archive)

Published Works

Aboites, Luis. *El agua de la nación: Una historia política de México, 1888–1946*. Mexico City: CIESAS, 1998.

——. *La irrigación revolucionaria: Historia del sistema nacional de riego del río Conchos, Chihuahua, 1927–1938*. Mexico City: CIESAS, 1988.

Aboites Aguilar, Luis. "The Transnational Dimensions of Mexican Irrigation, 1900–1950." *Journal of Political Ecology* 19, no. 1 (2012): 70–80.

Adams-Campbella, Melissa, Ashley Glassburn Falzetti, and Courtney Rivard. "Introduction: Indigeneity and the Work of Settler Archives." *Settler Colonial Studies* 5, no. 2 (2015): 109–16.

Ariel de Vidas, Anath. *El trueno ya no vive aquí: Representación de la marginalidad y construcción de la identidad teenek (Huasteca veracruzana, México)*. San Luis Potosí, MX: El Colegio de San Luis, 2013.

Armitage, Derek, Fikret Berkes, Erik Kocho-Schellenberg, Aaron Dale, and Eva Patton. "Co-management and the Co-production of Knowledge: Learning to Adapt in Canada's Arctic." *Global Environmental Change* 21, no. 3 (August 2011): 995–1004.

Assies, Willem. "David versus Goliath in Cochabamba: Water Rights, Neoliberalism, and the Revival of Social Protest in Bolivia." *Latin American Perspectives* 30, no. 3 (May 2003): 14–36.

Banco de Mexico. *Industria, Tomo 1*. Mexico City, MX: Departamento de Investigaciones Industriales, 1955.

Banister, Jeffrey. "Are You Wittfogel or against Him? Geophilosophy, Hydro-Sociality, and the State," *Geoforum* 57 (November 2014): 205–14.

———. "Patria Fugáz: The Troubled Birth of Hydraulic Populism on Sonora's Río Mayo, 1910–1934." *Journal of the Southwest* 57, no. 1 (Spring 2015): 103–44.

———. "Río Revuelto: Irrigation and the Politics of Chaos in Sonora's Mayo Valley." PhD diss., University of Arizona, 2010.

Bantjes, Adrian. *As if Jesus Walked on Earth: Cardenismo, Sonora, and the Mexican Revolution*. Wilmington DE: Rowman & Littlefield, 1998.

Barkin, David, and Timothy King. *Regional Economic Development: The River Basin Approach in Mexico*. Cambridge: Cambridge University Press, 1970.

Barlett, Peggy F. "Reciprocity and the San Juan Fiesta." *Journal of Anthropological Research* 36, no. 1 (1980): 116–30.

Barth, Fredrik. *Ethnic Groups and Boundaries: The Social Organization of Culture Difference*. 2nd ed. Long Grove IL: Waveland Press, 1988.

Beals, Ralph. *The Aboriginal Culture of the Cáhita Indians*. Berkeley CA: University of California Press, 1943.

———. *The Contemporary Culture of the Cáhita Indians*. Washington DC: Smithsonian Institution, U.S. Government Printing Office, 1945.

Bennett, Vivienne, Sonia Dávila-Poblete, and María Nieves Rico, eds. *Opposing Currents: The Politics of Water and Gender in Latin America*. Pittsburgh: University of Pittsburgh Press, 2005.

Boyer, Christopher. *Becoming Campesinos: Politics, Identity, and Agrarian Struggle in Postrevolutionary Michoacán, 1920–1935*. Palo Alto CA: Stanford University Press, 2003.

———, ed. *A Land between Waters: Environmental Histories of Modern Mexico*. Tucson: University of Arizona Press, 2012.

———. *Political Landscapes: Forests, Conservation, and Community in Mexico*. Durham NC: Duke University Press, 2015.

Boyer, Christopher, and Emily Wakild. "Social Landscaping in the Forests of Mexico: An Environmental Interpretation of Cardenismo, 1934–1940." *Hispanic American Historical Review* 92, no. 1 (February 2012): 73–106.

Brooks, Cassandra, and Lisa Brooks. "The Reciprocity Principle and Traditional Ecological Knowledge: Understanding the Significance of Indigenous Protest on the Presumpscot River." *International Journal of Critical Indigenous Studies* 3, no. 2 (2010): 11–28.

Carlos, Manuel L. "Enclavement Processes, State Policies, and Cultural Identity among the Mayo Indians of Sinaloa, Mexico." In *Ejidos and Regions of Refuge in Northwestern Mexico*, edited by N. Ross Crumrine and Phil C. Weigand, 33–38. Tucson: University of Arizona Press, 1987.

————. *Politics and Development in Rural Mexico: A Study of Socio-Economic Modernization*. Westport CT: Praeger Publishers, 1974.

Cave, Albert A. *Prophets of the Great Spirit: Native American Revitalization Movements in Eastern North America*. Lincoln: University of Nebraska Press, 2006.

Champagne, Duane. "Rethinking Native Relations." In *Indigenous Peoples and the Modern State*, edited by Duane Champage, Karen Jo Torjesen, Susan Steiner, 3–23. Lanham MD: Alta Mira Press, 2005.

Cipolla, Craig N. *Becoming Brothertown: Native American Ethnogenesis and Endurance in the Modern World*. Tucson: University of Arizona, 2013.

Collier, George. *Fields of the Tzotzil: The Ecological Bases of Tradition in Highland Chiapas*. Austin: University of Texas Press, 2012.

Comisión del Río Fuerte. *Datos hidrométricos, climatológicos y de azolve de la cuenca del río Fuerte hasta 1952*. Mexico City, 1952.

Comité para la Defensa de la Cultura Mayo de Huites. *Primer encuentro de poblaciones indígenas desplazados y efectadas por la construcción de presas*. Mexico City, 1996.

Crumrine, N. Ross. *The Mayo Indians of Sonora: A People Who Refused to Die*. Tucson: University of Arizona Press, 1977.

————. "Mechanisms of Enclavement Maintenance and Sociocultural Blocking of Modernization among the Mayo of Southern Sonora." In *Ejidos and Regions of Refuge in Northwestern Mexico*, edited by N. Ross Crumrine and Phil Weigand, 21–32. Tucson: University of Arizona Press, 1987.

Cruz, Roberto. *Roberto Cruz en la Revolución Mexicana*. Mexico City: Editorial Diana, 1976.

Dean, Janet. "The Violence of Collection: Indian Killer's Archives." *Studies in American Indian Literatures* 20, no. 3 (2008): 29–51.

De La Cadena, Marisol. *Earth Beings: Ecologies of Practice across Andean Worlds*. Durham NC: Duke University Press, 2015.

Doolittle, William E. "Intermittent Use and Agricultural Change on Marginal Lands: The Case of Smallholders in Eastern Sonora, Mexico." *Geografiska Annaler. Series B, Human Geography* 70, no. 2 (1988): 255–66.

Eckstein, Salomón. *El ejido colectivo en México*. Mexico City: Fondo de Cultura Economíca, 1966.

Eisenstadt, Todd A. "Usos y Costumbres and Postelectoral Conflicts in Oaxaca." *Latin American Research Review* 42, no. 1 (2007): 52–77.

Ekbladh, David. "Mr. TVA: Grass-Roots Development, David Lilienthal, and the Rise and Fall of the Tennessee Valley Authority as a Symbol for U.S. Overseas Development, 1933–1973." *Diplomatic History* 26, no. 3 (2002): 335–74.

Endfield, Georgina, *Climate and Society in Colonial Mexico: A Study in Vulnerability*. Hoboken NJ: Wiley-Blackwell, 2008.

Erasmus, Charles. *Contemporary Change in Traditional Societies. Vol. 3, Mexican and Peruvian Communities*. Champaign: University of Illinois Press, 1967.

————. *Man Takes Control: Cultural Development and American Aid*. Minneapolis: University of Minnesota Press, 1963.

Escobar, Arturo. *Territories of Difference: Place, Movements, Life, Redes*. Durham NC: Duke University Press. 2008.

Evans, Sterling. "Baja and Beyond: Toward an Environmental and Trans-Regional History of the Tomato Industry of Baja California." In *Farming across Borders: A Transnational History of the North American West*, edited by Sterling Evans, 148–66. College Station: Texas A&M University Press, 2017.

————. *Bound in Twine: The History and Ecology of the Henequen-Wheat Complex for Mexico and the American and Canadian Plains, 1880–1950*. College Station: Texas A&M University Press, 2013.

————. "La angustia de La Angostura: Consecuencias socioambientales por la construcción de presas en Sonora." *Signos históricos* 8, no. 16 (July–Dec. 2006): 46–78.

Fallaw, Ben. *Cárdenas Compromised: The Failure of Reform in Postrevolutionary Yucatán, Mexico*. Durham NC: Duke University Press, 2001.

Fiege, Mark. *Irrigated Eden: The Making of an Agricultural Landscape in the American West*. Seattle: University of Washington Press, 2000.

Figueroa, Alejandro. *Por la tierra y por los santos: Identidad y persistencia cultural entre yaquis y mayos*. Mexico City: Consejo Nacional para la Cultura y las Artes, 1994.

Figueroa, José Maria, and Gilberto López Alaniz. *Encuentros con la historia, Choix, tomo 1*. Culiacán: Gobierno del Estado de Sinaloa, Revista Cultural Presagio, 1990.

————. *Encuentros con la historia, Sinaloa*. Culiacán: Gobierno del Estado de Sinaloa, Revista Cultural Presagio, 1990.

Flavier, J. M. "The Regional Program for the Promotion of Indigenous Knowledge in Asia." In *The Cultural Dimension of Development: Indigenous Knowledge Systems*, edited by D. M. Warren, L. J. Slikkerveer, and D. Brokensha, 479–87. Dunsmore Rugby, UK: Intermediate Technology Publications, 1995.

Gálvez, Xóchitl, and Arnulfo Embriz Osorio. "Los pueblos indígenas de México y el agua." In Sandre Osorio and Murillo, *Agua y diversidad cultural en México*, 11–24.

García Becerra, José Antonio. "La pena de muerte en la legislación del estado de Sinaloa." *Ingeniera hidraulica en Mexico* 21, nos. 1&2 (1967): 9–440.

Garcia Canclini, Nestor. *Hybrid Cultures: Strategies for Entering and Leaving Modernity*. Minneapolis: University of Minnesota Press, 2005.

Gill, Mario. *La conquista del valle del Fuerte*. Culiacán: Universidad Autónoma de Sinaloa, 1957.

Gillingham, Paul, and Benjamin T. Smith, eds. *Dictablanda: Politics, Work, and Culture in Mexico, 1938–1968*. Durham NC: Duke University Press, 2014.

Glantz, Susana. *El ejido colectivo de Nueva Italia*. Mexico City: Instituto Nacional de Antropología e Historia, 1974.

Gledhill, John. *Casi Nada: A Study in Agrarian Reform in the Homeland of Cardenismo*. Boulder: University of Colorado Press, 1991.

Gómez Martínez, Arturo. "El agua en la cosmovisión de los nahuas de Chiconte-pec." In Martínez Ruiz and Murillo Licea, *Agua en la cosmovisión de los pueb-los indígenas en México*, 101–16.

Graham, Jonathan. "A Tale of Two Valleys: An Examination of the Hydrological Union of the Mezquital Valley and the Basin of Mexico." In *Mexico in Focus: Political, Environmental and Social Issues*, edited by José Galindo, 31–80. New York City: Nova, 2014.

Grande, Carlos. *Sinaloa en la historia. Tomo 1.* Culiacán: Universidad Autónoma de Sinaloa, 1998.

Guss, David M. "The Selling of San Juan: The Performance of History in an Afro-Venezuelan Community." *American Ethnologist* 20, no. 3 (1993): 451–73.

Hageneder, Fred. *The Meaning of Trees: Botany, History, Healing, Lore.* San Fran-cisco: Chronicle, 2005.

Harvey, David. *The New Imperialism.* Oxford: Oxford University Press, 2003.

Hiraoka, Mario. "Aquatic and Land Fauna Management among the Floodplain Rib-ereños of the Peruvian Amazon." In *The Fragile Tropics of Latin America: Sus-tainable Management of Changing Environments*, edited by Toshie Nishizawa and Juha Uitto, 201–25. Tokyo: United Nations University Press, 1995.

Hu-Dehart, Evelyn. *Yaqui Resistance and Survival: The Struggle for Land and Auton-omy 1821–1910.* Madison: University of Wisconsin Press, 1984.

Instituto Nacional Estadística y Geografía. *Anuario estadístico de Sinaloa.* Mexico City: 2012.

Japama. "Proceso de potabilización." Video, 6:45, 2011.

Knight, Alan. "Cardenismo: Juggernaut or Jalopy?" *Journal of Latin American Stud-ies* 26, no. 1 (February 1994): 73–107.

Langa Herrero, Alfredo, and Francisco Rey Marcos, "La aplicación del derecho a la alimentación en las crisis humanitarias." In *Derecho a la alimentación y sober-anía alimentaria*, edited by José T. Esquinas Alcázar, 149–62. Córdoba, ES: Uni-versidad de Córdoba Press, 2008.

Lazcarro Salgado, Israel. "Las venas del cerro: El agua en el cosmos otomí de la Huasteca Sur." In Sandre Osorio and Murillo, *Agua y diversidad cultural en México*, 89–104

Liffman, Paul. *Huichol Territory and the Mexican Nation: Indigenous Ritual, Land Conflict, and Sovereignty Claims.* Tucson: University of Arizona Press, 2014.

López, Francisco, Ana Ramirez, and Ramón Martinez. *Los mayos de Huites despla-zados por la presa.* Mexico City: Instituto Nacional Indigenista, 1996.

López, Marcos. "In Hidden View: How Water Became a Catalyst for Indigenous Farmworker Resistance in Baja, California, Mexico." In *The Politics of Fresh Water: Access, Conflict and Identity*, edited by Catherine M. Ashcroft and Tamar Mayer, 188–202. Milton Park, Didcot, UK: Routledge, 2016.

López Aceves, Hugo Eduardo. "Los mayos de Sinaloa: Esbozo etnográfico y regional." *Cuicuilco* 14, no. 39 (2007): 11–33.

López Carrera, Alma Mirella. *Atlas yoreme del municipio de Ahome: Monografía de los centros ceremoniales*. Mexico City: Consejo Ciudadano para el Desarollo Cultural del Municipio del Ahome, 2013.

López Ramírez, Eduardo. "Los Ñuu Savii: Los que habitan donde moran las nubes." In Martínez Ruiz and Murillo Licea, *Agua en la cosmovisión de los pueblos indígenas en México*, 71–82.

Martínez, Isabel. "Aguas que nacen en el cielo y en la tierra: El yúmari en la Sierra Tarahumara, una danza para continuar el camino rarámuri." In Martínez Ruiz and Murillo Licea, *Agua en la cosmovisión de los pueblos indígenas en México*, 29–44.

———. "El agua en la cultura rarámuri ¿Hasta cuándo los pilares del mundo podrán sostenerlo?" In Sandre Osorio and Murillo, *Agua y diversidad cultural en México*, 141–50.

Martínez Ruiz, José Luis. "Los verdaderos dueños del agua y el monte." In Martínez Ruiz and Murillo Licea, *Agua en la cosmovisión de los pueblos indígenas en México*, 129–44.

———. "Zitlala: La Santa Cruz, los tlacololeros maiceros y los jaguares de la lluvia y del monte." In Martínez Ruiz and Murillo Licea, *Agua en la cosmovisión de los pueblos indígenas en México*, 83–100.

Martínez Ruiz, José Luis, and Daniel Murillo Licea, eds. *Agua en la cosmovisión de los pueblos indígenas en México*. Mexico City: Secretaría de Medio Ambiente y Recursos Naturales, 2016.

Matsui, Kenichi. *Native Peoples and Water Rights: Irrigation, Dams, and the Law in Western Canada*. Montreal: McGill-Queen's University Press, 2009.

Matthews, Andrew S. *Instituting Nature: Authority, Expertise, and Power in Mexican Forests*. Cambridge MA: MIT Press, 2011.

McCormick, Gladys. *The Logic of Compromise: Authoritarianism, Betrayal, and Revolution in Rural Mexico. 1935–1965*. Chapel Hill: University of North Carolina Press, 2016.

McGuire, Thomas. *Politics and Ethnicity on the Rio Yaqui: Potam Revisited*. Tucson: University of Arizona Press, 1986.

Mendoza García, J. Édgar. "El manantial La Taza de San Gabriel Chilac (puebla) y los manantiales de Teotihuacán (Estado de México) ante la federalización: Un análisis comparativo entre 1917 y 1960." In *Mexico in Transition: New Perspectives on Mexican Agrarian History, Nineteenth and Twentieth Centuries*, edited by Antonio Escobar Ohmstede and Matthew Butler, 225–58. Mexico City: CIESAS, 2013.

Messerli, Bruno, Martin Grosjean, Thomas Hofer, Lautaro Núñez, and Christian Pfister. "From Nature Dominated to Human Dominated Environmental Changes." *Quaternary Science Reviews* 19, nos. 1–5 (2000): 459–79.

Mestaz, James. "Sweetness and Water Power: El SICAE Sugar Cooperative and Mayo Struggles for Water, 1943–1955." *Journal of Latin American Studies* 52, no. 1 (February 2020): 1–25.

Mintz, Sidney W. *Sweetness and Power: The Place of Sugar in Modern History*. London: Penguin, 1986.

Mitchell, Timothy. *Rule of Experts: Egypt, Techno-Politics, Modernity*. Berkeley: University of California Press, 2002.

Mottier, Nicole. "Calculating Pragmatism: The High Politics of the Banco Ejidal in Twentieth-Century Mexico." *The Americas* 74, no. 3 (July 2017): 331–63.

Muehlmann, Shaylih. *Where the River Ends: Contested Indigeneity in the Mexican Colorado Delta*. Durham NC: Duke University Press, 2013.

Muñoz, María L. O. *Stand Up and Fight: Participatory Indigenismo, Populism, and Mobilization in Mexico, 1970–1984*. Tucson: University of Arizona Press, 2016.

Murillo Licea, Daniel. "Manejo y organización comunitaria del agua en los Altos de Chiapas: El caso del Paraje Tzotzil Pozuelos." In Sandre Osorio and Murillo, *Agua y diversidad cultural en México*, 25–38.

Nabhan, Gary Paul. *Enduring Seeds: Native American Agriculture and Wild Plant Conservation*. New York: North Point Press, 1989.

Nabhan, Gary Paul, and Andrew R. Holdsworth. *State of the Sonoran Desert Biome: Uniqueness, Biodiversity, Threats and the Adequacy of Protection in the Sonoran Bioregion*. Tucson: Arizona-Sonoran Desert Museum, 1999.

Nakayama, Antonio. *Sinaloa: Un bosquejo de su historia*. Culiacán: Universidad Autónoma de Sinaloa, 1982.

Neurath, Johannes. "El agua en la cosmovisión wixarika." In Martínez Ruiz and Murillo Licea, *Agua en la cosmovisión de los pueblos indígenas en México*, 45–58.

Ochoa Ávila, María Guadalupe, and Fabiola Arias. "Cuando Maamlaab y Junkil aab despiertan: Agua, identidad y tradición oral entre los teenek de la Huasteca potosina y veracruzana," In Martínez Ruiz and Murillo Licea, *Agua en la cosmovisión de los pueblos indígenas en México*, 59–70.

Ochoa Zazueta, Jesús Angel. *Los mayos: Alma y arraigo*. Los Mochis, MX: Universidad de Occidente, 1998.

——. *Bachomo: Los días del gato; Crónica indígena de la revolución*. Culiacán: Creativos 7, 2010.

O'Connor, Mary. *Descendants of Totoliguoqui: Ethnicity and Economics in the Mayo Valley*. Berkeley: University of California Press, 1989.

Olmsted, Frank Henry. *Report on the Properties of the United Sugar Companies, S.A.* Los Mochis, MX: 1924.

Olsson, Torre C. *Agrarian Crossings: Reformers and the Remaking of the US and Mexican Countryside*. Princeton NJ: Princeton University Press, 2017.

Orlove, Benjamin S., John C. H. Chiang, and Mark A. Cane. "Ethnoclimatology in the Andes: A Cross-Disciplinary Study Uncovers a Scientific Basis for the Scheme Andean Potato Farmers Traditionally Use to Predict the Coming Rains." *American Scientist* 90, no. 5 (2002): 428–35.

Padilla, Tanalís. *Rural Resistance in the Land of Zapata: The Jaramillista Movement and the Myth of the Pax Priísta, 1940–1962*. Durham NC: Duke University Press, 2008.

Peppler, Randy. "'Old Indian Ways' of Predicting the Weather: Senator Robert S. Kerr and the Winter Predictions of 1950–51 and 1951–52." *Weather, Climate, and Society* 2, no. 3 (2010): 200–209.

Pierotti, Raymond. *Indigenous Knowledge, Ecology, and Evolutionary Biology.* Milton Park, Didcot, UK: Routledge, 2012.

Pisani, Donald. *Water, Land, and Law in the West: The Limits of Public Policy.* Lawrence: University Press of Kansas, 1996.

Portelli, Alessandro. *The Death of Luigi Trastulli and Other Stories.* New York: State University of New York Press, 1991.

Privott, Meredith. "An Ethos of Responsibility and Indigenous Women Water Protectors in the #NoDAPL Movement." *American Indian Quarterly* 43, no. 1 (2019): 74–100.

Pueblos America. Accessed May 21, 2021. https://mexico.pueblosamerica.com/.

Quintero, Filiberto Leandro. *Historia integral de la región del río Fuerte.* Los Mochis, MX: El Debate, 1978.

Radding, Cynthia. *Wandering Peoples: Colonialism, Ethnic Spaces, and Ecological Frontiers in Northwest Mexico, 1700–1850.* Durham NC: Duke University Press, 1997.

Rahal, Sheryl Ann. "The Ghost Dance as a Millenarian Phenomenon." *Caliban* 3, no. 1 (1998): 171–81.

Restrepo, Iván, and Salomón Eckstein. *La agricultura colectiva en Mexico: La experiencia de la laguna.* Mexico City: Siglo Veintiuno Editores, 1975.

Rivero-Romero, Alexis, Ana I. Moreno-Calles, Alejandro Casas, Alicia Castillo, and Andrés Camou-Guerrero. "Traditional Climate Knowledge: A Case Study in a Peasant Community in Tlaxcala, Mexico." *Journal of Ethnobiology and Ethnomedicine* 12, no. 1 (2016): 1–11.

Robards, Martin, and Lilian Alessa. "Timescapes of Community Resilience and Vulnerability in the Circumpolar North." *Arctic* 57, no. 4 (2004): 415–27.

Robins, Wilfred William. *Ethnobotany of the Tewa Indians.* Washington DC: Smithsonian Institution, 1916.

Romero-Ibarra, María Eugenia. "La reforma agraria de Cárdenas y la agroindustria azucarera de México." *Historia agraria,* no. 52 (Dec. 2010): 103–27.

——. "La Sociedad Colectivo Agrícola Industrial, emancipación proletaria, expropiación y cooperativismo en la industria azucarera de México, 1930–1960." Presented at IX Congreso Internacional de Asociación Española de Historia Económica, 2008.

Romero Navarrete, Lourdes, Daniel Murillo Licea, and Teresa Rojas Rabiela. "La autogestión del agua de riego en comunidades indígenas de México." In *La economía social y solidaria en la historia de América Latina y el Caribe: Cooperativismo, desarrollo comunitario y estado, tomo II,* edited by Valeria Mutuberría Lazarini and Daniel Plotinsky, 235–52. Buenos Aires: Idelcoop, 2015.

Russell, Lynette. "Indigenous Knowledge and Archives: Accessing Hidden History and Understandings." *Australian Academic & Research Libraries* 36, no. 2 (2005): 161–71.

Salmond, Anne. "Tears of Rangi: Water, Power, and People in New Zealand." *HAU: Journal of Ethnographic Theory* 4, no. 3 (2014): 285–309.

Sanderson, Steven. *The Transformation of Mexican Agriculture: International Structure and the Politics of Rural Change.* Princeton NJ: Princeton University Press, 1986.

Sandre Osorio, Israel, and Daniel Murillo, eds. *Agua y diversidad cultural en México.* Montevideo: UNESCO, 2008.

Santiago, Myrna I. *The Ecology of Oil: Environment, Labor, and the Mexican Revolution, 1900–1938.* Cambridge: Cambridge University Press, 2006.

Schobert, Lorena. *Historia de una gesta obrero campesina, la SICAE.* Mexico City: Dirección de Investigación y Fomento de Cultura Regional, 1998.

Schwartz, Diana. "Displacement, Development, and the Creation of a Modern Indígena in the Papaloapan, 1940s–1970s." In *Beyond Alterity: Destabilizing the Indigenous Other in Mexico,* edited by Ariadna Acevedo and Paula López Caballero, 222–43. Tucson: University of Arizona Press, 2018.

Scott, Christopher A., and Jeffrey Banister. "The Dilemma of Water Management 'Regionalization' in Mexico under Centralized Resource Allocation." *Water Resources Development* 24, no. 1 (March 2008): 61–74.

Scott, James. *Weapons of the Weak: Everyday Forms of Peasant Resistance.* New Haven CT: Yale University Press, 1987.

Secretaria de Agricultura y Fomento. *Ley de aguas de propiedad nacional y su reglamento.* Tacubaya, Mexico City: 1930.

Secretaria de Agricultura y Ganadería, y Banco de Mexico, S.A. *Projections of Supply and Demand for Agricultural Products in Mexico to 1970 and 1975.* Mexico City, 1976.

Secretaria de Agricultura y Recursos Hidraulicos. *Memoria de la comisión del río Fuerte.* Mexico City, 1985.

Secretaria de Industria y Comercio. *Ejidal Census, Mexican Agricultural, Livestock.* Mexico City, 1960.

Sheil, Douglas, and Daniel Murdiyarso. "How Forests Attract Rain: An Examination of a New Hypothesis." *BioScience* 59, no. 4 (2009): 341–47.

Silva Rodríguez de San Miguel, Jorge A. "Rural Water Supply in Mexico." *Cuadernos de desarrollo rural* 13, no. 78 (2016): 123–41.

Simonian, Lane. *Defending the Land of the Jaguar.* Austin: University of Texas Press, 1995.

Spicer, Edward. *The Yaquis: A Cultural History.* Tucson: University of Arizona Press, 1980.

Taylor, William. *Magistrates of the Sacred: Priests and Parishioners in Eighteenth-Century Mexico.* Palo Alto CA: Stanford University Press, 1996.

Uriarte, Gabriel. *Sinaloa yoreme: Sus fiestas y sus danzas, entre el catolicismo y el Juyya Annia.* Culiacán: Dirección de Investigación y Fomento de Cultura Regional, 2003.

Valdez, Raul, Francisco Abarca, Fernando Clemente-Sánchez, Luis A. Tarango-Arambula, and Juan C. Guzmán-Arranda. "Wildlife Conservation and Management in Mexico." *Wildlife Society Bulletin* 34, no. 2 (2010): 270–82.

Vaughan, Mary K. *Cultural Politics in Revolution: Teachers, Peasants, and Schools in Mexico, 1930–1940*. Tucson: University of Arizona, 1997.

Vitz, Matthew. *A City on a Lake: Urban Political Ecology and the Growth of Mexico City*. Durham NC: Duke University Press, 2018.

Wakild, Emily. *Revolutionary Parks: Conservation, Social Justice, and Mexico's National Parks, 1910–1940*. Tucson: University of Arizona Press, 2011.

Weber, Max. "The Distribution of Power within the Community: Classes, Stände, Parties." *Journal of Classical Sociology* 10, no. 2 (May 2010): 137–52.

Wittfogel, Karl A. *Oriental Despotism: A Comparative Study of Total Power*. New Haven CT: Yale University Press, 1957.

Wolfe, Mikael. *Watering the Revolution: An Environmental and Technological History of Agrarian Reform in Mexico*. Durham NC: Duke University Press, 2017.

Worster, Donald. *Rivers of Empire: Water, Aridity, and the Growth of the American West*. Oxford: Oxford University Press, 1985.

INDEX

commercial agriculture, 144–45, 180
Commission of Ecology, 229
Committee of Ejidatarios and Small Property Farmers Affected by the Vessel of the Miguel Hidalgo Dam, 198, 200–201
communal harvesting, 63, 64
Compañía Explotadora de las Aguas del Río Fuerte (Water Utilization Company of the Fuerte River), 32–33
Compañía Irrigadora del Río del Fuerte (Irrigation Company of the Fuerte River), 52–56
compensation, monetary, 122
complicity, 153
concessions, 15
Confederación de Trabajadores de México (Confederation of Mexican Workers), 257n91
Confederación Nacional Campesina (CNC) (National Campesino Confederation), 82–83, 87–88, 197, 257n92
Confederación Regional Obrera Mexicana (CROM) (Regional Confederation of Mexican Workers), 67
contamination, water, 166–67, 185, 204–6, 220, 223, 273n54, 276n83
cooperative, 248n59. See also specific cooperatives
corn, 234. See also maize
Coronado, Loreto, 211
corruption, 69–70
Cortines, Adolfo Ruiz, 85, 144–45, 187
corvée (hydraulic army), 154–61
credit, 83–84, 86–87
crony capitalism, 159
crops, 11, 122, 234. See also agriculture
Crumrine, N. Ross, 27, 153–54, 164, 173
Cruz, Raymundo Enríquez, 110, 112
Cruz, Roberto, 78–79
Cuadros, Librado, 26, 120, 149, 155, 169

dams, 155, 156, 197, 207, 272n27, 272n30. See also Miguel Hidalgo Dam
dancing, 133
Defense of the Mayo Culture of Huites, 227–29
deforestation, 125–27

Departamento Agrario (Agrarian Department), 64, 94, 95, 110
Department of Ejido Affairs, 191
desiccation theory, 127
Díaz, Porfirio, 30, 32
diets, alterations to, 218
displacement, from dams, 197–99, 272n30
dispossession, land, 140–54, 174, 175, 197
dotación (grant), 15, 16–17, 149
drought, 128
Dupont, 234

Echamea, Rudolfo, 183, 210
Eckstein, Salomón, 63, 73
Ejidal Agrarian Organization (Organización Agraria Ejidal), 84
Ejidal Forestry Cooperative (Sociedad Cooperativa Forestal Ejidal) (SCFE), 105
Ejidal Land Defense Committee, 75
ejidatarios (land reform beneficiaries): animals of, 214–15; benefits of, 15; within Camajoa, 90–96; cash crops of, 64; Committee of Ejidatarios and Small Property Farmers Affected by the Vessel of the Miguel Hidalgo Dam, 198; contamination effects on, 204–6; cooperative of, 60, 63, 74; CRF and, 185, 187, 189, 190, 191, 193, 194–201; Defense of the Mayo Culture of Huites, 227–29; diets of, 218; within El Teroque, 82–90, 97, 135; employment of, 156–59, 194; harvest/water exchanges by, 193–94; hydraulic social mobilization of, 98; irrigation restrictions to, 128–29, 137, 140–54; within Jahuara, 105–15; land dispossession of, 140–54; within La Palma, 115–24, 169; within Los Goros, 51–52, 56, 77–82; Mayo farmers as, 16; mobilization of, 62; nature relationship of, 210–11, 215–18; options of, 148; regulations regarding, 17; relocation of, 197–99; SICAE and, 65–72, 75–77, 96, 190; statistics regarding, 50; tradition decline of, 266n26; vulnerabilities of, 140–54; weather predictions of, 129–31; Yuco Conti ceremony and, 101, 103, 131–34, 162. See also collectivists; independent ejidatarios; individualists

laborers, as hydraulic army, 154–61
La Florida, 165, *172*, 204
lagoon, Jahuara: crop production within, 107, *111*, 111–12
La Laguna, 65
La Misión, 7, *102*, 103
land dispossession, 140–54, 174, 175, 197
land policies, 4, 14–18
land theft, 151–52
language, of Mayo people, 12, 27
La Palabra, 93
La Palma: adaptation challenges of, 143; background of, 116; Cahuinahua Canal and, 144; canal building process within, 155; demographics of, 266n28; Ejidal Bank (Banco Ejidal) and, 116; *ejidos* within, 146–47; encroachment within, 149; favoritism within, 147; flooding within, 117; hydraulic social mobilization of, 123; irrigation concession application of, 244n3; map of, *115*, *150*; modernization within, 120; overview of, 115–24, 135; protests within, 119–20; San Juan ritual and, 169; Yoris within, 151
Las Vacas, 199
Law of Irrigation with Federal Waters, 15, 23–24
Law of Waters and National Property, 47
League of Users of the Fuerte River, 74–75
legislation, water, 32–35
Ley Federal de Trabajo (Federal Labor Law), 44
Liffman, Paul, 8
livestock, 11, 204, 214–18. *See also* animals
loggerhead turtle (*caguama*), 219
loggers, 106, 107
López, Bernabé, 72
López, Hugo, 25
Lorenzo Valdés and Company, 36, 37, 47
Los Goros: division within, 77–78; *dotación* for, 49–52; features of, 24; harvest/water exchanges within, 193–94; Indigenous *ejidos* within, 97; irrigation concession to, 49–52, 244n3; irrigation fees within, 193; irrigation infrastructure approach by, 39–48; land seizures within, 80–81, 175; letter from, 53–54, 55; location of, 25, 77; map of, *40*, *76*; petition from, 23–24, 35–36, 48–52,

56; power of water within, 77–82; property of, 250n95; property ownership within, 250n102; SICAE and, 77–82; water access within, 271n17; water significance to, 24–25
Los Goros Uno (Oro Pinto), 97
Los Mochis, 207, 209
Los Picachos, 198

Madero, Francisco, 30
maize, 3, 79, 257n90. *See also* corn
Mateos, Adolfo López, 144–45
Matthews, Andrew, 127
Maya people, 263n73, 263n74, 274n58
mayombo (people of the riverbanks), 25
Mayo people: adaptation by, 14–18, 28–32, 142, 168–69, 210–11, 220, 221–22, 225, 226–27, 232–35; alliances of, 6; celebrations of, 232; characteristics of, 245n17; collaboration by, 3; community of, 246n25; core understanding of, 9; cultural decline of, 213; culture of, 27–28, 229–32; diets of, 216–18; fishing by, 220; Fuerte River significance to, 25–28; gender reciprocity beliefs of, 245n13; identity of, 221–22; Indigenous identity of, 40–42; inequalities within, 8; irrigation viewpoints of, 179; language of, 12, 27; livestock of, 215; within Los Goros, 193; marginalization of, 6, 205–6; people groups of, 264n76; power structures within, 17; rain prediction practices of, 129–31; renaissance within, 134; resistance by, 246n31; revolt by, 28–32; rituals of, 229; river practices of, 204; river respect of, 205; San Juan ritual and, 169; spiritual life of, 51; technology integration by, 7; time-honored practices of, 108; transactions of, 154; villages of, 12–14; vision significance to, 1–2; Yoris versus, 45, 71
Mayo valley, 176–77. *See also specific locations*
Mazatec people, 199
Mejía, Felicitas, 166, 194, 233
Mejías, Mauricio, 129, 137, 167, 190–91, 205, 216
Messerli, Bruno, 141, 142, 143
mestizos, 27, 138–39, 245n16, 245n17
Mexican government: challenges with, 101–2; corporate preferences of, 123, 124–25, 138, 147; disregard for Indigenous ide-

Soto, Jesús, 147–48
Soto, Pablo, 148
Standing Rock Reservation, 234
sugarcane, 11, 13, 32–35, 69–70, 73–74, 88–
    89. *See also* United Sugar Companies
    (USCOS); *and specific agencies and cooper-*
    atives; specific growing locations

Tecaltepec Project, 188
technology, hydraulic, 142, 143, 144, 157, 226
técnicos, 9
Teenek, 244n10, 246n31
Tehueco, 101, *102*
tenábaris (leg rattles), 213, 230
tenachi (prayer teacher), 132, 264n76
Tennessee Valley Authority (TVA), 186
Tewa Indians, 274n62
Tico, Eugenia, 216
Tlaloc, 183–85, *184*
toads, 133–34
Topolobampo, 219
Toro, *198*, 199
Torres, José Luis, 94–95
Trade Union Federation of Workers and
    Peasants of Northern Sinaloa (Federación
    Sindicalista de Obreros y Campesinos de
    la Zona Norte del Estado de Sinaloa), 44
traditional ecological knowledge, of Indige-
    nous people, 260n26
transgenic corn, 234
trees, 211–12, 213, 274n62, 274n65

United Sugar Companies (USCOS): confis-
    cation and redistribution from, 65; favor-
    itism of, 247n44; governmental favoritism
    regarding, 33; irrigation strategy of, 34–35;
    Law of Irrigation with Federal Waters and,
    23–24; operation of, 32; property appraisal
    of, 33; working conditions within, 67;
    work of, 13, 14, 15
Uriarte, Gabriel, 28, 133

Valdés, Juan, 52–53, 54–55
Valdés, Miguel Alemán, 114, 186–87
Valdés, Rosario, 52–53, 54–55
Valenzuela, Gabriel, 223
Valenzuela, Juan, 125

Valenzuela, Julián, 101–5
Valenzuela, Roberto, 223
Villa, Francisco "Pancho," 31
Vitz, Matthew, 9
Viuda de la Vega, Sara Herrán, 125, 148,
    262n57
vulnerability, irrigation, 140–54

Wakild, Emily, 9, 64
water: access questions regarding, 2; charges
    regarding, 192–93; contamination of, 166–
    67, 185, 204–6, 220, 223, 273n54, 276n83;
    duality of, 273n39; exchanges regarding,
    158; healing powers of, 162; inequalities
    regarding, 140; lack of treatment of, 273n54,
    273n55; legislation regarding, 32–35; Mayo
    approach to, 244n9; piped, 209–10; pota-
    ble, 206–10; religion and, 264n76, 267n58;
    SICAE's monopoly of, 72–77; significance
    of, 24–25, 96–97, 183; using land to secure,
    48–52; as weapon, 104. *See also* irrigation
Watering the Revolution (Wolfe), 9
water laws, 14–18
water snakes, 216, 218
Water Utilization Company of the Fuerte
    River (Compañía Explotadora de las
    Aguas del Río Fuerte), 32–33
weirs, 177
Weiss, Andrew, 195
Where the River Ends (Muehlmann), 8–9
white guards, 67
Wilson, Jack, 269n77
Wittfogel, Karl, 159
Wolfe, Mikael, 9, 34
women, 210, 232, 274n57, 277n21
Worster, Donald, 159

Yaqui people, 156, 197, 243n29, 264n76,
    269n82, 273n54
Yaqui valley (Sonora), 65, 144, 269n82
Ynustrosa, Sabás, 124, 157
Yoremes. *See* Mayo people
Yoris: alliances of, 6; canal access of, 137–38,
    186; characteristics of, 243n39; deceit of,
    157–58, 160; defined, 257n87; dispossession
    tactics of, 149, 150–52; distrust regarding,
    114; domination of, 153–54; Ejidal Bank

In the Confluencias series:

The Enlightened Patrolman: Early Law Enforcement in Mexico City
By Nicole von Germeten

Strength from the Waters: A History of Indigenous Mobilization in Northwest Mexico
By James V. Mestaz

To order or obtain more information on these or other University of Nebraska Press titles, visit nebraskapress.unl.edu.

www.ingramcontent.com/pod-product-compliance
Lightning Source LLC
Chambersburg PA
CBHW020459270326
41926CB00008B/671